International TESOL Teachers in a Multi-Englishes Community

NEW PERSPECTIVES ON LANGUAGE AND EDUCATION

Founding Editor: Viv Edwards, *University of Reading, UK*
Series Editors: Phan Le Ha, *University of Hawaii at Manoa, USA* and Joel Windle, *Monash University, Australia.*

Two decades of research and development in language and literacy education have yielded a broad, multidisciplinary focus. Yet education systems face constant economic and technological change, with attendant issues of identity and power, community and culture. What are the implications for language education of new 'semiotic economies' and communications technologies? Of complex blendings of cultural and linguistic diversity in communities and institutions? Of new cultural, regional and national identities and practices? The New Perspectives on Language and Education series will feature critical and interpretive, disciplinary and multidisciplinary perspectives on teaching and learning, language and literacy in new times. New proposals, particularly for edited volumes, are expected to acknowledge and include perspectives from the Global South. Contributions from scholars from the Global South will be particularly sought out and welcomed, as well as those from marginalised communities within the Global North.

All books in this series are externally peer-reviewed.

Full details of all the books in this series and of all our other publications can be found on http://www.multilingual-matters.com, or by writing to Multilingual Matters, St Nicholas House, 31–34 High Street, Bristol, BS1 2AW, UK.

NEW PERSPECTIVES ON LANGUAGE AND EDUCATION: 108

International TESOL Teachers in a Multi-Englishes Community

Mobility, On-the-Ground Realities and the Limits of Negotiability

Phan Le Ha and Osman Z. Barnawi

MULTILINGUAL MATTERS
Bristol • Jackson

DOI https://doi.org/10.21832/PHAN5478
Library of Congress Cataloging in Publication Data
A catalog record for this book is available from the Library of Congress.
Names: Phan, Le Ha, author. | Barnawi, Osman Z., author.
Title: International TESOL Teachers in a Multi-Englishes Community: Mobility, On-the-Ground Realities and the Limits of Negotiability/ Le Ha Phan, Osman Z Barnawi.
Description: Bristol, UK; Jackson, TN: Multilingual Matters, 2022. | Series: New Perspectives on Language and Education: 108 | Includes bibliographical references and index. | Summary: "This book embarks on an ever-expanding array of language, academic mobility, neoliberalism, and accompanying rich scholarly debates, with a focus on the day-to-day work experiences of international English language teachers in Saudi Arabia's higher education"— Provided by publisher.
Identifiers: LCCN 2021061243 (print) | LCCN 2021061244 (ebook) | ISBN 9781800415461 (paperback) | ISBN 9781800415478 (hardback) | ISBN 9781800415485 (pdf) | ISBN 9781800415492 (epub)
Subjects: LCSH: English teachers—Saudi Arabia. | English language—Study and teaching—Saudi Arabia.
Classification: LCC PE1068.S28 P47 2022 (print) | LCC PE1068.S28 (ebook) | DDC 428.0071/0538—dc23/eng/20220211
LC record available at https://lccn.loc.gov/2021061243
LC ebook record available at https://lccn.loc.gov/2021061244

British Library Cataloguing in Publication Data
A catalogue entry for this book is available from the British Library.

ISBN-13: 978-1-80041-547-8 (hbk)
ISBN-13: 978-1-80041-546-1 (pbk)

Multilingual Matters
UK: St Nicholas House, 31–34 High Street, Bristol, BS1 2AW, UK.
USA: Ingram, Jackson, TN, USA.

Website: www.multilingual-matters.com
Twitter: Multi_Ling_Mat
Facebook: https://www.facebook.com/multilingualmatters
Blog: www.channelviewpublications.wordpress.com

Copyright © 2022 Phan Le Ha and Osman Z. Barnawi.

All rights reserved. No part of this work may be reproduced in any form or by any means without permission in writing from the publisher.

The policy of Multilingual Matters/Channel View Publications is to use papers that are natural, renewable and recyclable products, made from wood grown in sustainable forests. In the manufacturing process of our books, and to further support our policy, preference is given to printers that have FSC and PEFC Chain of Custody certification. The FSC and/or PEFC logos will appear on those books where full certification has been granted to the printer concerned.

Typeset by Nova Techset Private Limited, Bengaluru and Chennai, India.

Early praise for *International TESOL Teachers in a Multi-Englishes Community*

'In this exciting and incredibly accessible manuscript, written consistently with an international readership in mind, authors Phan Le Ha and Osman Barnawi have produced what I see as a brilliant, regionally contextualized approach to bridging theory and practice in the "multi-Englishes" TESOL context of Saudi Arabia. Making great use of scripts of conversations between the authors for the preface and opening to the introduction, in the twelve chapters, the authors cover a comprehensive range of topics, targeting international mobility, as well as realities, practicalities, and limitations of how far new approaches influencing TESOL in the region can go. They raise critical arguments from the international scholarship, along with excerpts from a series of insightful interviews they conducted with international teachers. This book is a must-read for all TESOL researchers and practitioners interested in contexts where international teachers are the cornerstone of ideological developments and reshaping of not only TESOL theory and practice, but of the region itself'.

Jim McKinley, University College London, UK.

'The authors skillfully expose, unpack and interpret complexities of contextualized professional identity negotiations of international TESOL teachers in the broader waves and entanglements of neoliberalism, transnational mobility, globalization, hybridity, and superdiversity. This book will set the tone and serve as an inspiring example for future projects focusing on the diversity and complexity of realities and perspectives in other parts of the world'.

Ali Fuad Selvi, METU Northern Cyprus Campus, Turkey.

'All of us – nomads, immigrants, refugees, teachers, students, company executives, academics and farmers – are in flow, in motion and on the move, argues International TESOL Teachers in A Multi-Englishes Community. This is true even if physically we stay put. Methodologically innovative, scholarly grounded, and intellectually dareful, this book tells the story of this mobility, its challenges as well as its possibilities, especially how it looks like when it meets such a nice field as TESOL. It dares to ask, what does it mean to live in a time and a place that are neither neutral nor without history? At some point, especially for TESOL teachers and learners, we would not know if the *stories told in the book belong to the authors or to the reader. This is the poetic of this book, you can't put it down until the end. It is highly recommended, namely for those who are interested in that space of métissage between TESOL, mobility, historicity and negotiability'.*

Awad Ibrahim, University of Ottawa, Canada.

'*International TESOL Teachers in a Multi-Englishes Community provides a compelling analysis of sociocultural, political, and economic implications of transnational TESOL teachers working in Saudi Arabia. For those who are interested in the on-the-ground work realities of English teachers, this is a must-read book. The increasing demand of TESOL professionals in the Global South makes this exceptional account of teachers' engagement with Saudi Arabia's Higher Education system and their navigation of local tensions, challenges and demands more pressing than ever. Power, tensions, challenges, but also hope, resignation, and trust feed the multiple stories documented in this book written by two exceptional scholars who are clearly ahead of their discipline. This piece of writing provides a unique understanding of the inner workings of the international TESOL industry and makes a genuine contribution to a more politicized and ethnographically informed field of TESOL and Applied Linguistics'.*

Alfonso Del Percio, University College London, UK.

Contents

Acknowledgements		ix
Preface: Putting Curiosities in Action: An Uneasy Journey of Exploration		xi
1	International TESOL Teachers: What is Missing on the Ground?	1
2	International Teachers of English in the 'New' Middle East: Saudi Arabia in Focus	14
3	Engaging (with) *Flavors* of TESOL: Mobility, Space, Place, Neoliberalism, Multilingualism and Emotion Labor	30
4	Unpacking Mobility Drive: Geographical, Personal, Financial, Professional and More	48
5	Unpacking Often-Hidden Layers of Factors behind International Mobilities	61
6	English, ELT and Perceptions of Peers and Students	73
7	On-the-Ground Realities: From Training, Experience and Perception to Actual Classrooms	88
8	Every Teacher is Different, Every Classroom Has its Own Dynamic	104
9	Examining the (Im)mobility of African American Muslim TESOL Teachers in Saudi Arabia *Sulaiman Jenkins*	121
10	Unpacking Hardly-Ever-Revealed Emotions, Pains and Complexities	140
11	A Much-Needed Conversation with Native-English-Speaking Caucasian Teachers: Emotion Labor and Affect in Transnational Encounters *Abdullah Alshakhi and Phan Le Ha*	157

12 International TESOL Teachers Working in the Saudi 'Trust House': (Re)conceptualization of Key Constructs	180
Afterword *Ryuko Kubota*	198
References	202
Index	224

Acknowledgements

Writing the acknowledgements is often emotional, as it prompts us to recall, reflect and reconnect with a long journey leading to the arrival of this book. We are thankful to many individuals we met in the process, who kindly allowed us into their mobility journeys that brought them to Saudi Arabia, without which this book could not have been possible. We found our work continuously enriched by their nuanced life and work experience, expertise, reflections, perspectives, positionalities and emotions. Their willingness to share with us their many complicated stories, multi-faceted encounters at work, and diverse viewpoints and observations was admirable. We were inspired by the numerous on-the-ground realities faced and endured by as well as being transformed by these international TESOL teachers.

And as we were writing the Acknowledgements we knew that we were reaching the final stage of this long journey; and hence our Acknowledgements have come with joy, delight and a great sense of relief.

We are grateful to each other's trust and unconditional support since the day we started working together in the early 2010s. We are blessed that our bonding has taken us on amazing journeys. This book is a solid proof of our intellectual bonding, mutual appreciation and friendship.

We thank our families, friends and many colleagues and students who have never stopped encouraging us in this 'ambitious and rather challenging endeavor', as many have said it. Recognising how busy our colleagues are these days with endless life and work commitments, we are moved by their willingness and keen interest in reading our manuscript, engaging with our ideas, and endorsing the work. We are grateful to the kind assistance provided by Ibro Him who patiently and thoroughly went through our in-text references and list of references to ensure we have everything in order. We thank Multilingual Matters and its production team for all the support and patience.

We hope our book will be a joy to read for many years to come. Our apologies in advance if we misunderstood or did not discuss sophisticatedly enough any scholarly ideas, viewpoints or arguments cited and presented in the book. We look forward to your engagement with our work. Thank you!

Phan Le Ha and Osman Z. Barnawi

Preface
Putting Curiosities in Action: An Uneasy Journey of Exploration

Since the publication of our joint articles entitled 'From Western TESOL classroom to home practice: A case study with two "privileged" Saudi teachers' (Barnawi & Phan, 2014) and 'Where English, neoliberalism, desire and internationalization are alive and kicking: Higher education in Saudi Arabia today' (Phan & Barnawi, 2015), many colleagues have contacted us sharing their concerns about numerous problems associated with English language education in the region. Some of these colleagues are from Saudi Arabia and are pursuing their Master's and PhD in the UK, Canada, the US and Australia. Their research topics are highly relevant to our work. Some of them are international teachers of English working in Saudi Arabia and other countries across the Arabian Gulf – United Arab Emirates (UAE), Qatar, Bahrain, Kuwait and Oman. These colleagues thanked us for having written about those critical topics which have been affecting their everyday life and work in varied ways. Some of them shared with us incidents whereby their academic integrity had been pushed to the bitter end. Others expressed positive attitudes towards the rapid change taking place in the region, seeing them as playing an increasingly important role in shaping such change. Others took up apocalyptic positions. Specifically, they felt that the traditional authorities such as the ministry of education, universities, higher education bodies and teachers' unions (e.g. Kingdom of Saudi Arabia Association of Language Teachers) do not have a vision for an alternative future and at the same time no longer have the power to critique, negotiate and/or openly resist the rapid change taking place in the region. The complex accounts shared by these colleagues invited us to explore healing policies, curricula and pedagogical practices relevant to the sociocultural environment of the region.

These colleagues have given us permission to include their accounts in this book, as they felt the need to reach out to us to contribute their own insights. We are thankful for this generous permission and sense of sharing. All of this has enabled us to bring together the data we have collected through semi-structured questions and classroom observations together with the data offered to us by these colleagues. This characteristic speaks to the heart of our book – negotiations and intercultural interactions – which we now invite you to accompany.

Phan Le Ha and Osman Z. Barnawi: Epistemological Curiosities and Questioning Existing Practices

My (Phan Le Ha) long-term project on transnational higher education, language issues and the internationalization of global higher education has taken me to many countries and territories, including the Gulf region. Therefore, when I (Le-Ha, given name) received an email from Osman Barnawi, a scholar based in Saudi Arabia, asking me to collaborate on writing projects in the broad field of teaching English to speakers of other languages (TESOL), I was thrilled. Hours of engaged conversations for years on so many topics and issues have resulted in our friendship, joint publications, joint projects and joint conference presentations. This book is one such endeavor.

Our years of interactions with so many moments of joys, skepticism, wondering, curiosity and astonishment, questions and observations have taken us from one intellectual journey to another. The snapshots of our email and phone conversations below are just a few highlights. They are in no particular order of importance or priority.

#Conversation 1

Phan Le Ha: I wonder why on the one hand the media and scholars out there keep criticizing the Gulf governments for being conservative and not open to Western ideals of democracy and gender equality, for example. But, you know, on the other hand, the media also highlights the Gulf countries' excessive investments in Western forms of education and English language teaching and learning. Countries like the UAE and Saudi Arabia are repeatedly reported as leading this trend.
And I read from an Australian newspaper that Arab universities were paying millions of dollars to recruit Nobel Prize winners and top Western professors for some short-term periods so as to boost the rankings of their universities. And another article published in *Science*[1] in 2011 mentioned over 60 eminent professors, mostly based in Western institutions, involved in this kind of money-for-academic-prestige arrangement. And the endorsement of more English and English medium of instruction (EMI) in the Saudi government's 2030 Vision, etc. All this has made me wonder how

	comfortably so-called Western forms of education and research as well as 'the idea of Western superiority' have secured a place in this often-perceived-to-be-the-most-conservative region in the world. How has the ideology of 'the West is the best' coupled with an 'English-only' mentality penetrated the policies, curricula, pedagogies and practices of higher education (HE) bodies in the Arabian Gulf countries? What are the roles of authorities such as policy makers, university administrators, educators and researchers in the region?
Osman Barnawi:	Very interesting questions, Le-Ha! You won't believe it if I tell you how governments in the Arabian Gulf region have been deliberately internationalizing their HE institutions by adopting EMI policies, attracting top international institutions to operate college campuses, franchising their academic programs, and aligning their vision/mission statements with international standards. The education market of the Arabian Gulf countries is packed with international institutions today. Also, within a very short period of time the Saudi government has invited over 37 international institutions like Lincoln College International, Laureate, Niagara College and Mondragon to operate college campuses in the country.
Phan Le Ha:	Well, how do governments in the region perceive higher education then? On what basis do they want to build the future of their own nations?
Osman Barnawi:	What is clear to me so far is that it is all through the Englishization of HE. The government wants people to have access to global knowledge, technology, information and job opportunities, while at the same time maintaining Islamic values, local traditions and culture in the HE setting.
Phan Le Ha:	If it is true that Saudi Arabia is very conservative, where boys and girls are segregated throughout the entire education system, and Islamic values and cultural traditions are strictly maintained in the HE curricula, then I wonder how international teachers working in Saudi Arabia interpret and negotiate such educational, sociocultural and religious demands in their respective institutions? [*As we were finalizing this book, a new policy recently introduced in Saudi Arabia has allowed female teachers to teach male students at the primary level*].[2]

Osman Barnawi: Well, I think these questions need further exploration. Did you know that the number of international English language teachers in Saudi HE colleges and universities is higher than that of Saudis? And that the vast majority of these teachers are non-native English-speaking teachers!!

Phan Le Ha: Very interesting to hear such information. But why are there more non-native English-speaking teachers employed in Saudi Arabia? Published scholarship has criticized the Gulf region for submitting to and promoting native-speakerism, as we both know. Oh well, we must study this phenomenon. It must be a lot more complex than just some generalizations about the region and its culture and religion, and so on and so forth.

Osman Barnawi: Indeed, there's so much going on on the ground that has hardly been examined.

#Conversation 2

Osman Barnawi: By the way, do you know any qualified teachers of English whom you could recommend to me? We're short of teachers because of the high turnover here. A lot of them are in SA for money, and so if any other institutions pay them higher, they'll go. This is my headache.

Phan Le Ha: So what information should I give potential candidates then?

Osman Barnawi: That we offer very competitive and attractive packages, as long as they're qualified. They get free housing and medical insurance plus lots of paid leave and high salaries.

Phan Le Ha: Oh I'd love to join you THEN. Would you employ me? But who knows, I may leave after a few months, hahahahahahaha ...

Both laughed out loud. Hmm. Ahhh. Many international teachers do actually fall into the general stereotype about being 'gold diggers' and 'going to SA for money.' There must be more to this classic generalization. Le-Ha kept wondering, while Barnawi's headache continued ...

#Conversation 3

Phan Le Ha: While collecting data for my transnational higher education project,[3] I came across a lot of media coverage of the Colleges of Excellence Project initiated by the Saudi government. I'd like to study this and hope you can help me.

Barnawi:	Of course I'd be very keen to join you. Many problems with the COE project, I think.
Phan Le Ha:	I wonder about the motives of those international HE providers involved in the COE project, and if there might be any on-the-ground politics of this transnationalization act. I can't wait to study this. We will need to draw on Arabic and English sources.
Barnawi:	We've been talking among ourselves about this COE project for months now. Many Saudi academics are not happy. Many students are not at all ready with all this EMI (English as medium of instruction) hype in the country. We all suffer.

This very COE idea resulted in our joint publication, 'Where English, neoliberalism, desire and internationalization are alive and kicking: Higher education in Saudi Arabia today' (Phan & Barnawi, 2015).

#Conversation 4

Barnawi:	Have you read the news about our Vision 2030 yet? I can't wait to tell you about it.
Phan Le Ha:	Yes yes yes. I have seen the whole world covering it.
Barnawi:	Unbelievable. We're still in shock, and happy at the same time. Wow, the whole country's gonna change drastically very soon now.
Phan Le Ha:	What changes are you expecting?
Barnawi:	Everything.
Phan Le Ha:	Women driving, finally?

See our recent joint publication, 'Saudi women are finally allowed to sit behind the wheel: Initial responses from TESOL classrooms' (Barnawi & Phan, 2020).

#Conversation 5 (2019): 'Riyadh Season this October – the spectacular comes to the spectacle'

Phan Le Ha:	Hey, is your Facebook bombarded with ad after ad about the '*Riyadh Season this October*'? It looks like the whole world is gathering in Riyadh for all kinds of shows, entertainments and parties. Is this for real?
Barnawi:	Oh yes, 100% real. This is real Saudi Arabia. Don't trust Western media.
Phan Le Ha:	Why didn't you tell me in advance? I could have changed my flight so I wouldn't miss the Riyadh spectacle.
Barnawi:	Don't worry, more and more events like this are coming.

As we were finalizing the manuscript, constant advertisements about upcoming concerts and entertainment shows that would take place in

October 2019 in Riyadh, the capital city of the Kingdom of Saudi Arabia, were constantly popping up on our Facebook pages. Notably, the huge news about the very first foreign band – which is also the current top K-Pop band from South Korea, BTS – performing in Riyadh had been attracting so much media coverage as well as debates on the internet regarding the band's giving in to the conservative society. What is more, hip-hop dancers, rock bands, magicians and entertainers from everywhere would also be coming to Riyadh in October to mark the Kingdom's opening up to the world through this series of landmark cultural and music events. Indeed, for the first time in the history of Saudi Arabia, events of this nature would finally come true. '*Riyadh Season this October – the spectacular comes to the spectacle*' – the advertisement on social media seemed more and more intensified and energized.

During the pandemic years of 2020 and 2021, there have been constant announcements from various authorities in Saudi Arabia about its higher education sector heading towards full privatization in the next 24 months. What is more, English will be introduced as the medium of instruction at primary level in no time, according to the latest mandate from the government. Demand for English and English-medium instruction will be rocket high with no limit. Should we be happy or concerned or both?

The Kingdom has been transforming fast and profoundly, so fast and profoundly that no serious scholars could afford not to take such transformations seriously and on complex terms in their work and scholarly inquiries. We are among such scholars. These transformations have followed our research and scholarship. This current book is a result of our long-term joint scholarly endeavor, which we hope you will enjoy reading.

Notes

(1) See https://science.sciencemag.org/content/334/6061/1344 (accessed 10 October 2019).
(2) See https://www.harpersbazaararabia.com/people/news/women-can-teach-boys-in-saudi-arabia (accessed 10 October 2019).
(3) Phan, L.H. (2017).

1 International TESOL Teachers: What is Missing on the Ground?

> **A Vignette**
>
> I met several teachers of English at an event held in the UK a few years ago. Among these teachers were Jane and Patrick (pseudonyms), who had been teaching English in Saudi Arabia and were back in the UK for different reasons. I told them about my research with international teachers of English in the Gulf, and they then shared with me their experiences working in Saudi Arabia. I took notes as the conversation was taking place as if it were our direct speech.
>
> Le-Ha: How long did you work in Saudi Arabia?
> Jane: I couldn't last long there. Only less than a year. I couldn't stay any longer. More than enough. It's draining and I'm still feeling that. So I just left. I basically walked away.
> Le-Ha: When did you return?
> Jane: Just last week.
> Le-Ha: What has made your experience so unpleasant and unbearable?
> Jane: It's students who are so lazy and have a great sense of entitlement. They are paid to go to university and they just don't care. So why do you care when they have that attitude? They come late, they sleep in class, they leave when someone calls, they don't do homework or they turn in very poor quality work. And their government gives a lot of benefits, but they just don't seem to care. They have servants at home. They don't want to work. At the end I found myself running after them to serve their needs that they don't even recognize. I couldn't convince myself any longer. I know many others who just teach, collect the benefits and couldn't care less. But it's not me. I didn't go there to collect money. I did have a good reason. I wanted to help students to learn English and with my training and expertise I thought I would be able to

	make a contribution. But I was wrong. They didn't need me. Their government wants them to learn English, but they simply don't care. I saw no reason why I should stay. And as you see now, I'm applying for jobs everywhere and hope to get one soon. I don't mind teaching in any language centers here. I just want to be useful.
Le-Ha:	*How about you, Patrick?*
Patrick:	*It's the same with me. The only difference is that I've not left the place yet. I'm still under contract but I'm here for a job interview and hopefully I'll get it, so I can finally move. I've been wanting to move for about two years now but I haven't found a better job in other places yet.*
Le-Ha:	*How long have you been teaching in Saudi Arabia?*
Patrick:	*About five years now. Things are not always bad, but what Jane has said about the students remains more or less unchanged over time, although I have only taught male Saudis and Jane taught female Saudis. You do have a few driven students from time to time but they are rare. You don't usually feel satisfied as a teacher because you kind of get the feeling that your students don't really learn and that you're helpless. You kind of find it uncomfortable too because you're paid a fat salary. At times I ask myself if it is necessary to have foreign teachers like us in Saudi Arabia. Don't get me wrong. Before going there, I had been teaching in some European countries and my salary wasn't high or anything like that, but I felt that the students did learn something and that English was actually necessary and that learning English was relevant. But in Saudi Arabia, I'm not sure if they really need English that much.*

What Jane and Patrick shared with me reminds me of the many conversations I've had with other international teachers as well as with Saudi teachers of English. In spite of the fever for English at all levels, ELT in Saudi Arabia seems to have so many problems. Yet, hundreds of international teachers come and go. Many don't want to leave. Many have returned and stayed, while others have left in anger and depression. ...

    A few years have passed since I met Jane and Patrick. And here I am in Saudi Arabia meeting with many English language teachers of different backgrounds. Everyone has a unique story and mixed emotions. Above all, they are spending so much time talking to me, knowing that I am interested and paying attention. I find myself deeply grateful. I know it's never easy for anyone to reveal difficult thoughts, feelings and seemingly politically incorrect opinions and perceptions ... I wish I could stay longer to visit female colleges and speak to international TESOL teachers teaching female Saudi students ... Next time, I promise myself ... (Phan Le Ha, Field notes)

These days there are millions of users of English in the Middle East countries, including Saudi Arabia. The heavy presence of expatriates in the region has resulted in English being used as a lingua franca, especially in countries like the UAE, Qatar, Bahrain and Saudi Arabia. English is used in industrial companies, shopping centers, restaurants, airports, hotels, hospitals and official local newspapers, to name just a few. It is also taught as a core subject in kindergarten, primary schools and secondary schools in these countries. Additionally, as we have argued elsewhere (Phan & Barnawi, 2015), governments in the Arabian Gulf countries have

> at various levels, adopted an English medium of instruction policy, imported English medium educational and training products and services, franchized international programs, offered generous financial support and incentives to overseas institutions to establish branch campuses locally, and undertook major initiatives worth billions of dollars to reform and internationalize their HE systems. (Phan & Barnawi, 2015: 548)

A report released by the ICEF Monitor (International Consultants for Education and Fairs) in 2016 details that:

- The United Arab Emirates is the global leader in English-medium school enrolment: 45,074 students are now enrolled in 548 international schools in the Emirates, a significant lead over Saudi Arabia's second-largest enrolment of 260,989.
- More broadly, ISC calculates that more than 4.3 million students are now being educated at over 8200 international schools worldwide; by 2026, enrolment is projected to reach 8.7 million.
- This has become an increasingly important recruitment channel for universities as nearly all students enrolled in English-medium K-12 schools intend to pursue undergraduate studies abroad.[1]

The implications of this wholehearted promotion of English in the Middle East countries, including Saudi Arabia and the UAE, are summarized by Al-Issa (2011) as follows:

> This has taken the shape of recruiting and hiring foreign ELT expertise to formulate English language and ELT education policies pertinent to their respective contexts, writing and designing new textbooks and materials, introducing state-of the-art educational technology into ELT, allocating more ELT time on the national curriculum, re-designing the existing initial and in-service teacher training and education programs, and establishing public and private colleges and universities, which offer a General Foundation Program (GFP) in which English language is a core subject, and teaching science-based subjects through English. (Al-Issa, 2011: 63–64)

As will be seen in concrete terms in the subsequent chapters, the presence of international TESOL (teaching English to speakers of other languages) teachers of hugely different backgrounds in the Gulf region in general and in Saudi Arabia in particular means that complex packages of mindsets, accents, linguistic and sociolinguistic resources, sociocultures, ideologies and speakers' repertoires and multiple identities are operating and existing there. Moving to Saudi Arabia, they have taken their languages, knowledge, pedagogies, practices, experiences, aspirations, expectations and personal and cultural belongings as well as pre-assumptions and stereotypes with them. They may also have been under pressure to accommodate to the new workplace and the host society. Under these conditions, these teachers may find that what works well in their home countries and/or in other places that they have been may not work well in the host country. Thus, they have to constantly negotiate and construct, deconstruct and co-construct their positionalities, identities and professional selves in order to be legitimate members of the host country.

International TESOL Teachers: What is Missing in the Picture?

To date, most of the literature on international language teachers' negotiations and intercultural interactions in the sphere of English language teaching (ELT) and TESOL have paid significant attention to Western-trained TESOL teachers' and would-be teachers' experiences in the English-speaking West (Alshakhi & Phan, 2020; Brutt-Griffler & Samimy, 1999; Chowdhury & Phan, 2014; Ilieva, 2010; Ilieva & Waterstone, 2013; Ilieva *et al.*, 2015; Inoue & Stracke, 2013; Liu, 1998; Park, 2013, 2018; Pavlenko, 2003; Phan, 2008) and to Western-trained TESOL teachers working in their home countries (Barnawi & Phan, 2014; Chowdhury, 2003; Le & Phan, 2013; Menard-Warwick, 2014; Pham, 2004). Scholars have also examined how teachers of English from the English-speaking West perceive, negotiate and enact their values and pedagogies while teaching in other countries (Adamson, 2004; Alshakhi & Phan, 2020; Block, 2007; Bright & Phan, 2011; Clarke, 2008; Hartse & Jiang, 2015; Phan, 2016; Widin, 2010). This body of literature is growing fast.

Under the intersection and entanglement of mobility, multinationalism, multiculturalism and multilingualism in TESOL and applied linguistics, scholars have critically examined the multilayers of international language teachers' negotiations and intercultural interactions in a wide range of contexts in relation to the concepts of hybridity, fluidity and multiplicity (McNamara, 2011; Menard-Warwick, 2014; Pennycook, 2010; Phan, 2008). As an example, building on two years' data (2005 and 2006), including interviews and classroom observations at a northern Chilean university and at numerous northern Californian community colleges and schools, Menard-Warwick (2014) explores how and in what ways both English as a foreign language (EFL) and English as a second language (ESL) teachers' lives, identities, ideologies and pedagogies are 'shaped by the historical contexts in which they are immersed' (Menard-Warwick, 2014: 2). Through comparative analysis, Menard-Warwick (2014) looks at the production of English language discourse in the 'faultlines,' both geographically and metaphorically. 'Discursive faultlines' in this study were described as pedagogical challenges and cultural differences or misunderstandings occurring in classroom interactions while teaching in international contexts (Kramsch, 1993; Menard-Warwick, 2009). The findings of this study demonstrate that time, place and space play crucial roles in the ways in which ESL and EFL teachers negotiate and construct their identities as well as make sense of their classroom pedagogical decisions.

The values allocated to the English language in a certain context (e.g. as a language of economic, linguistic and cultural capital, or the language of suffering and opportunities, etc.) always influence teachers' perceptions and status. While teachers in the case of Menard-Warwick (2014) see their linguistic capital as a way of belonging to 'the elite' in Chile and to the 'mainstream' in California in the USA, the Western-trained Vietnamese English teachers in Phan (2008) see themselves as being 'broad-minded' but with a strong sense of belonging to Vietnam as their homeland while exercising their newly acquired status as Western-trained teachers of English with an international stature.

In our earlier work, 'From Western TESOL classrooms to home practice: A case study with two privileged Saudi teachers' (Barnawi & Phan, 2014), for instance, we examined issues of knowledge construction, pedagogy and training in Western TESOL programs and their impacts on TESOL teachers' pedagogical decisions. Locating the study against the backdrop of some persistent claims that Western-trained academics may not be aware of the cultural politics of English and TESOL and hence tend to be (uncritical) carriers of Western ideas, we looked at 'two Saudi TESOL teachers' pedagogical enactments in their home teaching contexts after returning from their Western-based TESOL programmes' (Barnawi & Phan, 2014: 259). The findings of our study show that 'these teachers have never been passive in the entire process nor have they been naïve about the cultural politics of TESOL'. Capitalizing on their given privileged status as TESOL teachers in Saudi Arabia, 'they have appeared to proactively take advantage of being trained in the West to teach effectively ... with awareness and with a strong sense of agency.' We argue that this very aspect of agency invites further critical scrutiny in the professional literature. We further contend that in order 'to move beyond the mindset that positions periphery teachers at the receiving end of Western TESOL training and as the recipient of Western TESOL pedagogical experiments, it is no longer valid to assume the enlightening and educating role of such training' (Barnawi & Phan, 2014). A recent study by Lin and Shi (2021) on the identity construction of two Western-trained Taiwanese TESOL instructors further shows the importance of teacher agency in engaging with their training to make informed decisions about their classroom pedagogies. These instructors' translingual identity and professional legitimacy challenge the rigid native versus non-native and West versus non-West binaries often found in TESOL discourses.

To add further to the vast literature in TESOL regarding teacher identity and negotiation of values and pedagogies, the field has also seen many studies examining how native-English-speaking teachers of English from the English-speaking West perceive, negotiate and enact their values and pedagogies while teaching in non-English-dominant countries (Adamson, 2004; Block, 2007; Bright & Phan, 2011; Clarke, 2008; Hartse & Jiang, 2015; Phan, 2016; Widin, 2010). Drawing on their study with Western native-English-speaking teachers teaching English in Vietnam, Bright and Phan (2011) show how the discourses of colonialism still pervade and shape much of these teachers' ideology and practice, evident in the ways in which they position themselves, their colleagues and their students in relation to English and ELT. They found that 'these teacher participants continue to position themselves in ways that are problematic, precluding relationships with foreign colleagues and students that are based on respect and equality' (Bright & Phan, 2011: 116). Throughout this study, they explore that 'this perceived superiority was constructed in a variety of ways, from their status as "owners" of the English language, from the status of English as a de facto lingua franca, and from their knowledge and ownership of Western culture and pedagogy' (Bright & Phan, 2011: 131). Bright and Phan (2011) argue for the importance of incorporating critical dialogue and reflection in TESOL teacher training courses in order to develop a counter-discourse of Western hegemony among teachers. As they argue, it is a must that teachers can 'acknowledge the political implications of their work, understand the ways that they are positioned by the dominant discourses of English, and work towards the creation of new identities that are based on equality, inclusiveness, respect and an understanding of the complexity of all those we encounter' (Bright & Phan, 2011: 133).

Recent years have seen new research into international TESOL teachers working in so-called Global South contexts, such as Hillman *et al.* (2021) for Qatar, Hopkyns (2020) for the UAE, Alshakhi and Phan (2020) and Jenkins (2019) for Saudi Arabia, Phan (2017) and Hickey (2018) for Thailand, Kostogriz and Bonar (2019) and Poole (2019, 2021) for China, and Bunnell and Poole (2021) for China and the Middle East. These new studies have all engaged critically with various theories on mobility/ies, English, teacher identity and the internationalization of education, while providing in-depth contextualization of the very specific sites where the studies took place. They have identified, highlighted and discussed often-overlooked aspects of expatriate mobility, which include precarity and unpleasant experiences resulting from certain social class, racial, ethnic, religious and linguistic stereotypes. These studies have also discussed in what ways certain mobilities among these expatriate teachers seem to hinder their future mobilities as well as confine their future plans within limited options.

What we have discussed so far has confirmed the importance of examining international language teachers' on-the-ground life and work realities as they move to other countries to teach English or to teach in the medium of English. These teachers' negotiations and intercultural interactions in these contexts are still very much under-researched. By international English language teachers, in this book we refer to native-English-speaking teachers, non-native English-speaking teachers, and teachers who speak English as an international language, as an additional language, who come from any country and territory worldwide, from the conventional English-speaking Western countries like the USA, the UK, Australia, Canada and New Zealand to other English-dominant contexts like Nigeria, South Africa and Singapore, and to countries where English is only a foreign language like China, Vietnam and Oman. Specifically, absent from the existing literature are in-depth accounts of on-the-ground realities presented to, experienced and faced by international TESOL teachers of different backgrounds teaching English in non-English dominant contexts (Saudi Arabia, in the case of our book). In this very context, teaching and learning 'may represent many cultures that come together to create a vibrant learning which will embark on a journey of discovery and adventures' (Medina-Lopez-Portillo, 2014: 330–331), as every teacher engages in negotiations and intercultural interactions.

Teachers as Actors within Contradictory Policy Narratives in Saudi Arabia

As one of us observes elsewhere (Barnawi, 2018), within Saudi Arabia's current neoliberal English education policy direction,

> for young Saudis, dressing like Westerners in the streets with different haircuts or using English expressions while conversing in Arabic are seen as effective strategies for becoming competent English users. Ironically, however, their use of these 'technologies of the self' (Foucault, 1997) in learning English got them arrested by the moral police. (Barnawi, 2018: 68)

At the same time, this very neoliberal English education policy does not seem to be able to safeguard educational initiatives that are considered to be at odds with dominant Saudi cultural and religious values, as Barnawi (2018) shows in the example below:

> A branch of a Canadian-based college called Lincoln College, which operates a female campus in a conservative rural area in the northern region of Saudi Arabia called Al-Afl aj, was completely shut down owing to some socio-cultural and religious inappropriacies in its academic programmes that were reported by the local community to the governor of the Technical and Vocational Training Colleges and Institutes. (Barnawi, 2018: 68)

The former incident suggests that, '[g]uided by their pragmatic and instrumental positions, [young Saudis] are deliberately adopting Western culture through their dress codes and hairstyles, and by listening to hip-hop music, on the grounds that such a pragmatic usage of English will enhance their linguistic and intercultural competency simultaneously' (Barnawi, 2018: 67). On the contrary, the latter incident shows that ELT and its associated products, goods and services have been contested and negotiated by Saudi society and its students within their own capacities. In this very context, one can even say that '[Saudi students] are creating alternative discussions to the Western model of education and destabilising the hegemony of the West in the country' (Barnawi, 2018: 69).

We argue that, similar to other countries in the Arabian Gulf (e.g. Oman, the UAE and Bahrain), the current neoliberal English education policy direction in the Kingdom of Saudi Arabia (KSA) opens and restricts as well as creates and closes vibrant language teaching and learning opportunities and spaces (see also Phan, 2017; Phan & Barnawi, 2015). Indeed, policy and reform, regardless of how good and sophisticated, are always subjected to complex and contradictory social norms, values and changing aspirations in society. In the same vein, teachers of English in Saudi Arabia, local or international, often find themselves caught up in these multiple competing policy narratives, practices and interpretations, which have profound professional and personal implications. Likewise, the domain of ELT and TESOL is rarely simple and straightforward. For decades, scholarship on ELT and TESOL has been evoked and complicated by constant debates over the commercialization and cultural politics of English and its underlying manifestations including policy, curriculum, pedagogy, methodology, teacher and learner identity, native versus non-native teachers, and power relations. Teachers of English have a tough job as they navigate the above issues, problems and prospects.

So, 'what does it mean for [international TESOL] teachers to be at the heart of language policy [in the Saudi HE context]?' (Barnawi, 2021; Brown, 2010: 310; Hillman *et al.*, 2021; see also Pavlenko, 2008: 275). In the remaining chapters, we invite you to engage with complex, diverse and critical observations, perceptions and experiences shared by many international teachers participating in the several studies included in this book. These teachers have been generous in providing us with insights into the various negotiating strategies/options/improvisations they employed and justified to steer potentially conflicting English language teaching and practices in the wider spaces of Saudi higher education.

Navigating and Making Sense of On-the-Ground Reality Observations, Experiences and Interactions: TESOL Teachers in a Transnational World

Transnationalism, broadly speaking, 'refers to multiple ties, interactions, and activities that connect people, institutions, and cultural practices across the borders of nation-states' (Barnawi & Ahmed, 2021: 2; see also Vertovec, 1999, 2009). Although the field of TESOL has long been transnational, transnationalism in relation to TESOL has only begun to gain scholarly attention over the past two decades (e.g. De Fina & Perrino, 2013; Duff, 2015; Phan, 2008, 2016; You, 2018). In today's age of mobility (i.e. mobility of people, languages, ideas, knowledge and cultures), transnationalism activities, as manifestations of globalization and neoliberal free market ideologies, among others, operate in complex ways in different geographical locations. As Rizvi and Choo (2020) succinctly capture:

> globalization has given rise to unprecedented levels of mobility of people and ideas across national borders, [and] it has also drawn attention to the growing levels of cultural diversity in most communities, raising the possibilities of both cultural exchange and conflict. (Rizvi & Choo, 2020: 2)

We examine the mobility of international TESOL teachers, with different epistemological, ideological, linguistic, cultural and educational backgrounds, to teach EFL in Saudi Arabia, a less studied site. We look into how this very diverse group of teachers negotiate and (co)-construct their identities in their everyday practices and in relation to their work surroundings, whereby their pedagogical decisions and classroom interactions are also conditioned by contextual factors and collectively play important roles in shaping their professional identities (Jain *et al.*, 2021; Motha *et al.*, 2012; Toom, 2019). Likewise, we pay attention to the transnational aspects influencing these teachers' experiences as well as numerous encounters that are enabled and challenged by transnationalism, as vividly shown in Jain *et al.*'s (2021) recent edited volume on transnational identities and practices in ELT through the voices of practitioners in the field. Among these voices are Wahyudi (2021), speaking from the standpoint of a transnationally trained Indonesian TESOL scholar-practitioner returning home, and Savski (2021), who became a TESOL teacher in Thailand rather 'incidentally', following more of a personal call than a professional one. Built further on this body of work, we examine the multiple accounts from international TESOL teachers working in Saudi Arabia to understand how they negotiate and transcend boundaries while engaging with their respective institutions through teaching, researching and assuming administrative tasks. In light of the existing literature, we refer to international TESOL teachers and transnational TESOL teachers interchangeably.

While investigating how they enact their multiple professional roles and perform and construct their transnational identities in a context like Saudi Arabia that has its own expectations and requirements, we also aim to capture how certain transnational teachers feel that they are welcomed and/or marginalized on the basis of their race, color, accents, nationalities, religions and place of origin – something along the lines of Kubota's (2020) interrogation of what she calls 'epistemological racism' in language education, sociolinguistics and applied linguistics. Through detailed analysis of these teachers' lived experiences, we identify and theorize how the aforementioned pressing issues reoccur and are manifest in complex ways.

We also closely examine how students resist and/or stigmatize the linguistic repertoires of some teachers as unsophisticated or inappropriate, phenomena that are called raciolinguistic ideologies. These phenomena are viewed as 'subscription to monoglossic language ideologies, in which powerful allegiances to imagined linguistic norms persist regardless of whether anyone actually adheres to those norms in practice' (Flores & Rosa, 2015: 151). As an illustration:

> a raciolinguistic perspective seeks to understand how the white gaze is attached both to a speaking subject who engages in the idealized linguistic practices of whiteness and to a listening subject who hears and interprets the linguistic practices of language-minoritized populations as deviant based on their racial positioning in society as opposed to any objective characteristics of their language use. (Flores & Rosa, 2015: 151)

We engage with new scholarship on raciolinguistic ideologies both directly and indirectly, as shown in Chapter 9 which features writing from our guest, Sulaiman Jenkins, who is also an informant in our study. In this chapter, we (Jenkins, Phan and Barnawi) exemplify how raciolinguistic ideologies are produced and perpetuated, thereby contributing to racial and institutional tensions that in turn cause troubled emotions and struggles that individuals have to shoulder in order to get by and perform their professional duties. At the same time, we further discuss varied manifestations of raciolinguistic ideologies in subsequent chapters to add more insights to Jenkins' account.

We also engage with the scholarship on emotion, affect and emotion labor that has recently received much scholarly attention among TESOL and language education scholars. A significant body of work on emotion labor in language teaching has been produced by Sarah Benesch (2017, 2019, 2020). Drawing on prior work from others such as Ahmed (2004) and Hochschild (1979, 1983), Benesch sees emotion labor as 'the struggle between workplace feeling rules [policies] ... and employees' prior training and/or beliefs about appropriate workplace conduct' (Benesch, 2017: 1). Emotion labor is as much a social and cultural construct as it is an ideological and inter-individual and inter-personal domain, where power plays out (see Chapter 3 for a detailed theoretical discussion). Through 'different spheres of power: institutional, professional, and individual' (Benesch, 2017: vi), we show here and there in the book how international teachers in different Saudi HE institutions navigate institutional as well as classroom pedagogical tensions in their everyday practices, and the emotion labor they bear and exhibit, whether implicitly or explicitly. We have dedicated one chapter to examining in depth this aspect of transnational mobilities with a focus on the emotion labor of native-English-speaking Western teachers teaching at a Saudi university.

At the same time, the very presence of international teachers in Saudi Arabia means that many cultural elements, including values, attitudes, types of behavior and linguistic as well as ideological resources are represented and are constantly interacting 'to create a vibrant learning community' (Medina-López-Portillo, 2014: 330). In this regard, we have noticed that the ways in which the teacher participants negotiated their intellectual resources and intercultural competences with different parties, including between/within their peers (e.g. American-American or Indian, American and Malaysian), students and institutions in the KSA were unpredictable, complex and multilayered. Such negotiations, whether implicitly, explicitly, strategically or organically, entail the negotiation of academic workplace conditions and self and identity negotiation. They can be conceptualized as 'critical interculturality' and 'a never-ending process' (Li & Dervin, 2018: 13). Seen in this manner, 'individuals do not approach every interaction as a new encounter but rather, on the level of lived experience, draw upon frames of reference (experiences and identities) in order to (re)negotiate the familiar, new and unexpected' (Poole, 2019: 61).

Methodological Compass and Inspirations

The journey of international TESOL teachers in Saudi Arabia, which is full of discovery, opportunities, investment and adventures, by and large, requires an instrument containing a magnetized pointer which vividly captures multiple directions, on-the-ground realities, identities, ideologies and running themes. The data informing our book, hence, come from in-depth qualitative data collected from multiple sources allowing for 'concrete and complex illustrations' (Wolcott, 1994: 364). The rich qualitative data also offer us a holistic understanding of the ways in which international English language teachers from different backgrounds working in Saudi Arabia position themselves, negotiate, interact, make sense of their classroom pedagogies, and validate their values and perspectives in their day-to-day interactions (Creswell, 2007, 2018; Merriam, 1998; Stake, 1995).

Specifically, this book is first and foremost inspired by the findings of a major qualitative research study conducted by both authors (Phan Le Ha and Osman Barnawi) over a period of four years in Saudi Arabia. The data were gathered first through an open-ended survey, followed by classroom observations and then semi-structured interviews with international TESOL teachers teaching at several universities and colleges across Saudi Arabia, all of which were conducted between 2013 and 2017. The survey encompasses three major themes: (i) participants' educational background and experiences as well as their reasons for moving to the KSA to teach English; (ii) how they see the status of the English language in the KSA and how they position themselves within the Saudi context; and (iii) how they negotiate, interact, make sense of their classroom pedagogies, and validate their values, experiences and perspectives in their day-to-day interactions. More than 200 teachers took part in the survey, of whom 48 completed all the sections in the survey, while the rest completed only parts of it, mostly on themes (i) and (ii). In the survey we also asked if they would be willing to be interviewed to help the researchers obtain further insights into their professional experiences, as well as to have their classes observed by one of the researchers. Most of them agreed to be interviewed, but only six teachers agreed for their classes to be observed. To ensure confidentiality, we have used pseudonyms for all of the participants and universities/colleges, as well as the region of the KSA where we collected our data.

All the interviews and semester-long classroom observations were conducted between 2013 and 2017 by one of us (Barnawi), as the other researcher (Phan Le Ha) could not travel to Saudi Arabia during this period. The interviews focused in particular on the themes emerging from the answers the teachers gave in the survey. In some interviews, the participants also told us about other teachers' experiences, both pleasant and unpleasant. Prior to the classroom observations with these six teachers, Barnawi explained to the students in Arabic the purpose of his presence in their classrooms and obtained the consent of each student in their respective classrooms. Informed by our earlier research which also employed classroom observations for data collection (Barnawi & Phan, 2014), all the classroom observations in this study started in Weeks 3 and 4 of the spring or autumn terms to ensure that 'the learners were familiar with the purpose of the researcher's presence, and also with their teachers and their classroom teaching styles' (Barnawi & Phan, 2014: 266). Importantly, in order to ensure that examinations or other forms of summative assessment practices were not being observed, Barnawi collected the teaching schedules of the respective teachers in advance and then scheduled classroom observations accordingly.

It is important to note that because a co-education system does not exist in the KSA, only the classrooms of male teachers were observed. It is also worthy of note that, although the students in this study were homogeneous (all Saudis), their teachers were from different cultural and linguistic backgrounds. Hence, the study of variations in teaching and learning strategies, negotiations, classroom interactions and student–teacher relations were crucial in developing a nuanced understanding of negotiation and intercultural interactions of international TESOL teaching in the Saudi context (Burton & Robinson, 1999; Coleman, 1997). Throughout the course of the classroom observations, the second author (Barnawi) focused mainly on the pedagogical strategies, as set out in the aims of the study, employed by each teacher in order to 'negotiate learning, understanding, and cross-cultural adjustment' (Crabtree & Sapp, 2004: 107). He also took detailed notes and then developed these notes into field notes after each observation (Menard-Warwick, 2014; Watson-Gegeo, 1988).

Then, building on the data obtained from the classroom observations, both researchers (Phan and Barnawi) developed specific questions for the individual follow-up interviews with each of the six participants so as to elicit further information centered on the teaching strategies they each used and the pedagogical assumptions behind their practices. Barnawi interviewed each teacher two to three times in response to the data that emerged from the classroom observations. The individual interviews with the teachers covered three main areas: (i) the teachers' experiences as international TESOL teachers in Saudi Arabia; (ii) their classroom pedagogies and the underlying assumptions behind these practices; and (iii) cross-cultural issues and classroom interactions that the teachers noticed, brought up and experienced. All the interviews were audio-recorded and transcribed verbatim. Each interview lasted between two and two and a half hours. It is important to acknowledge that one of the major limitations of these classroom observations and interviews was the absence of students' views as well as classroom accounts of international female TESOL teachers. Only one female teacher from the USA participated, while the rest were male. Through our own observations and through conversations with many teachers teaching in Saudi Arabia, we could see that Saudi female teachers as well as international female teachers generally would not participate in studies conducted by male researchers because of religious restrictions and norms regarding gender relations and the role of women in society. We therefore have developed our follow-up project whereby one of us, Phan (female), will directly invite female TESOL teachers and female students to participate. We hope to share the outcomes of this project in a future publication.

Another source of data discussed in this book includes selective findings from a multi-site, multi-year qualitative research study that Phan Le Ha conducted with TESOL teachers teaching in global contexts, including Saudi Arabia. What is more, with their permission, we incorporated in several chapters anecdotes and accounts brought to us by international TESOL teachers who contacted us after having read our publications on Saudi Arabia (Barnawi & Phan, 2014; Phan & Barnawi, 2015). Some of these teachers offered to be interviewed and to respond to any questions we might have with regard to their teaching experiences in the Gulf region more broadly. To ensure confidentiality, we have used pseudonyms for all these teachers, and any other teachers and universities/colleges mentioned in our correspondence.

We have also created two special chapters in the book (Chapters 9 and 11), to feature two separate projects on international TESOL teachers in Saudi Arabia carried out by other colleagues (Sulaiman Jenkins and Abdullah Alshakhi, respectively) in collaboration with us. The outcomes of these two projects have already been published in two different journals, and we have sought permission to feature them in this book in order to offer a holistic picture of international TESOL professionals in Saudi Arabian higher education. This picture unfolds in greater depth in the chapters that follow.

Note

(1) See http://monitor.icef.com/

2 International Teachers of English in the 'New' Middle East: Saudi Arabia in Focus

Islam, Terror, English

إِنَّ الدِّينَ عِندَ اللَّهِ الْإِسْلَامُ ۗ....(19)[1]

The term Islam in Arabic means 'سلام', i.e. 'peace' in English. The actual religion in terms of the God is Islam – submission to his will. Islam is a religious practice revealed by the Prophet Mohammed Peace Be Upon Him since 1816 (Cook *et al.*, 2010). Central to this notion of Islam is 'peace' with the 'self' and the 'other'. The name of Islam is not attached to a particular ethnic group or society, nor is it related to a certain time or place. Instead, it is related 'to the central ideas of the religion' (Nasr, 2004). Today, Islam is considered to be the second largest religion in the world, after Christianity. According to a 2014 report released by the Pew Research Center,[2] there are 1.6 billion Muslims in the world, and this number is growing fast, especially across Europe and North America. It is expected that the number of Muslims will equal the number of Christians by 2050.[3]

At the same time, however, several acts of violence in the name of Islam and its faith, including suicide bombings, hijacks, kidnappings, bomb threats, the 9/11 attacks, Boko Haram attacks and ISIS attacks (Islamic States of Iraq and Syria) and the like, have put Muslim communities at the front line of global cultural, religious and sociopolitical debates. Although some researchers have offered a chronological list of violent acts performed by extremist Muslims from the 1980s to the present (e.g. Matthes *et al.*, 2020; Reynie, 2021), it was not until the late 1990s that the ideological formation of Islamophobia began to emerge in the global international discourse, including media outlets, according to the Center for Race and Gender at the University of California, Berkeley[4] and studies by scholars such as Kearns *et al.* (2019). Islamophobia, as Sheehi (2011) succinctly captures,

> is not a political ideology in itself nor is it an isolated dogma just as Islam itself is not a political ideology. Islamophobia does not have a platform or even a political vision. Islamophobia is something more substantive, abstract, sustained, ingrained and prevalent. (Sheehi, 2011: 6)

Despite the absence of a platform for the term Islamophobia (Alam, 2006; Hagopian, 2004; Kumar, 2012), its usage has recently increased dramatically in international sociopolitical discourses, starting in Western countries and then spreading to other regions. Specifically, Islamophobia has been widely circulated in international media outlets such as BBC, CNN and Fox News as well as social media such as Facebook, Twitter and the like, creating incessant fears and hostility against Muslim communities. As scholars like Drennan (2015), Dabashi (2008), Lane (2012) and Said (1997) have constantly argued, '[Islam's] historical analysis focuses on cultural and political derivations that lead up to Islamophobic manifestations.' Drennan (2015), for instance, observes that:

> France's history of colonialism in the Muslim realm led to resistance in, and immigration from, its former colonies. Previous colonialist tropes segued into ensuing reactions against Islam. The United States' history of anti-Muslim belligerence extending back to the Barbary Coast Wars provides another example. (Drennan, 2015: 7)

To date, Islamophobia, often presented as a both a political weapon and a cultural reality (Alam, 2006), has been consolidated and contested through the English language, partly as a matter of ensuring assumed global security. This, indeed, has several implications for teaching English in both Muslim and non-Muslim contexts. After the 9/11 attacks and other acts of violence performed by extremist Muslims, a group of governments led by the USA launched several rather aggressive attacks on the educational systems of Muslim countries worldwide. Central to these attacks is the accusation that Islamic discourses, coupled with Muslims' school curricula, the Islamic Madrassa system, traditional Quranic schools and textbooks are considered 'terrorist breeding factories' (Karmani, 2005: 263; see also Barnawi, 2018). In response to widespread international pressure and this allegation that Muslim school curricula were motivating doctrines of violence, Muslim governments in the Middle Eastern region and beyond, including Saudi Arabia, Qatar, Afghanistan, the Philippines, the United Arab Emirates (UAE) and Pakistan, have carried out several educational curricular reforms (as discussed in Barnawi, 2016, 2018; Barnawi & Phan, 2014; Glasser, 2003; Iqbal, 2003; Karmani, 2005; Phan & Barnawi, 2015; among others).

Specifically, Muslim countries have witnessed several reforms and cuts 'on the amount of religion [courses or programs] being taught at schools, colleges, and universities' (Karmani, 2005: 263), and have implemented 'a broader, more secular based curriculum' (Karmani, 2005: 263). These governments have included more English courses than ever in their school curricula. The calls for 'More English and Less Islam' were based on a perception that English could bring nations together, and at the same time promote democracy, freedom, tolerance, peace, justice, openness and civilization among Muslim communities and beyond (Barnawi, 2018;

Karmani, 2005; Said, 1997). Embedded in these calls is a belief that English can prevent Muslims from adopting radical views, and hence an assumption that global security can be realized. In a provocative article published in the *Washington Post*, entitled 'Putting English over Islam,' Glasser (2003) reports how the Royal family in Qatar is prioritizing more English courses over Islamic studies and Arabic courses in order to prevent radical views among its citizens. Likewise, Barnawi and Al-Hawsawi (2017) discuss the Saudi government's recent introduction of English courses all the way from primary school to university level, hoping to achieve modernization, peace and tolerance. Iqbal (2003, cited in Karmani, 2005) also documents the Pakistani government spending over US$255 million on adopting English subjects from primary school to university level, 'to wrest control of the country's 8,000 religious schools from the mullahs' (Karmani, 2005: 263).

In their enthusiasm to inculcate the message that English could prevent Muslims from adopting radical views, the Australian Defense Force, the US Department of Defense, the British Council and other international aid agencies have been constantly offering and funding hundreds of English courses in conflict countries such as Afghanistan (Tran, 2002), East Timor (Appleby, 2010) and other Gulf countries (see Barnawi, 2018; Nelson & Appleby, 2014; Rupp, 2009, for more details). Those agencies' primary goals are to obtain global security and to address conflicts within/between nations via English language teaching and learning. This is precisely what researchers like Woods (2005, cited in Nelson & Appleby, 2014) describe as 'The Fourth World War':

> a series of ongoing wars waged against ethnic insurgents, so called terrorists, and other forces considered anti-state. These wars rely on international cooperation between states that may have no common language, so English has been adopted as a means to improve interoperability among military and security forces [as well as nations] from diverse language backgrounds. (Woods, 2005: 95)

In 2016, British Prime Minister David Cameron promised his people that he would deport Muslim women to their countries of origin if they did not learn to speak English. Cameron told the BBC radio that 'poor English skills can leave people more susceptible to the message of groups like Islamic States in Iraq and the Levant' (Adam, 2016, n.p.). He further added that Muslim women 'would face a further test after 2 or 1.5 years in the country' and that their stay would not be guaranteed unless they improved their English (Adam, 2016, n.p.). The controversial proposed travel ban against Muslims from certain countries by US President Donald Trump has invoked and brought to the surface anxieties associated with Islamophobia.

Against the backdrop of the above scholarly and political debates, we (Phan and Barnawi) argue that, while having the potential to mediate relations, education in general and language teaching and learning in particular could be a major 'contributor to [intercultural] conflicts' (Kagawa, 2005: 490), ideologies, communication and contestations too. When Afghanistan was invaded by the Soviet Union, the US government funded and produced a series of school curricula that promoted violence, and textbooks with explicit images of jihad and war, in local Afghani languages such as Dari and Pashtu (see Karmani, 2005; Reuveny & Prakash, 1999, for more details about these issues). In this context, 'the purpose behind the textbook project was unmistakable: to produce an entire generation of jihadist warriors that would participate in the Afghan jihad against the Russian "infields" or as the Americans then saw it, the war against communism' (Karmani, 2005: 264). English language teaching and learning in contexts like this is hardly neutral. The 'calls for more English less Islam are inextricably tied to the shifting political alliance in the current international power struggle for greater control over the Middle East' (Karmani, 2005: 264) in general, and the Arabian oil-rich Gulf countries in particular.

Paradoxically, while the calls for more English appear to project Arabic as a language of violence as well as a language that fosters a militant Islamic mindset in the views of the West, as scholars like Coffman (1995), Said (2002) and Karmani (2005) have argued, today there are also hundreds of language schools that offer intensive Arabic language courses/programs/degrees in the USA, the UK, Australia, Canada and New Zealand. According to a report released by the Modern Language Association in 2014, enrolment in Arabic language courses at US colleges and universities is growing fast, due to the demand for critical-need languages that address US national security interests. The number of American students studying Arabic courses increased '12.9% from 2002 to 2006 and another 6.6% from 2006 to 2009,'[5] especially after 9/11 and the invasion of Iraq and Afghanistan.

At the same time, however, the number of people living in Western countries migrating to the Islamic States is also growing fast. According to scholars like Cottee (2015), 'it was estimated that around 4,000 people [including medical doctors, gifted students, former rappers, intellectuals, professionals and ordinary people] have left their homes in the West to migrate to ISIS. Many have become jihadist fighters in the apparent hope of achieving martyrdom' (Cottee, 2015: Para. 4). This phenomenon, according to Cottee (2015), speaks to a certain Western mentality that political sociologist Hollander (1981, 2017) identified and discussed in his classic work, *Political Pilgrims*, whereby many Westerners aspire for faraway foreign societies and ideals as a result of their critical stances against their own societies. The mass migration from the West to ISIS not only contrasts acutely with the notion of English as a language of peace, democracy, civilization and tolerance, but it is also indicative of the fact that acts of violence are not attached to any particular ethnic group, society, place or time. Although the intention of this book is not to address international cultural politics, conspiracy and wars, these conflicts indeed could have serious implications for international teachers working in a contested area like the 'New' Middle East region. It is important to note that the term 'New' Middle East was first coined by the former US President George W. Bush on 7 November 2003 after the US invasion of Iraq. It has been assumed that the New Middle East will 'be a region of mostly democratic countries allied with the United States' (Ottaway *et al.*, 2008: 1). Within such political/economic endeavors, as Ottaway *et al* (2008) put it:

> regimes that did not cooperate would be subjected to a combination of sanctions and support for democratic movements, such as the so-called Cedar Revolution of 2005 in Lebanon that forced Syrian troops out of the country. In extreme cases, they might be forced from power. (Ottaway *et al.*, 2008: 1)

The 'New' Middle East: Internal, Regional and International Structures

In the context of today's increasing Islamophobia, conspiracy, civil wars and ethnic conflicts, which all contribute to complicating the already complex cultural politics of teaching English to speakers of other languages (TESOL), English language teaching in the Islamic countries of the Middle East region, including the Arabian Gulf, could be a very challenging task for anyone. Over the past two decades, the Middle East region in general and the Arabian oil-rich Gulf countries in particular – Saudi Arabia, Kuwait, Qatar, Bahrain, UAE and Oman – have faced enormous social, political, economic, cultural, religious, ideological and epistemological challenges. As one of us (Barnawi, 2018) succinctly summarizes it:

> … the 9/11 event, the invasion of Iraq by the U.S. and its allies, the Arab Spring uprisings, the birth of ISIS (Islamic States of Iraq and Syria), the Yemen War of 2015, the GCC-Hezbollah religious and ideological conflicts, the Saudi, UAE and Bahrain versus Qatar conflicts, the ambivalent policy of the Omani government within the GCC, GCC-Iran conflicts, … and the North Thunder Military Drill of 2016 operated by the 20 largest Muslim nations in the world (and led by Saudi Arabia) on the one hand, and the global financial crisis of 2008, China's market crash of 2015, and recent tumbling oil prices in the world market, on the other hand, have ignited ideological, socio-political, geopolitical and economic debates in the Arabian Gulf region. (Barnawi, 2018: 20)

Central to these debates is the fact that the current sociopolitical, economic, intercultural and ideological changes in the region have necessitated the creation of 'New' *internal, regional* and *international* structures of the Middle East states.

At the internal level, the current challenges confronted by the Arabian oil-rich countries have led to the creation of 'New' consensual discourses in local media across the Gulf countries. Social media such as Facebook, Twitter and WhatsApp as well as local newspapers were loaded with posts and articles that echo collective concerns and responsibilities about the security of the region as well as calls for immediate collaboration in reporting suspicious acts in public to local authorities. There is now 'New' decentralization of English school curricula within the Gulf countries, whereby local schools, academic bodies, education directorates and higher education (HE) institutions have been granted full autonomy to import a wide range of Western prepackaged commercialized curricula, materials, series, textbooks, pedagogies and practices into their respective institutions (see, for example, Barnawi, 2018). It has been assumed that successful mastery of the English language within nation-states coupled with international education systems (mainly Western-oriented) could effectively contribute to building nation-states as well as competing in the global market economy. There have also been 'New' initiatives from governments in the Gulf region to remove several Islamic books from local school and universities. For instance, in 2015 the Saudi government pulled out around 80 books produced by the Muslim 'Brotherhood' from the libraries of local schools and universities.[6] Officials gave local schools two weeks to remove books by religious authors who represent Muslim Brotherhood ideologies such as Yousuf Al Qaradawi, Sayyed Qutb and Hassan Al Banna; at the same time these officials warned schools not to take or accept any gifts in the form of Islamic books. Kuwaiti officials and law makers have even gone one step further and called for the renaming of 'Hassan Al Banna Street' by putting 'the name of a local resident who was killed during the invasion of the country by Iraq in 1990.'[7] At the Riyadh International Book Fair in 2018, a publisher's stall was completely shut down for selling banned Muslim Brotherhood books. The Supervisor of the Fair, Abdul Rahman Al Asem, commented that '[throughout our inspections], we discovered that the publisher was hiding the books and selling them secretly.' As a result, the necessary measures were taken, and 'the stall was shut down.' He further commented that, 'There is solid coordination between the heads of the various fairs in the Gulf Cooperation Council (GCC) and any publisher banned in any member country will also be banned in the others.'[8] At the same time, 'New' long-term economic visions are now being introduced by each government in the Arabian Gulf countries to respond to internal, regional, international and global challenges. These long-term economic visions include 'Saudi Vision 2030,' 'Kuwait Vision 2030,' 'Bahrain Economic Vision 2030,' 'UAE Vision 2021' and 'Oman Vision 2040.' In his recent book entitled *Neoliberalism and English Language Education Policies in the Arabian Gulf*, Barnawi (2018) argues that:

> Analysis of the long-term plan 'vision' documents for the six GCC countries revealed that [GCC] governments have made strong reference to

globalisation, the internationalisation of education, a knowledge-based economy, international benchmarking and the like in order to realise their neoliberal policy formulations. It was also found that there was a radical shift in educational values across the six GCC countries – moving from education as a social good to education as an economic good. The six Arabian Gulf countries now compete among each other for the status of intellectual hub in the region. (Barnawi, 2018: 168)

At the regional level, the Arabian oil-rich countries have devised 'New' safeguards designed to control public goods, 'New' cuts in education, social services and welfare subsidies, 'New' aggressive spending on military and intelligence services, and a 'New' value-added tax system in the region. At the same time, they are also committed to a 'New' 'desire for the Englishization, internationalization, privatization and "mallification" of education, and English medium of instruction (EMI) programmes at all levels'. While facing '"New" sociopolitical and economic relations within/between the oil-rich countries and their Western counterparts, "New" societies in the Arabian Gulf region have appeared to have more collective concerns about securing the future of their nations than ever before' (see Barnawi, 2018: 21, for more accounts of these issues).

At the international level, the Arabian oil-rich countries have pronounced a 'New' statement (i.e. consensual discourse) that labeled Hezbollah in Lebanon a terrorist group in 2016,[9] thereby intensifying the tensions/conflicts between Sunni Muslims and Shiite Muslims as well. At the same time, however, there have been 'New' calls for unity between the Arabian Gulf countries and other Muslim states across the globe. For example, the President of Turkey, at the 2016 Summit in Istanbul, called for unity among these countries so as to read conspiracy, bridge differences and fight terrorism.[10] In the middle of all these 'New' initiatives and happenings, there is also a 'New' growing gap between the USA and the Arabian oil-rich Gulf countries, owing to changing oil politics and US politics towards the Middle East region's conflicts.[10]

Within these intersecting internal, regional and international structures in the 'New' Middle East region, including the Arabian Gulf region, English plays a vital role in that it 'is integral to the globalization processes that characterize the contemporary post-Cold War phase of aggressive casino capitalism, economic restructuring, McDonaldization and militarization on all continents' (Phillipson, 2001: 187). At the same time, as one of us has argued (Barnawi, 2018) in the case of the GCC region:

The authorities' enthusiasm rapidly to harmonise Islamic traditions, values and culture as well as social governments with Western neoliberal values and strategies has caused intensifying ideological debates within and between religious clerks, officials, scholars, language educators, policymakers, families, learners and the society at large, particularly in regard to accepting and respecting the shared vocabulary between English educational policy and economic politics in the Arabian Gulf region. (Barnawi, 2018: 22)

In this account, international teachers working in a country like Saudi Arabia would face several 'challenges of classes that are not only metaphorical contact zones, but are also situated in literal conflict zones' (Nelson & Appleby, 2014: 309). This is particularly true after the recent formation of an alliance of 34 Muslim nations led by the Saudi government, together with the establishment in 2017 of a global center, Etidal, by the Saudi government in order to address the Islamic world's issues including intercultural communication conflicts, ideologies and terrorism, to name a few. Before we elaborate these challenges further in the subsequent chapters, the role of the Kingdom of Saudi Arabia (KSA) in the 'New' Middle East and beyond is discussed.

The Role of the Kingdom of Saudi Arabia in the 'New' Middle East and Beyond

The KSA plays an influential role in the 'New' Middle East region and beyond. It is the guardian of Islam's two Holy Mosques: Makkah and Madinah. As such, it is globally committed to spreading and maintaining the Islamic faith in collaboration with other Muslim countries around the world. Over the past two decades, the KSA has played a leading role in addressing sociopolitical, economic, cultural and ideological challenges confronted by the region and beyond.

Within the Middle East region, when Iraq invaded Kuwait in 1990 under the regime of Saddam Hussein, the Saudi government accommodated all of the Kuwaiti Royal family and its government leaders and citizens. When the Iraqi government refused immediate withdrawal from Kuwait after several warnings from the UN Security Council, it was the Saudi government that led Operation Desert Storm, in collaboration with an international coalition and forces from 32 countries, including the USA, Britain, France, Kuwait and Egypt, to free Kuwait from Iraq's attacks (Atkinson, 1993; Finlan, 2003; Hiro, 1992). When Bahrain's uprising erupted in 2011, it was the Saudi government that led the Peninsula Shield Force, in collaboration with five other countries in the Gulf Cooperation Council region, to protect the Al-Khalifa ruling family and at the same time to restore peace in Bahrain (Held & Ulrichsen, 2012). When the Houthis, an armed religious-political movement and allies of former President Ali Abdullah Saleh, broke peace in Yemen and caused a civil war in 2014–2015, the contested President of Yemen, Abd Rabbu Hadi, fled his country and went to Saudi Arabia. To restore peace in Yemen, it was the Saudi government that led Operation Decisive Storm, in collaboration with nine Arab states, including the UAE, Bahrain, Kuwait, Sudan, Egypt, Jordan and Morocco (Mazzetti & Kirkpatrick, 2015; Schwartz *et al.*, 2015). The Saudi government also led the Arabian oil-rich Gulf countries to stop Iran's ongoing intervention in Arabian affairs in 2015 and at the same time to preserve the security of the region (Kinninmont, 2015b).

Internationally, the Saudi government has played a major role in addressing the sociopolitical, economic, cultural and ideological challenges confronted by Muslim countries worldwide. During the long Israeli-Palestinian conflict, the Saudi government has condemned the Israeli occupation of Palestine, providing financial aid and support worth $240 million every year to Palestinian people, and calling on international communities to ban Israel from attacking civilians in Palestine (Turki, 2014). It also established the King Abdullah bin Abdulaziz International Centre for Interreligious and Intercultural Dialogue in 2005 in order 'to promote the use of dialogue globally to prevent and resolve conflict, to enhance understanding and cooperation … [as well as] … to foster dialogue among people of different faiths and cultures that bridges animosities, reduces fear and instills mutual respect.'[11] The Saudi government, in 2015, also formed an alliance of 34 Muslim nations to address issues such as intercultural communication conflicts, extremist ideologies and terrorism, to name a few. In 2017–2018, it established a global center called Etidal in order to fight extremist ideology: 'a flag bearer rallying all the international community that extremist has become an ominous and prevalent epidemic. Continuously there are new breeds of extremist groups that now act globally across geographic boarders and gaining followers from across cultures.'[12] The above accounts demonstrate the important role that the KSA has consistently played in the Middle East region and globally.

English Education in the KSA: The Epistemology of Land

English education in the KSA, the land of two holy mosques for about 1.6 billion Muslims in the world, has long been controversial, owing to sociopolitical, cultural, religious and economic reasons as well as tribal customary practices. Saudi Arabia has relatively more conservative cultural traditions and beliefs that originate from Islam; consequently, its education system in general and language teaching and learning in particular have been affected by Islamic interpretations (Barnawi & Al-Hawsawi, 2017). Although the country has been governed under Islamic Sharia law, different tribal traditions, cultural values, customs and norms of local communities have simultaneously continued to reshape and challenge English education across the country. Specifically, different customary laws or what is called '*Urf*' in Arabic – practices that have public acceptance – usually hold a strong position in rural as well as urban areas. Central to these customs, cultural traditions and practices are, as Maisel (2009) outlines:

> property law (tribal territories, or *dirah*), personal law (collective responsibility, marriage regulations), inheritance (women's share), criminal law (murder, honor crimes), and conducting raids. While '*urf*' stands for the nomadic, orally transmitted, and secular world of pastoral Bedouin

tribes, *Shari'a* is the agent for settled communities and states with their agricultural bases economy and divine, written codex. (Maisel, 2009: Para. 13).

Since the establishment of its education system in 1925, religious courses are predominant components of curricula, pedagogies and practices in the KSA. Additionally, boys and girls are segregated in the education system from the early years of schooling up to HE levels (Barnawi, 2011, 2018). At the same time, English as a foreign language was first introduced in Saudi public schools in 1937, and was taught four times a week (45 minutes each session), as Al-Hajailan (1999) and Zafer (2002) point out. As Barnawi and Al-Hawsawi (2017: 203) show, 'owing to the shortage of qualified Saudi EFL – English as foreign language – teachers [those days], English was taught mainly by teachers from neighboring Arab countries, namely, Egypt, Syria, Palestine, Jordan and Sudan.' At HE level, Arabic was the medium of instruction in engineering, business and management and science programs, while English was taught as a general subject throughout these programs.

Over the past two decades, however, the evolving sociopolitical, cultural and economic challenges faced by Saudi Arabia, including the 9/11 attacks, the global financial crisis of 2008, the 'Arab Spring Scenario,' the birth of ISIS, and Saudi Economic Vision 2030 and other policy reforms, have had great impacts on the epistemology of language education across the country. After the 9/11 attacks, for instance, the Saudi government experienced international pressures, particularly from the USA, calling for major reforms to be made to Saudi education policy so as to foster 'more liberalism, and counterbalance the extremist ideology allegedly encouraged by some components within the Saudi curriculum, especially religious education' (Habbash, 2011: 34). In response to these pressures, in 2004 the Saudi Ministry of Education (MoE) introduced English language as early as Grade 6 of primary school. It also, in 2011, introduced English as a core subject in the fourth grade of primary school. These critical decisions have created incessant tensions between liberal Saudis and the conservative wings. Barnawi and Al-Hawsawi (2017) summarize these tensions and reactions as follows:

> Many parents have become resentful of the idea of teaching English to youngsters on the grounds that their children should master proper Arabic in the early stages of their education in order to be able to read and understand Arabic; an important tool to access Islamic text such as the Holy Quran and the Holy *Hadeeth* (the sayings and heritage of the Prophet Mohamed peace be upon him). Others even claim that there is a conspiracy to destroy the Arabic language in the country and the Islamic heritage associated with it. (Barnawi & Al-Hawsawi, 2017: 205)

In addition to the global forces confronted by the country there are deep-rooted local socioeconomic problems that have forced the government to take action. While there are over 9 million foreign workers constituting the engine of Saudi economy (Barnawi, 2011, 2016, 2018; Phan & Barnawi, 2015), the alarmingly high unemployment rates among young Saudis (30%), in particular, have led the government to undertake several major initiatives and projects to build local capacity. Specifically, in its quest towards the development of human capital as well as a knowledge-based economy, the Saudi MoE has undertaken several major initiatives worth billions of dollars to reform its education system in various ways and forms. Like other countries in the Arabian oil-rich Gulf region, the Saudi MoE has adopted top-down internationalization policies to promote national, institutional and individual competitiveness in response to the increasing globalization of English. Saudi universities and colleges are now revising their mission statements to ensure a commitment to internationalization, franchising international programs to their local people, cultivating partnerships with foreign institutions, launching joint programs and adopting international curricula, among other endeavors (see, for example, Barnawi, 2018; Phan & Barnawi, 2015). As such, the Technical and Vocational Training Cooperation (TVTC), the largest sector in Saudi Arabia which runs all the Technical Colleges (over 35 branches), Girls' Higher Training Institutes (17 branches) and Vocational Institutes (70 branches) across the country, 'is now adopting international curricula, syllabi, instructional strategies and assessment practices,' and has adopted English 'as the medium of instruction in most of its programmes' (Barnawi & Al-Hawsawi, 2017: 211).

A further example of the Englishization and internationalization of education in the KSA can be seen in its latest major project entitled 'Colleges of Excellence.' The primary goal of this project (with an investment of more than $1 billion) is to restructure the entire technical and vocational training and education sector of the country. The government has invited international training providers to bid to set up college campuses across the country. In under two years, almost '37 international branch campuses ha[d] been established under the Colleges of Excellence project' (Phan & Barnawi, 2015: 546) by the Saudi government. There are now many international training providers operating college campuses across the country, including Lincoln College, GIZ-Festo Training Services llc, TQ Education and Training, Laureate International Universities, Hertfordshire London College, Australian Aviation, Riyadh College of Excellence and Niagara College. Consequently, Western prepackaged materials, products, goods and services coupled with an English-only mentality have become the loudest story across Saudi society.

What is more, the King Abdullah University of Science and Technology (KAUST), established in 2009, is another prime example of the country's endeavors to Westernize local education. It is public knowledge that 'King Abdullah himself has offered $10 billion of his own money to launch this graduate-level science-and-technology university called KAUST with international standards' (Barnawi, 2011; Barnawi & Al-Hawsawi, 2017: 212–213). Remarkably, KAUST has already established collaborative ventures with more than 27 leading international academic institutions across the world so as to promote its global outlook (Corbyn, 2009; Wilkins, 2010). The King Abdullah Scholarship Program (KASP) is another major policy initiative which aims to promote human capital development and economic growth among Saudis through Western forms of education and English-medium instruction (EMI). Based on the slogan, 'Your Career, Your Scholarship' (which is an extended version of the earlier KASP published in 2014–2015), education in the KSA has become 'increasingly tied to Western political-economic constructs of the knowledge economy in policy and national strategy' (Patrick, 2014: 236). Since its establishment in 2005, its ambition has been to put the country on the front line in the global market economy and at the same time to internationalize education policy, curricula and pedagogy across the country. Today, thousands of young male and female Saudis travel to Western countries like the UK, Australia, New Zealand and the USA with their families in order to pursue their education under the KASP. In the USA alone, its universities have seen students from Saudi Arabia enroll in record numbers, as is evident in published reports such as the 2016 report released by the International Consultants for Education and Fairs (ICEF) Monitor.

> At its inception in 2005, there were just over 3,000 Saudi students in the US, a country that has been the primary destination for KASP-funded students in the years since and that saw its Saudi enrolment swell to just under 60,000 students in 2014/15 (for a nearly 2,000% increase over the last ten years). For the past five years in a row, Saudi Arabia has been the fourth-largest sending country for the US. (ICEF, 2016)

In 2019, the Saudi Minister of Education announced that 'Foreign universities [are] to open branch campuses in Saudi Arabia' (Al-Kinani, 2019). He added that such a decision could (i) 'create a variety of educational opportunities for those wishing to join the international universities' and (ii) increase competition among universities.[13] Additionally, 'it would also be instrumental in raising the efficiency of spending, developing financial resources and human capabilities for universities in line with the Kingdom's Vision 2030.'[14] Embedded in the new Saudi policy directions are Western-inspired educational values coupled with instrumental agendas and HE practices. The Saudi government is striving to build a global and influential knowledge hub that will help upgrade its education system, and at the same time to address the socioeconomic order of the country within a short period of time, in collaboration with international partners. This ambitious global vision together with such urgent expectations has led the government to offer full autonomy and financial and logistic support to local institutes to invite top world-class universities and colleges around the world to benchmark their academic programs. Saudi institutions have also sought international accreditations for their own programs, signing memoranda of understanding with international HE bodies in North America, Europe, Asia, South East Asia, Africa, Australia and New Zealand. For instance, King Abdul Aziz University, in 2018, celebrated the news of being ranked number one in the Arab world and among the top 200 universities in the world according to Quacquarelli Symonds (QS). On its official website, it celebrates the news as follows:

> It is now recognized as a world-class prestigious university brought about by its international outreach and collaboration in research, innovation, accreditations and rankings. It does this while it continues to maintain its traditional commitment to deliver outstanding education and community service.[15]

These rapid changes within the Saudi education system have reshaped the epistemologies of education in general and language teaching and learning in particular in various ways. Western forms of education paired with an English-only mentality are often seen as desirable educational policies and practices (Barnawi, 2016, 2018; Phan & Barnawi, 2015), thereby challenging both the linguistic and the cultural autonomy of Saudis. English language has been projected 'as gatekeeper to positions of prestige in society' (Pennycook, 1995: 39) as well as the primary language to gain access to education and socioeconomic opportunities. Hence, 'marketing social reproduction' (Bourdieu, 1991a, 1991b) in the country has become inevitable, thereby imposing 'English as a terrain where individual and societal worth are established' (Piller & Cho, 2013: 23). Under the current English education epistemology in the KSA, Saudis with less access to English language, scientific resources and Western forms of education are more likely to suffer in the job market. As one of us has argued, 'English has often been referred to as "the way to go" by administrators, teaching staff and students [and the society at large]. More English means more income, a more internationalised outlook, and better opportunities at all levels' (Phan, 2017: 26).

International TESOL Teachers' Mobility into Saudi Arabia: What is at Stake?

> What happened in the last 30 years is not Saudi Arabia. What happened in the region in the last 30 years is not the Middle East. After the Iranian revolution in 1979, people wanted to copy this model in different countries, one of them is Saudi Arabia. We didn't know how to deal with it. And the problem spread all over the world. Now is the time to get rid of it.
>
> We are simply reverting to what we followed – a moderate Islam open to the world and all religions. 70% of the Saudis are younger than 30, honestly we won't waste 30 years of our life combating extremist thoughts, we will destroy them now and immediately. (Saudi Arabia's Crown Prince, Mohammed bin Salman, 2017)[16]

The above statements were pronounced by the Saudi Crown Prince, Mohammed bin Salman, in the presence of top local officials and investors as well as the frontrunners of global financial institutions (e.g. International Monetary Fund, World Bank, etc.) and international investors (e.g. Amazon, Blackstone, Google, etc.), at the inauguration of 'an independent $500 billion megacity,' dubbed NEOM in the country. During the course of the inauguration, the Saudi Crown Prince also announced the appointment of Klaus Kleinfeld – a Western business leader – as Chief Executive Officer (CEO) of this historic national transformation plan. Klaus Kleinfeld was the former CEO of Siemens AG, Arconic and Alcoa Inc. This appointment has put Saudi Arabia on a new footing. Central to this ambitious plan, which evolved out of the Saudi Economic Vision 2030, is to: revert to a moderate Islam; move from oil-based economy (rentierism) to a knowledge-based economy (developmentalism); attract foreign investors to the country; create job opportunities for Saudi women; and push the boundaries of the country in the global market economy. This strategic vision is realized in collaboration with international investors from Asia, Africa, North America and Europe, who are promoting every opportunity to generate revenues for their own organizations as well.

Given all the complications and complexities plus the increasing intensification of knowledge economy discourses and the growing desire for more Western-inspired pedagogies that we have laid out thus far, neoliberal free market ideologies have been given all that they need to continue to challenge and reshape HE policy, curricula, pedagogies and practices in Saudi Arabia in particular and in the Arabian Gulf region in general (Barnawi, 2018; Phan, 2017; Phan & Barnawi, 2015). The 'neoliberal preoccupation of [teaching and] learning English as an international language' (Kubota, 2014: 486) and a language of 'university corporations' (Piller & Cho, 2013) has created incessant demand for English language teachers as well as for English-medium programs in the world market economy (De Costa *et al.*, 2020, 2021; Kirkgöz & Karakaş, 2021; Macaro *et al.*, 2017; McKinley *et al.*, 2021). In this picture, many teachers of English from India, Pakistan, Malaysia, Nigeria, the Philippines, Jordan, Turkey, Morocco, Tunisia, Sudan, South Africa, China, Singapore, the USA, the UK, Australia and Canada, etc., are working alongside their local counterparts in the Middle East, including the oil-rich Arabian Gulf region (i.e. Saudi Arabia, Qatar, Oman, Bahrain, UAE and Kuwait). This vastly diverse group of international TESOL teachers deserves more scholarly attention, particularly in relation to issues of religious tensions, socioeconomic mobility, employability, transnationality, territoriality, and sense-making of contested values and practices.

Indeed, thousands of international language teachers with different linguistic, racial, religious, ideological and cultural backgrounds have entered the TESOL profession and have been working in all corners of the world, owing to increasing globalization, immigration and translocal mobility. These 'teachers are social and cultural transmitters' (Taylor & Sobel, 2011: 5) who, building on their personal, professional and academic experiences, negotiate and transmit knowledge in the host country (which is Saudi Arabia in the case of our book), as well as making significant contributions to pedagogy, teaching, learning and knowledge at a global level, as we will demonstrate in more depth in the subsequent chapters.

While this is happening, actors (e.g. students, administrators, program directors and other academic leaders) in the host country/institution are neither passive nor naïve in the face of these international TESOL teachers. Rather, they resist, value, negotiate and appropriate those very personal, cultural, professional and academic experiences being brought to their classes and/or institutions by these international TESOL teachers. At the same time, international TESOL teachers with different cultural, racial, ethnic and linguistic backgrounds (e.g. Indian versus Jordanian, American versus Sudanese) are also negotiating their interpersonal as well as intra-personal, cultural, professional and academic experiences within/between each other while teaching in the host country. In such complex layers of teaching environments, 'teachers need to know the growing importance of cultural sensitivity and understanding for effective intercultural communication' (Taylor & Sobel, 2011: 5), and at the same time strive to move beyond what De Jong and Harper (2005: 102) call 'just good teaching' and 'being "nice"' (Nieto, 2010: 264) to students, local authorities, academic leaders and administrators in the host country. Put simply, under these conditions, respect, tolerance, recognition and negotiation of cultural, ideological, religious and linguistic differences among actors (e.g. students, international TESOL teachers and administrators) have become key to pedagogical, work and life fulfillment.

There is so much at stake, but there are also unknown satisfactions waiting ahead. Indeed, the journey of international TESOL teachers, with mixed backgrounds, working in Saudi Arabia is full of discovery, opportunity, potential challenge, investment and adventure. In this book, we invite you to explore with us the ways in which international English language teachers from different and mixed backgrounds working alongside one another in Saudi Arabia position themselves, negotiate, interact, adjust, make sense of their classroom dynamics, and validate their senses of selves and pedagogies in their day-to-day observations of their institutions and interactions at work. We attempt to offer insights into these experiences and processes in the chapters that follow.

Notes

(1) Quran: Aal-i-Mran, 19.
(2) Pew Research Center at http://www.pewresearch.org/
(3) See https://www.pewresearch.org/religion/2015/04/02/religious-projections-2010-2050/

(4) Center for Race & Gender at the University of California, Berkeley at http://crg.berkeley.edu/
(5) See http://monitor.icef.com/2014/12/arabic-language-studies-booming-us/
(6) See http://www.globalmbwatch.com/2015/12/01/saudi-arabia-to-pull-books-by-muslim-brotherhood-ideologues-from-libraries-and-schools/
(7) See https://gulfnews.com/world/gulf/saudi/muslim-brotherhood-books-pulled-out-of-saudi-schools-1.1629853#.Vl27uqIJD74.twitter
(8) See https://gulfnews.com/news/gulf/saudi-arabia/riyadh-book-fair-stall-shut-down-over-muslim-brotherhood-books-1.2191273
(9) See http://www.wsj.com/articles/gulf-cooperation-council-labels-hezbollah-a-terrorist-group-1456926654
(10) See http://time.com/3864061/these-5-facts-explain-the-troubled-u-s-arab-relationship/
(11) See http://www.kaiciid.org/who-we-are
(12) See https://etidal.org/
(13) See https://www.arabnews.com/node/1576231/saudi-arabia
(14) See http://saudigazette.com.sa/article/581232
(15) See https://www.timeshighereducation.com/world-university-rankings/king-abdulaziz-university
(16) see https://www.theguardian.com/world/2017/oct/24/i-will-return-saudi-arabia-moderate-islam-crown-prince

3 Engaging (with) *Flavors* of TESOL: Mobility, Space, Place, Neoliberalism, Multilingualism and Emotion Labor

In this chapter we critically engage (with) what we call *flavors of TESOL*, which refer to several key theoretical developments in TESOL. These developments intersect with and are informed and driven by theories, concepts and debates surrounding the mobility aspects of TESOL professionals. The experiences of the international TESOL teachers we focus on in our work are at the heart of our scholarly engagement. We, in particular, situate international TESOL teachers' (im)mobilities in our close examination of space and place, of the rising and intensifying neoliberalism in language and education, of ongoing debates on race, ethnicity, native–non-native teachers and multilingualism more broadly, and of more recent scholarship on emotion labor in language teaching. These theoretical and conceptual grounds are not only intertwined but in various ways cast different logics onto the ways in which these teachers negotiate and position their multilayered (inter)cultural interactions and pedagogical decisions.

Space and Place in the Mobility of International TESOL Teachers

> We now see that the mobility of people [e.g. international English teachers into a particular space] also involves the mobility of linguistic [sociocultural, ideological, epistemological, pedagogical] and sociolinguistic resources, that 'sedentary' patterns of language use are complemented by 'trans-local' forms of language use, and that the combination of both often accounts for unexpected sociolinguistic [and other cultural belongings] effects. (Blommaert & Dong, 2010: 367)

In this context of celebrated mobility, what are often undermined are the consequences of mobilities and the underlying immobilities and inequalities that individuals and communities are subject to and/or find themselves in. What is more, mobility is not always a given, a choice, but can be a situation, a condition or an accident that carries precarities and unknown risks (Collins & Ho, 2018; Hoang, 2020; Poole, 2019), all of which need to be questioned rather than uncritically promoted. We (the authors) constantly remind ourselves of this very aspect of mobility and of its much less explored companion – immobilities. As our writing continues, (im)mobilities also unfold.

The mobilities of people coupled with the mobility of their linguistic, sociocultural, ideological, epistemological, pedagogical and sociolinguistic resources are rather complex and at the same time fluid and contingent (Phan *et al.*, 2020). Such a complex and multilayered phenomenon, thus, requires 'more holistic objects of analysis' (Blommaert, 2010: 366), as well as demands that we constantly rescale our epistemological, theoretical, methodological and conceptual tools. The above observation from Blommaert and Dong (2010) also rejects the traditional paradigm of investigating issues of English language education, including language resources, policy, curricula, pedagogies, practices, negotiations, intercultural interactions and social status, in a binary and fixed manner. Instead, Blommaert and Dong (2010) and other scholars such as Jenkins (2019), Lee (2022), Nonaka (2018), Phan (2008) and Windle *et al.* (2020) urge us to investigate issues of language education 'in-motion, with various spatio-temporal frames interacting with one another' (Blommaert & Dong, 2010: 368) so as to enrich and sharpen our epistemological, methodological, theoretical, conceptual and pedagogical understandings of the mobility of people and language in a given space and time.

This very paradigm of investigation also necessitates the incorporation of a theoretical understanding of on-the-ground realities when exploring the ways in which international English language teachers of different backgrounds working alongside one another in Saudi Arabia, a non-English-dominant context, position themselves, negotiate, interact, make sense of their classroom pedagogies and validate their values in their day-to-day intercultural interactions. This is because particular forms of mobility occur in specific 'spaces where actual people live and interact with one another' (Blommaert & Dong, 2010: 367). Importantly, there are differences in the distribution of variables within 'one locality or across localities such as schools, institutions, cities, regions' (Blommaert & Dong, 2010: 367), communes and towns. Furthermore, TESOL international teachers in particular and specific spaces 'naturally represent a wide array of social, cultural roles and identities: as teachers ... as gendered, and cultural individuals, as expatriates or nationals, as native speakers (NSs) or nonnative speakers' (Duff & Uchida, 1997: 451). The epistemologies, ideologies and pedagogies that are 'foregrounded depend in large measure upon the institutional and interpersonal contexts in which individuals find themselves, the purpose of their being there, and their personal biographies' (Duff & Uchida, 1997: 451).

With this in mind, space is 'metaphorically seen ... as [a] layered and stratified' concept, and as such 'every horizontal space (for instance a neighborhood, a region, a country, [an institution]) is also a vertical space, in which all sorts of socially, culturally, and politically salient distinctions occur' (Blommaert & Dong, 2011: 368). In other words, as Fu Tuan (1977, cited in Creswell, 2004) puts it, 'space' is linked to movement, whereas 'place' is related to 'pause':

> [w]hat begins as undifferentiated space becomes place as we get to know it better and endow it with value. ... The ideas 'space' and 'place' require each other for definition. From the security and stability of place we are aware of the openness, freedom, and threat of space, and vice versa. Furthermore, if we think of space as that which allows movement, then place is pause; each pause in movement makes it possible for location to be transformed into place. (Tuan, 1977: 6)

Indeed, in the context of mobility, including that of the international TESOL teachers reported in our research, mobility at any given places and spaces embeds and enables various forms of desire and aspirations and anxieties, as well as constant interactions of linguistic, sociocultural, ideological, epistemological, pedagogical and sociolinguistic resources. This phenomenon also embeds complexities and requires meaningful scholarly interpretations of the intermingling and intersectionality of space and place. Specifically, on the one hand, for the international TESOL teachers from hugely mixed backgrounds moving to Saudi Arabia (i.e. place) to work, moving to Saudi Arabia could mean moving to a place full of potential waiting to be explored and utilized; in the process they would occupy and cultivate a certain space. Saudi Arabia (i.e. place), on the other hand, is also a 'pause' that has its own expectations, values, cultural traditions and norms within the given space. These 'interaction orders' (Agha, 2006; Collins & Slembrouck, 2007) within/between space and place are unpredictable, complex and multilayered, owing to social, cultural, political, epistemological and ideological differences in the 'order of discourses' (Foucault, 1997) among different actors. Within this epistemic logic, it is impossible to talk about space without talking about place, and vice versa. Thus, space and place are not mutually exclusive; they are interdependent.

International TESOL teachers, with mixed backgrounds, working in the Saudi context (there are so many sub-contexts underneath the so-called Saudi context) have to constantly negotiate their intellectual resources, cultural and religious values and intercultural competence with different parties, including between/within peers (e.g. American-American or Indian, American and Malaysian), students, institutions and the society at large.

At the same time, they have to be careful not to use language pedagogies and practices that might be seen as being culturally inappropriate in Saudi classrooms. They also have to be constantly mindful of self-negotiation and the visible and invisible presence of others in order to accommodate the varied intellectual, religious and (inter)cultural needs of multiple parties. Under these conditions, as Blommaert and Dong (2010) capture:

> [t]he movement of people across space is therefore never a move across empty spaces. The spaces are always someone's space, and they are filled with norms, expectations, conceptions of what counts as proper and normal (indexical) language use and what does not. Mobility, sociolinguistically speaking, is therefore a trajectory through different spaces – stratified, controlled, and monitored ones – in which language 'gives you away'. (Blommaert & Dong, 2010: 368)

Differences in social, cultural, political, ideological, linguistic and classroom pedagogical practices among international teachers from different backgrounds working in the Saudi Arabian context (i.e. place) can be classified into various 'indexical ascriptive categories' (Gumperz, 1982: 58). These categories not only define but, in many cases, question their identities, professional experiences, roles, race, gender, intellectual resources and intercultural competence in social and educational settings, as we shall demonstrate later in the book.

The Mobility of International TESOL Teachers under Neoliberalism and Increasing Academic Capitalism

As shown earlier, international language teachers' pedagogical and cultural negotiations and their intercultural interactions have been examined in close relation to hybridity, fluidity and multiplicity in varied contexts (McNamara, 2011; Menard-Warwick, 2014; Park, 2018; Pennycook, 2010; Phan, 2008). Such examinations have also had to take into serious consideration the neoliberal capitalist aspects of language, language policy and knowledge generation and increasing competition in the current global HE landscape (Barnawi, 2018; Flores, 2013; Flubacher & Del Percio, 2017; Hamid & Rahman, 2019; Kabir & Chowdhury, 2021; Kubota, 2014; Naidoo & Williams, 2015; O'Regan, 2021; Phan, 2017).

Neoliberalism, by and large, is 'a theory of political economic practices that proposes that human well-being can best be advanced by liberating individual entrepreneurial freedoms and skills within an institutional framework characterized by strong private property rights, free markets and free trade' (Harvey, 2005: 2). An emphasis on free markets and on how individuals' attributes and economic success could be cultivated and optimally developed under this free market umbrella is another core element of neoliberalism (Kubota, 2014). Scholars including Fazal Rizvi and Bob Lingard (2010), Henry Giroux (2009, 2014), Ryuko Kubota (2014) and Steven Klees *et al.* (2012) have criticized the promotion of neoliberalism in international organizations and governments' education policies around the world. These strong critics of neoliberalism have condemned it for destroying education as a public good and as a human right when so-called free markets and individual opportunities remain accessible to only a select few in societies rather than to those in need of support. As Giroux (2009: 31) puts it, 'everything either is for sale or is plundered for profit' under neoliberalism. At the same time, the increasing privatization of public services, which is promoted to create 'a flexible workforce, and [to increase] individual and institutional accountability for economic success,' has been seen as the main cause of 'reducing social services and producing disparities between the rich and the poor' (Kubota, 2014: 485).

Higher education (HE) and English language teaching (ELT) are not exempt from the spread of neoliberalism. Neoliberal ideals, at varied levels, have penetrated HE and ELT across the board, leading to the ever more aggressive commercialization of so-called Western products, ideologies, practices, methodologies, models and pedagogies (Altbach & Knight, 2007; Chowdhury & Phan, 2014; Chun, 2016; De Costa *et al.*, 2020; O'Regan, 2014, 2021). All these have contributed to the consolidation of the English language and English-medium instruction, as well as the controversial values and discourses that come with them (Barnawi, 2018; Chun, 2016; De Costa *et al.*, 2020, 2021; Pennycook, 1998/2017; Phan, 2017; Phillipson, 1992, 2010). Governments' and individuals' investments in education are driven by these discourses that favor English as a global language, essential for internationalization and economic success, a highly regarded language of global academe, and the main language of international scholarly research and publications.

At the same time, with the continuing expansion of HE bodies and the increasing embracement of neoliberalism in education policy, reform and practice worldwide, academic capitalism as a frequently used term has entered and somewhat pervaded much of academia (cf. Ball, 2016; Naidoo & Williams, 2015). Academic capitalism is understood as the ways in which contemporary HE institutions are aggressively transforming 'their basic functions of teaching, research, and service into revenue generating operations' (Saunders, 2007: 2). In the spheres of TESOL and applied linguistics, academic capitalism is gradually attracting attention and has been examined from various perspectives, including the experiences of EFL students as well as teachers as neoliberal subjects, the commercialization of English language textbooks and language testing, and the like (Barnawi, 2018; Chowdhury & Phan, 2014; Kubota, 2014; Park, 2013). Under the global capitalist economy, neoliberalism encourages the immigration and translocal mobility of TESOL teachers across national borders. As Hardt and Negri (2000) capture,

> Circulation, mobility, diversity, and mixture are its very conditions of possibility. Trade brings differences together and the more the merrier! Differences (of commodities, populations, cultures, and so forth) seem to

multiply infinitely in the world market, which attacks nothing more violently than fixed boundaries: it overwhelms any binary division with its infinite multiplicities. (Hardt & Negri, 2000: 150)

Given these happenings, international English teachers' movements into a particular context 'must be understood in relation to the material conditions of our capitalist economy' (Gao & Park, 2015: 78). These material conditions include negotiations and intercultural interactions. Through examining international English language teachers' movements, negotiations and intercultural interactions in Saudi Arabia (place), for instance, one can capture and document the social 'restructuring of space' (i.e. movements) (Gao & Park, 2015; Harvey, 1993; Ong, 2007) and the cultural politics of place in dialectical ways. As a matter of fact, the intersectionality between space and neoliberalism is still underexplored within the field of TESOL (e.g. Barnawi, 2016; Gao & Park, 2015), and if this critical research gap continued to be left unaddressed and neglected, this problem would prevent us from developing/deepening our understanding of crucial aspects of the social and cultural politics of English education under the neoliberal economy (Block *et al.*, 2012; O'Regan, 2014, 2021; Park, 2021; Park & Wee, 2012; Phan, 2021; Shin & Park, 2016; Simpson & O'Regan, 2018). Thus, in the remaining chapters, we attempt to respond to this critical research gap. We will present complex accounts of international English language teachers of different backgrounds who have been working alongside one another in Saudi Arabia, a non-English-dominant context, with regard to how they position themselves, negotiate, interact, make sense of their classroom pedagogies and validate their values in their day-to-day intercultural interactions.

Under the neoliberal globalized economy, different countries across the world attribute different social meanings and political, economic and cultural values to English language learning today. At the same time, 'academics [including TESOL teachers], as a key part of the global transfer and production of knowledge, have become important to governments and universities that compete internationally' (Kim, 2017: 981). In the same vein, academics are exposed 'to new contexts that can lead to new knowledge creation' (Kim, 2017: 981), as cross-border academic mobility and migration take place. As such, the mobility of international teachers can either be facilitated or hindered or both, depending on the spatial differences between actors in given social and educational contexts (Park, 2013).

In a context like Saudi Arabia, for instance, English education has been increasingly seen as what Gao and Park (2015: 78) describe as 'a spatial project of linguistic investment,' in which the Saudi government is constantly and even aggressively spending billions of dollars to promote mass literacy in English language education (Barnawi, 2018). This aim has been realized through introducing English courses at primary school level, adopting English medium of instruction policies and practices across local HE institutions, internationalizing HE bodies, and constantly importing

Western products, goods and services (Barnawi, 2018; Phan & Barnawi, 2015). Today, becoming a competent English language user in Saudi Arabia, where there is a foreign workforce of over nine million people driving the engine of the economy and where learning/knowing English is becoming more important than learning/knowing Arabic, means that you are more likely to have access to better job opportunities.

Seeing the acquisition of the English language as cultural and economic capital and attaching instrumental values to the learning of English have led to the creation of a mass English education market across the country. It is also under these conditions that international publishers such as Pearson, Cengage, McGraw Hill, Cambridge University Press and Oxford University Press have invaded the Saudi market with their commercialized textbooks, prepackaged teaching materials, exams and assessment practices, labeled as 'Kingdom of Saudi Arabia Version,' 'Middle Eastern Version' and 'Arabian Gulf Version' (Barnawi, 2018). Ironically, these English education materials being imported into the Saudi market by these international publishers are based mainly on the 'communicative language teaching' (CLT) and task-based learning (TBL) approaches, which are often inappropriate for the immediate needs of Saudi EFL learners, as scholars like Barnawi (2011, 2018), Barnawi and Phan (2014) and Phan (2014) have thoroughly discussed and documented. Additionally, these English education materials, including curricula, syllabi and assessment practices, are based on the *Common European Framework of Reference for Languages: Learning, Teaching, Assessment* (CEFR; Council of Europe, 2001), a framework that is still ineffective, even in the context for which it was originally designed (see, for example, Bérešová, 2017; Foley, 2021).

At the same time, the increasing movement of international teachers of mixed origins (e.g. a person whose mother is English and whose father is Pakistani) into contexts like Saudi Arabia 'means increased mobility across markets of accents and speech varieties' (Blommaert & Dong, 2010: 369), of pedagogies, cultures, repertoires and the like. However, according to Blommaert and Dong (2010: 369), 'what works well in one place can backfire elsewhere.' Earlier work shows how mobility is often dictated by material conditions such as economic background/status or 'issues of cultural and social integration,' which largely limit 'options of movement for less privileged people' (Gao & Park, 2015: 81). Importantly, the promise of the mobility of international teachers in a particular place may be a false one, since it is not guaranteed that their movement would simultaneously secure economic and linguistic benefits for the host country. This is particularly true for the current turn of multinationalism, multiculturalism and multilingualism in the field of TESOL which constructs the mobility of international teachers 'in complex material conditions and inequalities that make up the sociolinguistic and socioeconomic landscape of neoliberalism that we live in' (Gao & Park, 2015: 80). We address these issues in detail below.

Multinationalism, Multiculturalism and the Multilingualism Turn in the Age of TESOL Teachers' Mobility

TESOL, as a profession and a field of study, is expanding more and more rapidly as the endorsement of English as an international/global language is getting stronger and stronger, almost globally. The field of TESOL, in many ways, has brought together language teachers from different backgrounds, races, religions, cultures and ethnicities to co-create a very dynamic field which has produced cutting-edge scholarship and has helped inform policy, pedagogy and practice around the world. These professionals also constantly co-construct knowledge that is central to language education, policies, curricula, pedagogies and research. The TESOL International Association is perhaps one of the largest professional associations globally, with members coming from almost every country in the world. As a matter of fact, thousands of multinational, multilingual and multicultural individuals have become TESOL teachers and educators in different parts of the world. With globalization and the demand for English enabled by the global neoliberalism-driven English fever, these teachers often move from one country to another in order to seek better teaching positions and to diversify their experiences. Such movements have greatly contributed to the expansion and growth of TESOL. As a field, a profession and a professional entity, TESOL is truly global in many ways, and it is committed to diversity and inclusivity, at least in principle. This global orientation of TESOL is evident in its credo, as Liu and Berger (2015: 3) show:

> [TESOL enjoys] professionalism in language education, interaction of research and practice for educational improvement; accessible, high quality instruction; respect for diversity, multilingualism, and multiculturalism; respect for individual language rights; and collaboration in the global community …. (TESOL International Association)

However, this very field, TESOL, contains many limitations and inherent problems, as pointed out in numerous scholarly works (Barnawi & Phan, 2014; Chowdhury & Phan, 2014; Kiczkowiak & Lowe, 2021; Kubota & Lin, 2009; Motha, 2014; Park, 2018; Selvi, 2014; Simpson & O'Regan, 2018; Yazan & Rudolph, 2018; and so on). Since its inception in 1965, the field of TESOL has been 'a pedagogical site and institution for educating the racial and linguistic Other' (Luke, 2004: 25). It has been argued that 'the TESOL field is implicated in neo-colonial relations of power and the work of teacher educators in this field can be seen as securely in the service of mobilizing global capital' (Ilieva & Waterstone, 2013: 16). At the same time, scholars such as Canagarajah (1999), Golombek and Jordan (2005), Holliday (2005) and Kubota and Lin (2006) argue that a major feature of neo-colonial discourses is the hegemonic attack on non-native English-speaking teachers (NNESTs). This is coupled with an inequality in power relations in the field of TESOL. The discourses in which NNESTs are compared unfavorably with native-English-speaking teachers (NESTs) in the field of TESOL have taken various forms and were examined in depth in earlier scholarship. In the hiring of international English language teachers, for instance, it has been found that NESTs continue to have a privileged status in the market economy (e.g. Amin, 1997; Golombek & Jordan, 2005) across Western and non-English speaking countries. Racial discrimination against NNESTs in the TESOL profession has been captured and documented in job advertisements, accents, textbooks in use across periphery countries (Mahboob *et al.*, 2004; Matsuda, 2002; Selvi, 2010; Sulaiman Jenkins, 2019), standards of language proficiency (Canagarajah, 1999; Holliday, 2005), in their significantly low representation as invited and keynote speakers at TESOL conferences (Kiczkowiak & Lowe, 2021), and in research publications (Kubota & Lin, 2006), among other types of epistemological racism (Kubota, 2020), thereby marginalizing multinational, multilingual and multicultural teachers who come from non-English speaking nations and cultures.

At the same time, poststructuralist and postcolonial scholars argue that the monolingual ideologies and discourses that have long dominated the field of TESOL are no longer in vogue. They have been replaced by 'multinational', 'multilingual' and 'multicultural' perspectives (e.g. May, 2014; Pennycook, 2010). In this regard, multinationalism is 'thematically concerned with multilevel governance, constitutional devolution and federalism' (Meer, 2015: 1487). It often foregrounds issues of identity, rights, history, justice and citizenship in a given social and educational space (McEwen *et al.*, 2012; Miller, 1995). It also pays close attention to governments or countries 'that have restructured themselves to accommodate significant sub-state nationalist movements' (Kymlicka, 2011: 282), such as the professional mobility of teachers. Multilingualism, on the other hand, is defined both as 'an individual' as well as 'a social phenomenon'. As Cenoz (2013) states:

> [i]t can be considered as an ability of an individual, or it can refer to the use of languages in society. Individual and societal multilingualism are not completely separated. It is more likely that the individuals who live in a multilingual community speak more than one language than for individuals who live in a monolingual society. (Cenoz, 2013: 4)

Indeed, there are various elements that have contributed to the emergence of multilingualism as an individual as well as a social phenomenon in various social and educational settings; these include 'globalization', 'technologies' and the 'transnational mobility' of populations (Barnawi & Ahmed, 2021; Cenoz, 2013; Conteh & Meier, 2014; De Costa *et al.*, 2020; Jain *et al.*, 2021; Kubota, 2014; Phan, 2017). Thus, it is important to recognize and examine the many opportunities as well as conditions that have both enabled and forced international teachers of English to move from one destination to another. Likewise, it is important to acknowledge that teachers of English and their workplace have also been expected and been under pressure to respond to and accommodate a highly mobile, multilingual, multicultural and multiracial student body that is constantly growing in number. As Han (2011) puts it:

> [w]ith increasing numbers of people moving across regional and national borders in search of better work and life opportunities in the globalized new economy, many societies and their institutions face the challenges of regulating and serving unprecedentedly diverse populations, with linguistic diversity an integral and important dimension. (Han, 2011: 383)

Multiculturalism, a slippery concept that originated in Canada in 1968, has been defined and interpreted differently by different multicultural theorists in various historical, political, social and educational settings. Conceptually, it evolved 'from an immigrant settlement programme, with pragmatic objectives, into an ideology' (Jupp, 1995: 208) that labels societies as multicultural, multi-ethnic and multilateral. Scholars like Kymlicka (2010: 97) define multiculturalism as 'a feel-good celebration of ethno-cultural diversity, encouraging citizens to acknowledge and embrace the panoply of customs, traditions, music and cuisine that exist in a multi-ethnic society'. For Hall (2000: 20), multiculturalism refers to 'the strategies and policies adopted to govern or manage the problems of diversity and multiplicity which multicultural societies throw up'. Other scholars (e.g. Jandt, 2020) also see multiculturalism as representing and encompassing diversity – 'a reality that has been in existence since the time of early human civilizations' (Hall, 2000). In this view, diversity refers to lifestyles, cultural traditions, norms, pedagogical practices, 'technological acquisitions, concepts, value representations, behaviours and institutions, explanations, interpretations, value rankings and traditions' (Marga, 2010: 106).

Heckmann (1993), in contrast, argues that multiculturalism is a multilayered concept in itself and cannot be used to clarify the discourse of diversity and heterogeneity among societies. For Heckmann, multiculturalism is defined in seven different ways in the contemporary literature. First, it refers to 'the changing ethnic composition of the population'; thus, it has become a descriptive category. Second, multiculturalism is used in a normative cognitive way to describe the inevitable need for immigrants; one has to accept the reality of this need and face the consequences. Third, multiculturalism is used to describe attitudes and norms; we have to tolerate and respect differences and learn from errors. Fourth, 'multiculturalism is an interpretation of the concept of culture: there are no "pure", original cultures. Each culture has incorporated elements of other cultures; cultures are the result of interaction with one another; culture is continuous process and change' (Heckmann, 1993: 245). For instance, cultural differences between international teachers with mixed backgrounds working in Saudi Arabia should be regarded as learning opportunities for all concerned parties. Fifth, multiculturalism is used to describe an attitude that sees immigrants' culture (e.g. food or clothing) as something that enriches the culture of the host country. Sixth, multiculturalism is seen as 'a political-constitutional principle' in which issues of ethnic identity are seen as primary pillars of the state organization, the distribution of resources and the practice of pluralism. Seventh, multiculturalism is used 'as a well-intended, but illusory concept which overlooks the necessity for a common culture, language, and identification to enable societal and state integration and stability' (Heckmann, 1993: 245).

More recently, Ubani (2013) contends that multiculturalism can be broadly divided into two categories: (i) descriptive and (ii) normative.

> Multiculturalism, in a descriptive sense, refers to the existence of different cultures and communities within a society. When multiculturalism is used in a normative sense, it is used to designate the set of normative and political responses and to present an increasing sociocultural diversity in contemporary society. (Ubani, 2013: 196)

Since TESOL, as a profession, field of study and international professional organization, is intended to respond to the needs of people from a diversity of linguistic, ideological, social and cultural backgrounds in a particular society, multiculturalism could act in a normative sense as well as a political response.

Alongside embracing multiculturalism, there has recently been a marked increase in scholarly engagement in and promotion of multilingualism in the fields of TESOL and applied linguistics. It is important to note that there is no clear-cut division between the term multilingualism and its associated terms such as bilingualism and trilingualism in the professional literature (see, for example, Aronin & Singleton, 2008; De Groot, 2011). We therefore treat multilingualism as a generic term that includes bilingualism and trilingualism throughout our book. Scholars have examined multilingualism from different perspectives at both individual and societal levels as well as at the intersection of the individual and the social. Some scholars have examined the cognitive outcomes of multilingualism among individuals (Bialystok *et al.*, 2008), individual multilingual brains (De Groot, 2011), as well as cross-linguistic interaction (Lin & Li, 2012; Paradis, 2007). Other scholars, on the other hand, have looked at multilingualism on a societal level (e.g. Gardner & Martin-Jones, 2012), including globalization and mobility of the population and multilingual identities (Pavlenko & Blackledge, 2004), multilingual classroom practices (Block, 2008a, 2008b; Canagarajah & Liyanage, 2012), and multimodality and new technologies (Shohamy & Gorter, 2009). For post-structuralist scholars, multilingualism is seen as 'a more nuanced and complex situation in which the market saturation of English has opened up opportunities for other languages' (Kubota, 2014: 475). Individual multilingualism in this case is linked to 'plurilingualism,' which pays close attention to 'the individual as the locus and actor of contact' (Moore & Gajo, 2009: 138). Through various experiences as well as exposure to different language situations, an individual can master more than one language during the course of his or her life. In the case of multilingualism as a social phenomenon, learners experience one of two cases: (i) additive multilingualism, in which an additional language (e.g. English) is added to the 'linguistic repertoire' of the learning when acquiring their first language (e.g. Arabic); or (ii) subtractive multilingualism, in which a new language replaces the first language of learners (see Cenoz, 2013; De Groot, 2011; Kramsch, 2009, for more accounts of these issues).

Nevertheless, these different orientations to multilingualism have also been criticized by many scholars (e.g. Cenoz, 2013; Cummins, 2007), for they seem to support what Harris (1998) describes as a 'segregationist' stance, in which the elements, varieties and uses of a language are treated 'as autonomous entities with clear linguistic boundaries' (Kubota, 2014: 476). Put differently, instead of looking at the relationship among the various elements of a language, segregationist views of multilingualism 'consider languages as discrete, fixed, and independent entities and imply that multilinguals are expected to be like two or more monolinguals' (Cenoz, 2013: 10). In this view, code-meshing and code-switching (Canagarajah, 2011a) are seen as problematic, since they are indicative of a student's lack of competence.

At the same time, other researchers have adopted a 'holistic' approach (also called plurilingualism) to examine multilingualism in the fields of TESOL and applied linguistics (Block, 2007; Cenoz, 2013; Cook, 1992; Moore & Gajo, 2009). This pluralistic orientation to language teaching and learning 'regards multilingual linguistic practices as products of language users' multiple repertoires that are employed in a contingent and flexible manner rather than an aggregate use of languages that are separated along structural boundaries' (Kubota, 2014: 477). From a holistic point of view, researchers like Cenoz (2013) argue that:

> the characteristics of multilingual speakers [are] ... different from those of monolingual speakers. Multilingual speakers use the languages at their disposal as a resource in communication, and as their repertoire is wider, they usually have more resources available than monolingual speakers. (Cenoz, 2013: 11)

This viewpoint shows that multilinguals are 'hyperlingual' (Block, 2007), and that the resulting hybridity and fluidity they possess will always allow them to negotiate meanings, posit their voices and construct their identities in a language classroom in a 'fluid' as well as a heterogeneous manner (Block, 2007; Cogo, 2012; Kubota, 2014). Several terms associated with multilingualism, including hybridity (Rubdy & Alsagoff, 2014), world

Englishes (WE; Kachru *et al.*, 2006), English as a lingua franca (ELF) translingual approach (Horner *et al.*, 2011) and multiliteracies (Cope & Kalantzis, 2009) are seen as counter-discourses to monolingualism and native-speakerism in the profession of TESOL.

Overall, multilingualism is a multi-faceted term, and researchers have examined it from various directions in order to address particular social and educational phenomena. In our book, however, we will capture and document the ways in which both monolingual and multilingual international teachers of English interact and at the same time negotiate their linguistic and intellectual resources as well as their intercultural competencies in their current workplace in Saudi Arabia. These international teachers teach mostly non-English speaking Saudi students but in their everyday work environment they interact mostly with peers who are speakers of English from many other countries; therefore, we would like to refer to their work and social space as *a multi-Englishes-speaking community*. By *a multi-Englishes-speaking community*, we refer to international teachers, including native-English-speaking teachers, non-native English-speaking teachers and teachers who speak English as an additional language. These teachers are of different racial, cultural, linguistic, social, religious and ideological backgrounds, who interact, negotiate and transform their linguistic and intellectual resources as well as their intercultural competencies in a given social and educational setting. In the case of what we discuss in this book, Saudi Arabia is the focal point.

Emotion and Affect, Emotion(al) Labor and Affective Practice

The scholarly inquiry pursued in this book has also opened up an avenue for us to engage with a recurring line of scholarship on emotion and affect which has recently received much attention among scholars in language education, applied linguistics and TESOL (see, for example, Barcelos & Aragão, 2019; Benesch, 2017, 2019, 2020; De Costa *et al.*, 2018, 2019; Prior, 2019; Schuman, 2019; Song & Park, 2019; Viete & Phan, 2007). We bring into the conversation a different angle on transnational academic mobilities, that is, *transnational emotion labor*, as we examine the on-the-ground working realities of international TESOL teachers in Saudi HE. We observe that these teachers engage in complex interactions with themselves, their professional training and experience, their students and the institutions where they work, and the broader cultural, social and religious surroundings of Saudi Arabia. Such interactions, expressed in varied forms and intensities, are a manifestation of 'emotion labor' – discussed extensively by Benesch (2017, 2019, 2020), among others. Such emotion labor shouldered by English language teachers remains under-researched and, therefore, demands more scholarly investigation.

The remainder of this section was originally published in an article that Phan Le Ha co-authored with Abdullah Alshakhi on the emotion labor of transnational TESOL teachers working in Saudi higher education (Alshakhi & Phan, 2020). We acknowledge that Phan Le Ha has solely written this section and has sought permission from Sage to reproduce it here.

Emotional labor refers to the self-regulation, self-management and commodification of emotion as one is expected to observe and follow workplace rules, guidelines, protocols, procedures, terms, norms, policies and mandates (Hochschild, 1979, 1983). These workplace standards assume and expect particular behaviors, consumption and displays of emotion that are deemed to be appropriate, acceptable, desirable and professional, which Hochschild (1983) theorizes as workplace *feeling rules* (cited in Benesch, 2019: 531). Workplace feeling rules and their underlying connotations vary according to contexts and each specific workplace; and power is often at the core of such rules and connotations. Studying and conceptualizing emotional labor, hence, ought to recognize the role of power and the sociopolitical dimension of the (work)place so as to understand the multiple layers of factors and pressures shaping teachers' emotion labor. Drawing on carefully discussed scholarship on this area, Benesch (2017, 2019, 2020) argues for the conceptualization of what she terms 'emotion labor' as being discursive and socially shaped by wider sociopolitical and institutional norms, power relations and practices. While we largely engage with Benesch's conceptualization and theorization of emotion labor in this book, we also bring into the conversation other related theoretical discussions that place emotion labor in complex relationships with emotion, affect and emotional capital, as elaborated below.

Emotion and affect are interdisciplinary, complex and contested concepts, bearing multiple theoretical underpinnings and conceptual foundations within and across disciplines (Ahmed, 2004; Al-deen & Windle, 2016; Benesch, 2019, 2020; Bigelow, 2019; Prior, 2019; Wetherell, 2015). Scholars in applied linguistics and language education, for the past decade, have been raising concerns about the lack of scholarly attention to emotion and affect as well as the under-theorization of these constructs, and have thus called for an 'affective turn' (see Prior, 2019: 516, for more details). This 'affective turn' has resulted from sustained critiques of certain works on psychology and on language and learning theories that fixate on the cognitive and bodily inherent traits of emotion and affect. Likewise, the 'affective turn' counters works that detach emotion and affect from social, cultural and political histories and conditions.

The 'affective turn' in applied linguistics and language education takes place alongside the re-emergence of affect 'as a key site in social and cultural research' (Wetherell, 2015: 139). In thoroughly reviewing several highly influential lines of scholarly works on affect and emotion, Wetherell (2015) shows how certain theorizations contribute to the categorization and hierarchization of emotions and affects into rigid establishments such as strong and weak, positive and negative, and low and high. Such establishments often characterize individuals, communities and groups into stereotypes that could sideline critical questions of inequality, ethics and gender politics. They also risk leading research on affect to a dead end because of their inherent biases and flaws. These categorized and hierarchized establishments of affect cannot help explain complexly diverse emotional responses either. Wetherell (2015) praises Ahmed's (2004) widely cited cultural politics of emotion and representation for its rigorous and sophisticated engagement with the cultural politics and relationality of affect and recognizes its tremendous scholarly contributions that speak to scholars in multiple fields. Nonetheless, Wetherell (2015) has pointed out flaws in Ahmed's analytical framework, particularly its hard-to-understand depersonalization of emotion and affect, given Ahmed's highly sophisticated conceptualization of emotion. This problem, as Wetherell argues, leads to emotion/affect floating out there and being detached from the person/body/mind. So, to move scholarship on emotion/affect forward, Wetherell (2015) offers her theorization of *affective practice* as follows, which we find helpful for our study:

> … [A practice approach emphasizes] relationality and negotiation, attentive to the flow of affecting episodes. A practice approach positions affect as a dynamic process, emergent from a polyphony of intersections and feedbacks, working across body states, registrations and categorizations, entangled with cultural meaning-making, and integrated with material and natural processes, social situations and social relationships. (Wetherell, 2015: 139)

Wetherell's (2015) critique of Ahmed (2004) echoes Prior (2019) and Schuman (2019), who are also critical of approaches to emotion that rely almost exclusively on sociocultural, political, historical and contextual factors and that simultaneously disregard human minds and undermine their complexities. The critiques from these scholars, to some extent, apply to Benesch's (2020) justification for using emotion labor instead of emotional labor – the more commonly used term.

> My use of 'emotion labor' rather than the more commonly used 'emotional labor' is due to the negative connotation of 'emotional,' a term often used to suggest that someone, especially a woman, is behaving in an overwrought and socially undesirable manner. Furthermore, by linking 'emotion' and 'labor,' I am emphasizing the relationship between emotions and power rather than qualifying the labor as emotional. (Benesch, 2020: 39)

Benesch's critiques of emotional in emotional labor appear to be a little at odds with Al-deen and Windle (2016), who affirm the importance of emotional labor in their study with Muslim Iraqi immigrant mothers' involvement with their children's education in Australia. Firmly located in a

Bourdieusian framework of capital and in the emerging scholarship on emotional capital, Al-deen and Windle (2016: 111) show 'how emotional labor is situated differently in relation to cultural, institutional and market hierarchies for a particular group of mothers who have moved between social fields through the process of migration'. Importantly, they indicate that these mothers all see their emotional labor as a domestic and moral responsibility concerning their involvement in their children's education. Nevertheless, whether or not their emotional labor is recognized as capital depends on the relationships between emotional capital and other forms of capital that these mothers possess, accumulate, display and reflect on. By analyzing these mothers' emotional labor in relation to emotional capital and discourses on motherhood, neoliberalism, and Islam and Muslims, Al-deen and Windle (2016) point to the complex nature of emotional labor, showing a wide range of emotions expressed, enacted, adopted and cultivated by their female participants in transnational space. Importantly, their focus on emotional labor does not suggest that labor is emotional but, instead, solidifies the need to engage critically with a range of emotions in the context of transnational migration and neoliberalism. We find their work relevant to what we aim to examine in this book as well.

Among ongoing interdisciplinary conversations on emotion and affect, we also find Benesch (2019, 2020) highly pertinent to our study. Specifically, Benesch's (2019) theorization of emotion labor from a sociopolitical stance, much influenced by Ahmed (2004), highlights the multiple roles of social practice, power and human agency in studying emotion. These constructs take into account the dynamic, dialogic and multi-directional entanglements of emotion/affect which occur and are generated not only in specific and personalized but also in more general contexts, settings and situations. It questions social discourses and explains systemic racism and privilege. It places blames for wrongdoings on institutions and their policies, rules and regulations rather than on individuals. We also see this line of argument evident in Benesch (2020) on emotion labor and activism, although Benesch (2020) does not refer to Ahmed (2004).

For Benesch (2020), emotion ought to be conceptualized as being discursive and socially constructed, whereby prejudice, power, hierarchy, inequality, injustice and agency should be identified and addressed. She argues that emotion is driven and generated by certain institutional, cultural, social and historical circumstances, and emphasizes the relationship between emotions and power. Benesch (2020) shows how the English language instructors at her own university in the US expressed a sense of ambivalence when it came to high-stakes standardized testing. Specifically, these teachers acknowledged the inevitable aspect of testing ('*discourse of inevitability*'), but also indicated problems associated with this kind of test, noting their students' immigrant backgrounds and their likely unfamiliarity with certain elements of the test ('*discourse of unfairness*') (Benesch, 2020: 33). Intertwined with this sense of ambivalence, these teachers recognized issues with discrimination and exclusion embedded in their university's practices that prevented non-native students of English from 'pursuing their degrees in a timely manner' (*'discourse of injustice'*) (Benesch, 2020: 35). Benesch (2020) then sees teachers' emotion labor as a powerful source of activism which could be engaged with, mobilized and invited to bring about positive changes to the system, and to demand equity and justice as well as academic freedom for both teachers and students. Hence, instead of handling emotion privately to adjust to the institutional demands and to come to terms with the ambivalence discussed above, teachers can come together and communicate their emotion labor in a productive and empowering manner for the betterment of pedagogy, teaching and learning.

However, up to this point, we feel that there is a missing element: *the inter-individual*. Specifically, Phan Le Ha's recent work engages with and builds on Vološinov's (1929/1986, 1929/2017) theorization of ideology to examine affect/emotion displayed in personal and artistic encounters with English (Phan & Bao, 2019).

> For Vološinov, ideology and power are lived and felt, integral to the processes of living and feeling, which are social, inter-personal and inter-individual. He viewed the individual psyche as having a social origin, and as such one's inner voice is never detached from the social individual. The inner voice, the individual and the inter-individual interact and communicate through signs whose meanings are shaped by multiple and changing contexts. (Phan & Bao, 2019: 240)

Seeing 'ideology and power as lived and felt' does not reject the metaphysics and metanarratives of contexts and meaning-making, while making prominent 'a politics of the self' that anchors in the self's complex and dynamic social, inter-personal and inter-individual multiplicities, moments, experiences, encounters, responses and articulations (Phan & Bao, 2019: 241). Through emphases on the social inter-individual and its multifaceted dialogues with others and with its immediate and far-out contexts, as the authors reflect on their personal and professional experiences with English, Phan and Bao (2019) share some common ground with and complement Ahmed's (2004) cultural politics of emotion, Benesch's (2019, 2020) theorization of emotion and emotion labor, Al-deen and Windle's (2016) discussion of emotional labor and emotional capital, and Wetherell's (2015) affective practice framework. We use *emotion(al) labor* throughout the book to signify the complex intertwinedness explained above.

Thus far we have introduced and discussed a number of theoretical concepts and debates that we consider important and relevant to what we aim to examine and put forward in the book. While we are making every effort to engage them in our presentation and make sense of the multiple accounts collected from varied sources, we acknowledge that we are not aiming to bring every single concept and debate into every chapter of the book. Rather, some concepts and debates are more pertinent in some chapters than in others, and they are not meant to be juxtaposed for the purpose of comparing their importance in understanding the on-the-ground realities of international TESOL teachers working in Saudi Arabia. At the same time, we do not intend to test any theories or to interpret the data under any particular framework or theoretical concept; rather, our purpose is to theorize the on-the-ground realities experienced, perceived and expressed by the many international TESOL teachers we have encountered. We seek to bring fresh ideas, insights, empirical evidence, and different conceptualizations and theorizations into the already well-established fields of TESOL, language education and applied linguistics.

4 Unpacking Mobility Drive: Geographical, Personal, Financial, Professional and More

Preface

In this chapter and those that follow, readers may feel overwhelmed by the many details about so many teachers that we will include and refer to. Readers may also wonder why we did not just focus on some key informants and told in-depth stories about them so as to highlight featured findings and to emphasize key arguments. Readers may find us a bit 'greedy' and seemingly 'unorganized' when we introduce almost every teacher out of the 48 participants that took the time to engage with us throughout the course of our study. We acknowledge that we are aware of potential criticisms of this on-the-surface unwise decision. Personally, we are indebted to all the participants and felt it was important to feature each and every account.

The purpose of this chapter and the rest of the book is not to select a few participants' narratives on transnational mobilities and what such mobilities have entailed. Rather, we would like to first introduce the participants and their mixed professional, educational, ethnic, linguistic, cultural, racial and experiential backgrounds as we engage with their mobilities and their life stories and circumstances prior to Saudi Arabia that have led to their relocation to this country. These hugely rich backgrounds, we believe, will help readers when reading the subsequent chapters to make sense of the many pedagogical decisions these teachers made and did not make in their classrooms as well as their aspirations to (dis)engage themselves in the workplace, and their future trajectories expressed from the very location they were in, be it their institutions, their programs or their appointments.

Likewise, it is our deliberate decision to showcase the busy and crowded volume of details about these teachers in this chapter and the subsequent chapters. We hope this sense of crowdedness and intensity will help readers imagine the 'superdiversity' (Blommaert, 2013) of the TESOL 'messy marketplace' (Blommaert, 2010) in Saudi Arabia and what was going on in this marketplace as projected and conveyed by and seen through these teachers' accounts. We are hopeful that readers will follow us around and jump on and off our TESOL high-speed train to enter seemingly endless doors to grapple a tale here and there about different teachers. While we recognize that traveling on a high-speed train may make it difficult for passengers to appreciate in depth certain scenes during the journey, we would also like to use this high-speed train metaphor to portray the endless speedy flow of international TESOL teachers in and out of Saudi Arabia, a complex land of promise, as we call it.

We also aim to evoke imagination among readers about these teachers' transnational mobilities and many directions, twists and turns that they come across and against, because the on-the-ground realities they have faced and lived do not constitute a sense of coherence and continuity and do not necessarily follow any particular pattern that can be generalized via the storyline of some key informants' accounts. However seemingly fragmented and incoherent these abundant accounts may appear in our here and there extracts and retellings, we have genuinely tried to capture these teachers' everyday interactions at work, with students and colleagues, the multiple tasks and assignments they performed, and their varied perceptions of and attitudes towards the TESOL profession and their own professional lives. Very importantly, featuring the lived experiences of 48 participants (and those of other teachers from other studies and those who contacted us independently) has allowed us to capture rich, complex and contradictory accounts of the mobilities of international TESOL teachers and their on-the-ground realities in Saudi Arabia, which is a super highway of the TESOL marketplace, yet remaining under-studied.

International TESOL Teachers in the Saudi Market: Who Are They?

Generally speaking, like academic mobility in general, international TESOL teachers' (im)mobility is 'subject to national particularities and institutional contingencies – including informal, implicit rules of the game as well as legal rules and conditions of employment' (Kim, 2017: 982). There are also other factors that are inherent in and arising from the very act of mobility, as we show in each chapter and collectively throughout the book. At the same time, the different social meanings and cultural values attributed to a particular group of TESOL teachers, together with their different language varieties, nationalities, qualifications, attitudes, behaviors and ways of speaking serve as particular forms of 'a semiotic resource through which spatial difference is constructed and through which mobility may be facilitated or restricted' (Gao & Park, 2015: 79). Taking these arguments into consideration, we have been curious to learn about the demographic and layered mobilities of international teachers teaching English in Saudi Arabia, particularly those teaching at higher education institutions (HEIs).

Although the participants in this study numbered 200, in this chapter and those that follow we focus primarily on the responses from 48 participants who completed all the sections in the survey, and among these 48 participants on six of them who also allowed us to observe their classrooms and then participated in the follow-up interviews. The findings of our study show that international TESOL teachers in Saudi Arabia come from a variety of countries including the English-speaking West, countries in the Middle East and Africa, as well as Asia, the Caribbean and other European countries. While many participants are bilingual/multilingual and with years of teaching experience, the rest do not see themselves as being able to function in languages other than English, but they all have had at least some limited experience learning another language at some point in life. Therefore, in light of the current scholarship on language education, bilingualism and translanguaging (for instance, Canagarajah, 2011b; García & Li, 2017; García & Lin, 2017), these teachers could potentially draw on their linguistic repertoire and language learning experience to make a difference in their classroom teaching and pedagogy, regardless of how limited this might be.

Among the participants, the number of English language teachers originally from Asia who do not necessarily identify English as their first or native language is significantly higher than that of teachers who identify themselves as native-English-speaking (NES) teachers. As shown in Figure 4.1, out of the 200 teachers who responded to our survey: those that identified themselves as native-English speakers from Inner Circle

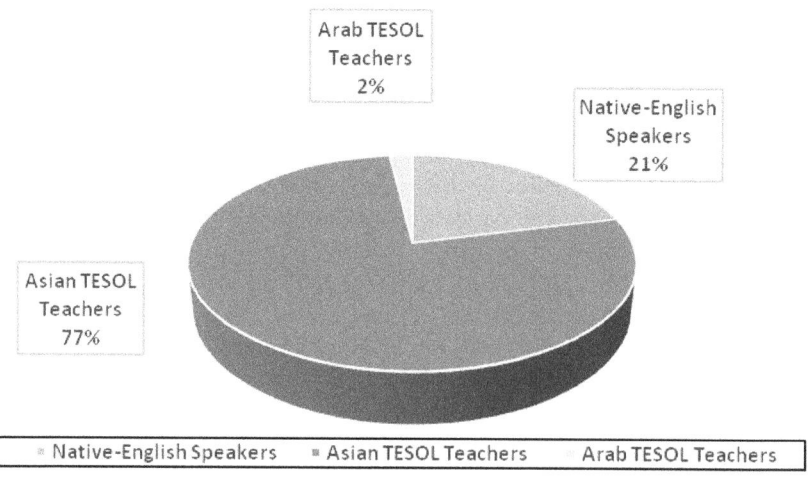

Figure 4.1 The demographic of international TESOL teachers in Saudi HEIs

countries occupy around 21% of the teaching positions; Arab teachers from neighboring countries such as Sudan, Jordan and Egypt account for 2%; and the remaining 77% are made up of almost all non-native English-speaking (NNES) teachers from Asia plus one teacher from the Caribbean.

Although we recognize and agree with the many limitations associated with labeling teachers of English as native and non-native teachers that earlier work has identified and discussed (Davies, 2003; Holliday, 2005; Llurda, 2005; Mahboob, 2010), we would also like to acknowledge that the participants used these labels to refer to themselves and others. They did not seem to use these labels in any negative light but rather as a neutral term without any indication of superiority or inferiority regarding self-worth. However, they showed varied degrees of awareness and criticality of the use of these labels by employers, institutions, recruitment agencies, students and the general public if such use embedded or implied discrimination and mistreatment of teachers. The subsequent chapters delve into these aspects in more depth. We (Phan and Barnawi) find ourselves, on different occasions, employing these terms to self-position as well. As a matter of fact, we have, in many cases, described ourselves as non-native teachers of English because we both learnt other languages before learning English as a foreign language at school in our home countries – Vietnam and Saudi Arabia, respectively. We have, as well, actively engaged in scholarly discussion and debates on critical issues underlying the native–non-native divide and dichotomization discourse deeply rooted in ELT and TESOL at all levels (e.g. Barnawi, 2018; Barnawi & Phan, 2014; Phan, 2004, 2008).

We (Phan and Barnawi) have, therefore, decided to refer to our participants overall as *international TESOL teachers*, but have also used the terms *transnational teachers*, *native-English-speaking* and *non-native English-speaking teachers* where necessary to tease out multiple layers of the data collected and of the ways in which the participants described their own and others' experiences and positionalities. All in all, together with the participants, we have been traveling within and across all these labeled and labeling spaces with an open mind, expecting the unexpected.

In this chapter, we focus in particular on NES international TESOL teachers, and the next chapter is dedicated to those participants who identify themselves as NNES teachers.

NES International TESOL Teachers: Saudi Arabia as Response to Financial, Personal and Religious Pursuits and Future Mobilities

As is evident in the data, the NES teachers working in Saudi HEIs have acknowledged that the main reason for their moving to Saudi Arabia to teach English was to escape financial hardship in their home countries. For some, there were religious motives as well as the irresistible financial benefits they would gain during their employment. There were also some teachers who perceived the Saudi market as a sort of layover where they could save money and then travel around the world.

It was noted in the data that the overwhelming majority of NES teachers teaching English in Saudi HEIs do not hold relevant degrees in English language teaching and learning, nor do they have much experience of learning a second or foreign language. These teachers can be divided into two categories: teachers with 'starter pack survival' (Hobbs, 2013: 174) qualifications (this will be explained below); and teachers with degrees *relevant* to English language teaching and considered *qualified* by the profession. By relevant degrees we are referring here to qualifications related specifically to English language teaching and learning, such as three-year or four-year BA degrees and/or postgraduate/MA degrees in English language teaching (ELT), English as a second language (ESL), English as a foreign language (EFL), linguistics, applied linguistics and TESOL.

As shown in the data, the teachers with 'starter pack survival' (Hobbs, 2013: 174) qualifications have obtained at least a Bachelor's degree in non-TESOL areas such as music, political sciences, computer sciences, sociology, business administration, public accounting, finance, law and criminology, and communication. To apply for ELT positions in Saudi Arabia, they supplemented these BA degrees with starter pack survival courses such as the 'TESOL Certificate', 'CELTA – Certificate of English Language Teaching to Adults' and 'DELTA – Diploma in Teaching English to Speakers of Other Languages'. For them, the requirements for the teaching job are generally rather easy, and therefore what they have supplied the employers with seem to have been sufficient to secure them attractive teaching positions in the Saudi market.

Many of these teachers, in their responses provided in the survey and in follow-up interviews, seemed to think that they can successfully teach Saudi students to improve their linguistic and communicative competency on the sole basis that they are native speakers of English plus the certificates(s) they have obtained from some short-term training in TESOL. What is more, some of these teachers have also been placed in various management and leadership positions in Saudi HEIs, including those of 'a program and curriculum leader', 'a research and development coordinator' and a 'program coordinator', to name a few.

NES international TESOL teachers with 'starter pack survival' qualifications

Let us first introduce you to some of our 'starter pack survival' (Hobbs, 2013: 174) qualifications teacher participants whose multiple interests, aspirations and calculations were depicted and expressed during the data collection period.

Adam, an African-American teacher who holds a Double Bachelor's of Science in Sociology and Education and a certificate in TESOL from an institution in Philadelphia, USA, was working as a university EFL teacher in Saudi Arabia when he participated in our study. He had had two years of teaching English at several centers and weekend schools for troubled youth and Muslim communities in the USA prior to taking his current job. **Adam** acknowledged that this very experience had contributed to making him qualified for the job. In his words, *'it was very easy for me to get the job of English teacher here.'* Additionally, his religion, Islam, was the main reason he gave for moving to teach in the Kingdom of Saudi Arabia (KSA). In addition to his teaching position, **Adam** had been appointed as one of the administrative consultants, *'helping to run the day-to-day operations of academics and [design] course outline and proposals'* at the institution where he worked.

Daniel, who holds a BA in Political Science and a CELTA from his home country, the USA, had had several years of teaching experience. After learning about his current job through the Davis ESL Café, he moved to the KSA, *'to save up money and travel around the region.'* Apart from the fact that *'the visa process was onerous,'* it was not difficult for him to get the job at all, as he reported.

Johnson, also from the USA, holds two Bachelor's of Science degrees, one in Business Administration and the other in Public Accounting, as well as a postgraduate TESOL Diploma. He was a teacher of computer science before moving to the KSA:

> *I taught computer science classes in Florida to business owners who were installing micro-computers in their businesses. I also taught ESL classes in South Korea on a full-time basis without a break from July 2004 until I arrived in Saudi Arabia and started teaching at XXX University in 2011.* (**Johnson**)

He gave the following justifications for his move to the KSA:

> *The cost of living in South Korea became prohibitively expensive, and the government increased the employment taxes on foreigners without telling them about what they were doing. I chose Saudi Arabia because there were no taxes.* (**Johnson**)

Johnson also commented that the hiring process in Saudi Arabia was one of quality, fairness and professionalism, while acknowledging that in the current environment it would be very hard for those without the relevant TESOL qualifications to get a job in the country.

> *I was very fortunate to be in the right place at the right time with sufficient qualifications to be accepted as a teacher for my present position. Now that the staffing situation has stabilized, I doubt if an ESL teacher without an English degree would be considered for a teaching position. I considered the hiring process thorough, comprehensive and fair. I never considered the hiring decision to have been made in an arbitrary or haphazard manner. I considered the process to have been professional.* (**Johnson**)

Sarah – the only female participant in our study – holds a PhD in Educational Administration from a university in New York, in her home country, the USA, and a TEFL certificate. She had 15 years' working experience prior to coming to the KSA owing to the availability of a *'better environment for children'* and a *'better salary.'* She learned about her current job through a personal contact and found it *'easy to get a job here.'* In addition to teaching, she had been appointed as the 'Research and Professional Development Liaison' officer at her institution.

Peter, who holds an MA in the Philosophy of Mind and Language, had seen Saudi Arabia as his long-term home. He reported that he had worked as teacher in various different places in the KSA for 20 years before settling in his current institution. For him *'financial gain'* and *'enjoyment'* were the primary reasons for coming to work in the KSA. He also learned about his current post from recruitment websites. He served as a writing tutor at the Writing Centre of his school alongside his teaching post. **Peter** found it rather easy to get a job in the KSA. For him, *'it was the usual process,'* he said.

Tim perhaps holds the most qualifications and certificates, all from his home country, the USA: a PhD in Rhetoric & Intercultural Communication; an MA in Rhetoric & Intercultural Communication; a BA in Speech Communication; the CELTA Teaching Certificate; and an online MA TEFL Teaching Certificate. Prior to taking up his current position at an institution in the KSA, he had been employed as 'a Communication and Culture professor' at a college in Daejeon, South Korea. He learned about his current job via the internet, and described his move to the KSA as follows:

> *I came to Saudi Arabia to land some of the highest-paying jobs for teaching English anywhere in the world.* (**Tim**)

Tim also felt that it was *'easy to get the job'*; by the time he participated in our study he had been serving as an academic coordinator at his institution, in addition to teaching.

Another case is **Simon**, who has a Bachelor of Law LLB (Hons) and Master's of Science in Criminology from a major research university in the UK. He shared his experiences of moving to the KSA as follows:

> *My brother works in Dammam and recommended that I come over here as the pay was very good for the hours worked. This was very appealing as the job market in the UK is very competitive. Also, Saudi Arabia appealed to me straight away, as I am used to the lifestyle here as well as the pilgrimage being round the corner. I applied through Tefl.com and the agency got in contact.* (**Simon**)

It is clear that all the teachers we have introduced above had enjoyed some teaching experience elsewhere prior to Saudi Arabia and that their prior teaching experience was considered favorably by their employers. In other words, their prior teaching experience worked to their advantage although they did not have the relevant ELT qualifications/degrees required by the profession. However, for those NES teachers who had almost no relevant work experience prior to moving to Saudi Arabia, it was not always easy or straightforward to get jobs in the country. Specifically, **James**, who has a BA in Music from an institution in the UK and a CELTA, felt that it was difficult for him to get a job overseas including his current post: '*I had to apply for many jobs first.*' He left his previous job at a finance firm in the UK and moved to the KSA because of '*the good salaries and interest in teaching adult learners.*' He was grateful to the agency that had offered him his current job.

NES international TESOL teachers with relevant qualifications

It should be mentioned, however, that there are also NES teachers with relevant degrees working in Saudi HEIs, and some such teachers took part in our study. Like almost every other teacher surveyed, these teachers cited reasons such as financial gain, economic returns and job scarcity in their host countries as the primary reasons for their move to Saudi Arabia. At the same time, they felt that securing a teaching position in the Saudi market was never a difficult task. Instead, through personal contacts and recruitment agencies which are constantly on the lookout for NES teachers, they not only secured teaching positions, but also acquired leading positions at their respective institutions. Examples of these cases are presented below.

Mario, who holds a BA in English from the California Commission on Teacher Credential, thought that getting an English teaching position in the KSA was '*a piece of cake*' and '*a timely job offer*,' since he had '*no teaching experience at all*' in the USA. He had been teaching English in Saudi Arabia for five years when we interviewed him.

Likewise, **Dan**, a Canadian teacher with an MA in TESOL, described his mobility and becoming-a-teacher journey in the KSA as follows:

> *I became a teacher by accident. I finished university with an English Literature degree, which is pretty useless for getting a job, but I found that I could use it to get a job like teaching English. I wanted to travel, so I found a job in Korea (in 1995 it was the easiest place to get a job).* (**Dan**)

He added,

> *I learned about my current position as I was researching information to present to my previous school in order to get a raise and computers in the classrooms. I compared my previous job's benefits to my present job's benefits and decided to switch schools.* (**Dan**)

Ben, who has an MA in Linguistics from a prestigious university in Montreal, Canada, speaks three languages: French, Amharic and English. Although he did not have any teaching certificates or diplomas, he stated that,

> *… teaching was part of my experience as a language learner since I speak more than one language. I was a language student for years and I draw*

upon this experience to be a better language teacher. I know what teaching strategies worked for me because I have been on both sides of the teaching process. (**Ben**)

After learning about his current post at the '*job fair of the 2005 TESOL Arabia Conference,*' **Ben** decided to move to the KSA in order to '*experience teaching ESL in the Arab world.*' Notably, he felt that it was never difficult for him to get a job in the KSA: '*my BA and MA studies in Canada prepared me well for this teaching position. I had teaching and research experience in Canada and Ethiopia.*' He was serving as the course coordinator for writing portfolio and technical report writing at his current institution when he participated in our study.

David holds an MA in TESOL from his home country, the USA. He taught ESL at an American school before moving to the KSA for '*better payment.*' He came across his current job through his friends. It was '*very easy*' to get a job in the KSA, **David** reported. He said happily, '*I am now course coordinator, in addition to my teaching duty.*'

Webber, from the UK, holds an MA in Applied Linguistics and a CELTA certificate. He had no teaching experience at all; however, through personal contacts he moved to the KSA in order to '*earn money*' and '*live an easy life.*' He also believed that 'it was easy to get a job' in Saudi Arabia.

Likewise, **William**, from Ireland, who holds a Master's degree in English Literature and a CELTA certificate, had no prior teaching experience in his home country. He described his experience as follows:

> *I decided to become an English teacher owing to the economic climate in Ireland, and the need to work abroad. I initially intended to teach for 1 year, but have found the job very enjoyable, and as a result have stayed with it. I came to the Middle East to earn a higher salary.* (**William**)

He also mentioned that, '*I learned about the current position through online advertisements (Dave's ESL Cafe).*'

The same experience was shared by **Berry**, a Canadian teacher with an MA in TESOL and a TEFL Diploma from one of the best universities in Toronto, Canada. He described his decision to move as follows: '*budget cutbacks forced me to look for other work; with a family to feed I did what I could.*' **Berry** then added,

> *I had pretty well made up my mind that Saudi Arabia was my next destination – it was about as far from my comfort zone (culture, religion, language) as I could imagine, so to my contrarian mind it was the obvious choice. It was while I was studying for my TESL diploma that I met a fellow Canadian, and he put my name forward with the XXX institution. And here I am.* (**Berry**)

Notably, TESOL teacher recruiting websites such as seriousteachers.com, Dave's ESL Café, Hire Pro LLC and Interlink are also targeting native speakers who are not only qualified to teach overseas, but also badly needed in non-English-dominant countries such as the Arabian Gulf region in general and Saudi Arabia in particular. Many NES teachers in Saudi Arabia have been recruited via local recruiting agencies such as the Quality Education Holding Company, Learn4Life and V2, which subcontract to and support Saudi universities, colleges and schools. These agencies operate as mediators in the Saudi market in order to fulfil the conflicting needs of local HEIs and businesses. While some Saudi HEIs are serious about their hiring requirements, others are just 'dying' to hire someone with a degree in any field plus a CELTA, a DELTA or a Cert-TESOL to teach English. From the data we have collected, the participants have reported inconsistencies and internal contradictions in many of the job advertisements being posted by online recruitment agencies and recruiting services like those mentioned above. The problems the teachers have identified include what we show in the following two job advertisements for multiple TESOL positions[1] posted by a recruiting agency called CBES which represents the aviation industry and a Saudi university:

Advertisement 1

We are seeking innovative and resourceful male and female ESL Instructors for a leading operator in the aviation industry. This position offers an excellent salary and benefits. Interviews will be held on 20th November in Washington DC for US Nationals. If you cannot attend an interview in Washington, an alternative arrangement may be offered. For candidates based in KSA, the interviews will be held within KSA.

Requirements:
Native of USA/Canada/U.K./Australia/New Zealand
CELTA/TEFL/TESOL
BA/MA English/Linguistic/TESOL/Education or minor English
Minimum three years of ESL teaching experience

Advertisement 2

Male and Female ESL Instructors needed in Riyadh and Dammam Saudi Arabia!
Duration: Minimum one-year contract
Availability: ASAP
CBES recruits on behalf of universities in Saudi Arabia. CBES are experts in providing support to secure a great teaching job overseas. We offer comprehensive support and have many years of extensive experience in this industry.

> Who are we looking for?
>
> (1) A teacher with a positive attitude
> (2) Native of USA [Any native available in Saudi Arabia can also be considered]
> (3) BA or MA in any field [Preferably an English major]
> (4) TEFL, TESOL or CELTA
> (5) No criminal record
> (6) No major illnesses
> (7) Minimum two years' teacher experience

What is noticeable in the first job advertisement is the flexibility and the NABA-only mentality (North America, Britain and Australia) in the hiring requirements of the aviation industry. This institution is also quite rigorous in its requirements, i.e. it will only hire teachers who hold relevant degrees (e.g. BA/MA in English/Linguistics/TESOL) with adequate teaching experience. The second job advertisement, by contrast, asks for teachers with a positive attitude, who are native speakers from the USA and who hold a BA or MA in any field plus certificates such as TEFL, TESOL or CELTA. As one of us has argued elsewhere, such short training courses as CELTA and DELTA 'do not encourage a critical approach to EFL instruction, nor [do they] pay explicit attention to language awareness' (Barnawi, 2018: 16). Instead, they tend to produce 'teachers with a rationalized efficient method that is universally appropriate: McTeachers with McQualifications' (Anderson, 2005, cited in Chowdhury, 2008: 34). This raises the question of how NES teachers who have only gone through such short training courses as CELTA and DELTA could be regarded as having a positive attitude and would be able to negotiate cultural and pedagogical issues and approaches with their students and peers.

Relevant TESOL Qualifications without Teaching Experience versus Starter Pack Survival Qualifications with Teaching Experience: Digging beyond the Surface

We have also noticed a somewhat uncomfortable reality from the data reported thus far. The brief accounts from the abovementioned teachers have raised several points for further discussion. First, the NES teachers with the 'starter pack survival' qualifications seemed to assume that their limited training in ESL/TESOL/EFL would not be a problem if they wanted to work as a teacher of English in a foreign country, in this case Saudi Arabia. Except for **Johnson**, who had moved to Saudi Arabia after years of EFL teaching experience in South Korea, all the other teachers had little teaching experience in English before moving to the KSA, but most of them had some teaching experience in other subject matters. Although these teachers made no effort to conceal the reasons behind their relocation to Saudi Arabia, and at the same time were honest about the kinds of easy-to-get certificates they had obtained to secure their current jobs, we should not lose sight of the fact that local HEIs in Saudi Arabia have been (pro)actively legitimizing such certificates by hiring these teachers directly or subcontracting them through local recruitment agencies.

Second, the data clearly show that all the surveyed NES teachers are very highly educated and most of them have graduated from reputable universities in English-speaking Western countries. They also seemed to possess sophisticated skills, expertise and knowledge, as is evident in the degree majors they have obtained. They do not seem to fit the category of unemployed, poorly educated or low-educated, unqualified and on-welfare backpacker teachers of English that has been highlighted in some of the literature (Bailey & Evison, 2020; Coskun, 2013; Evison & Bailey, 2019; Medgyes, 2011a; Mullock, 2009; Sarıgül, 2018; Stanley, 2013). Indeed, while these international TESOL teachers have all been attracted to the financial and benefit packages offered to them in Saudi Arabia, it is important to note that their 'academic mobility and migration are more often shaped by the intellectual centre/periphery relationships rather than merely directed by pure economic incentives [on their side]' (Kim, 2017: 984). Therefore, their economic incentives need to be put in perspective and ought to be understood in relation to the employer–employee dynamics and their own aspirations as teachers.

Third, those teachers with relevant teaching qualifications for TESOL/ESL/EFL like **Mario**, **Dan**, **Webber** and **William** have had little or zero teaching experience prior to their relocation to Saudi Arabia, whereas most of the teachers without the relevant teaching qualifications whom we featured earlier had at least some teaching experience or years of education-related work experience in other countries. In the existing literature, the former have always been projected as the *ideal teachers of English*, whereas the latter have been the target of criticism, merely based on the qualifications tag. There is little evidence in the existing literature to show that the former are better teachers in real-life classrooms, although hypothetically they should be, given the training they have received and the theories and knowledge they have been introduced to. In the same vein, it tends to be taken for granted that the latter are not qualified, and therefore they are deemed 'bad teachers' despite their rather impressive educational backgrounds and rich experience teaching/working in multiple settings.

Indeed, the geographical mobility of the international TESOL teachers featured thus far, as well as what accompany them in terms of qualification, expertise and experience, can be seen as being 'indexical of an ideal neoliberal subject' (Gao & Park, 2015: 81). In the context of increasing competition among teachers of English for employment in many countries around the world, the neoliberal project manifests in numerous forms. For example, using Turkey as a case study, Sarıgül (2018) argues that given the increasing competition within the TESOL field plus the high number of people who know and can access English these days, it is no longer easy or even possible for those without proper and relevant qualifications and relevant experience to be employed as teachers of English in many countries, including Turkey. Coskun (2013) conducted a study on 'Turkey to Hire' 2011 – a project from the Turkish government to recruit 40,000 NES teachers from Inner Circle countries to collaborate with local teachers to teach English in Turkey starting in 2012, so as to enhance the level of English among Turkish learners and hence leverage Turkey's international competitiveness. The study showed severe criticism against this project from different stakeholders before it was even implemented. The group that resisted this project the most strongly as expressed in the media was pre-service Turkish teachers of English. To explore their resistance, Coskun (2013) investigated 240 such teachers and found out that 189/240 held negative views towards the planned hiring because of 'employment and pedagogic concerns' (Coskun, 2013: 8). Specifically,

> Two sub-themes emerged under the theme of employment concerns: the fear of being replaced by the NEST [native-English-speaking teacher] and the perceived unequal treatment of the NEST and the NNEST [non-native-English-speaking teacher] in terms of salaries. Under the theme of pedagogic concerns, there appeared three sub-themes that are the poor teaching qualities of the NEST, the perceived drawbacks of co-teaching and the cost-effectiveness of the project. (Coskun, 2013: 8)

Coskun (2013) reports a strong sense of 'distrust [among the teacher participants] in the pedagogical teaching qualifications of their native English-speaking counterparts' and in the quality of teaching conducted by NESTs (Coskun, 2013: 9).

The findings from Coskun (2013) and Sarıgül (2018) have made us wonder to what extent the Saudi market could still accommodate a variety of expertise, experience and qualifications from its teachers of English that are not necessarily directly relevant to the requirements of ELT. We also wonder if this new reality has been a result of serious attempts to counter so-called *bad practice* in TESOL and ELT or simply a stepping stone to bring neoliberal ideals up to full speed.

We, nevertheless, would like to put forth that it is too simplistic to assume a clear-cut divide in terms of expertise, knowledge and teaching efficiency between those teachers with the necessary qualifications and those without. In the chapters that follow, we will show more complex insights into and nuances about the on-the-ground teaching realities and everyday language classroom happenings that we have observed and obtained from these teacher participants.

Note

(1) See http://www.seriousteachers.com/index/0/137/teaching-job-offers-from-saudi-arabia

5 Unpacking Often-Hidden Layers of Factors behind International Mobilities

NNES International TESOL Teachers: An Overview of their Multifold Mobilities

Following the previous chapter, let us now introduce you to our other teacher participants from various countries in Asia, from the Caribbean and from the neighboring countries in the Middle East, who make up 79% of our data sample. These teachers referred to themselves as non-native English-speaking (NNES) teachers. This number is significantly higher than that of native-English-speaking (NES) teachers (only 21%) in the Saudi higher education (HE) market that have participated in our study. Strikingly, our data indicate an increasingly warm welcome from the Saudi side given to NNES teachers in the Saudi market. These English language teachers do not necessarily identify English as their first or native language, and most of them speak at least three languages. Almost all of them have the relevant proper TESOL qualifications, while some started their employment in Saudi Arabia with CELTA and DELTA certificates.

Financial gain as the driving factor

The majority of these NNES TESOL teachers cited reasons such as *'financial gain'*, *'better salary'* and other materialistic reasons to justify their relocation to the Kingdom of Saudi Arabia (KSA). The teacher participants from neighboring countries like Jordan, Sudan and Egypt cited religion as a primary reason for their move, in addition to financial gain. There were also some teachers who cited issues such as security and culture as the primary motives for their relocation to the KSA. As will be shown below, while some teachers see their move to the KSA as a strategy to *'negotiate their values'* and *'invest in their qualifications'*, others see it as a way to *'escape from political crisis at home'*, *'gain new experience'*, *'explore new culture'* and as an *'affirmation of their values as non-native TESOL teachers'*. For almost all of these teachers, it was quite easy to get jobs in the KSA, and indeed some of them had worked at several institutions within the KSA, as well as moving across the Gulf region and the Middle East. Some of them had moved to the KSA from other teaching jobs in their home countries or in countries outside the Gulf region.

Chris, originally from Saint Lucia in the Caribbean, has a BA in Communications and Social Sciences from a private university in New York. He also has a TESL Certificate from International House, Toronto, Canada. After teaching Social Studies, English, French, Literature and History in Saint Lucia, he moved to the KSA in order to have an *'opportunity to travel throughout Africa, the Middle East and South Asia'*. He learned about his current position via job ads posted on the internet. He felt that getting the job in the KSA *'was very easy! Since I did my ESL Certificate with International House Toronto, Canada, it was therefore easy to get a job with International House, Saudi Arabia'*.

Sumah from Jordan holds a BA in English Language Teaching and has several years of teaching experience in his home country. Following his friends' advice and in order to experience living and working in the KSA, Sumah moved to the KSA because of *'the high salary'* as well as the *'religious status of Makkah and Madina'* and *'other personal reasons'*. Prior to his current job, he had worked in another institute in Saudi Arabia and he appeared proud of the experience he had accumulated.

> *When I applied for this job I had had four years' teaching experience from XXX, which is a renowned institute in Saudi Arabia. First, that place's reputation is accepted in Saudi Arabia as the premier workplace. Second, XXX equips its staff with the latest technology and aids needed for teaching. Finally, there is continuous professional development for the employees on pedagogies and learning theories.* (Sumah)

Ameer, who holds a BA in English from Damascus University, Syria, had over eight years of teaching experience in Jordan, Yemen and Syria before coming to Saudi Arabia. He learned about his current job from the internet. He, however, believed that *'it was difficult'* to get his current job in the KSA. Similar to **Sumah**, he cited cultural and religious reasons for moving to teach in the KSA: *'Close to Makkah and Madina'* and *'the culture of Saudi Arabia is close to the culture of my country (Jordan)'*. He is now 'Moodle Committee Chairman' as well as 'External Exam Committee Vice Chairman' at his workplace.

At the same time, it is evident from the data and from what the participants have elaborated in our further communications, that for the majority of Asian teachers such as those from the Philippines, Malaysia, India and Pakistan, the main reason for their moving to the KSA has been financial gain, in addition to other benefits and opportunities to grow professionally and to gain more experience. For instance, **Dong** has an MA from the University of the Philippines, his home country, and moved to the KSA for monetary reasons: *'it was the highest pay offer from among the available* *options*'. He declared that it was easy to get his current job: '*I sent in an application then got called for an interview three months later. I was offered the job on the very day of the interview.*' In addition to his teaching post, which he has held for over eight years, he is also a committee coordinator.

Likewise, **Roy**, who holds an MA in Teaching English Language from one of the top universities in the Philippines as well as an MA in Applied Linguistics from one of the premier universities in the UK, learned about his current job from friends and then moved to the KSA. He cited the following reasons for his relocation: '*very important financial and professional considerations prompted me to teach English in Saudi Arabia.*' He also added that:

> *it was not really difficult to get this teaching job in the KSA because I have prior teaching experience at the XXX and 13 years of university teaching and research publication experience at two major universities in the Philippines.* (Roy)

Alex has an MA in Language Education, a PhD in Language Studies for Teachers from his home country, the Philippines, and a TESOL certificate. After having taught English courses for eight years in his home country, he moved to the KSA because of the '*attractive salary and fringe benefits*'. He learned about his current job through an advertisement on a website and he reported that it was not difficult to get the job.

Aris from the Philippines holds an MA in English Language Teaching and a PhD in English Language Teaching and Education Management. Prior to moving to the KSA based on '*friends' recommendations*', he had taught for 16 years in tertiary education/universities in the Philippines, Vietnam and Cambodia and had worked simultaneously as a consultant for ELT/EFL/ESL/IELTS. It was mainly '*financial gain*' and '*professional development*' that brought him to the KSA. He also articulated that,

> *It was not difficult because I had the qualifications, knowledge and experience. Qualifications that matched the demands of ELT, knowledge which is helpful in understanding the learners and experience which is vital in the teaching-learning environment.* (Aris)

Raqib, who speaks Sindhi, Urdu and English and holds a PhD in TESOL and Applied Linguistics from a highly reputable research-intensive university in the UK, left his home country, Pakistan, in order to get a '*better monetary package.*' He described his experience as follows:

> *I saw the advertisement on the internet and applied for the job. Subsequently, interviews took place in my country and I was offered the position of Assistant Professor in the Department of Applied Linguistics at XXX.* (Raqib)

Abbas, who has an MA in Applied Linguistics and an MSC in International Relations from his own country, Pakistan, had taught at several universities in Pakistan. After 15 years of teaching, he left Pakistan and moved to the KSA for the following reasons: '*to liberate myself from bureaucracy, [and to find] financial reward and spiritual solace in the Kingdom.*' He came across his current job through '*a job fair at a conference.*' Like the other participants quoted above, he felt that '*it was easy to get jobs*' in the KSA.

Shah, who speaks Urdu, English, Punjabi and Hindko and holds an MA in EFL as well as a Diploma in TESOL, moved to the KSA because of '*good salary, good quality of life and Harman*'. He had worked as a lecturer at a university in Islamabad, Pakistan for several years before being introduced to his current job by his '*friends*'. He mentioned that it was '*absolutely easy*' to get a job in the KSA and has now been teaching foundation English courses for over 10 years.

Feroz was a Lecturer in English in the Air Force in Pakistan and had taught general English to the Air Force cadets for several years before moving to the KSA in order to '*earn enough money to start a doctorate and pay for my doctorate study.*' He learned about his current job in a local Pakistani newspaper, and got the job rather easily, as he described:

> ... it was not difficult in the sense that it was my very first attempt at a job in the KSA, and since I was successful, I would say it was easy. I did not face any difficulty in securing the job, though the visa process is pretty long and complicated. (Feroz)

Likewise, **Kurshaid** from Pakistan, who holds an MA in English Literature and a TESOL Diploma, moved to the KSA in order to find a '*better income.*' He had seven years' teaching experience before successfully obtaining his current job. He said: '*I got this job after a comprehensive written test and face-to-face interview.*'

Noor from Pakistan speaks English, Urdu, Punjabi, Hindi and Hindko and has an MA in English Literature. He also has a CELTA from the British Council in Sharjah in the UAE. After teaching in Pakistan for several years, he decided to move to the KSA for '*financial gain.*' In addition to his teaching duties, he is now 'Chairman of the Assessment Committee' at his institution.

Maher is a Sudanese doctor with an MA in Applied Linguistics and a PhD in Critical Applied Linguistics:

> I had been teaching linguistics, English literature, English for Specific Purposes – ESP (medical English, scientific English, technical English), and general English for 13 years before I came to KSA. (Maher)

Maher stated plainly that '*better payment*' and a '*better environment*' were the main reasons for coming to the KSA. However, he said that getting a job in the KSA was not difficult. As he stated, '*all the contract procedures (getting the job and coming here) were clear and smooth*'. It was through '*friends*' that he learned about his current job, and this was his '*fifth year*' in the KSA.

Likewise, **Ahmad**, a Sudanese lecturer with an MA in Applied Linguistics from a Sudanese university and a TEFL Higher Diploma from a university in Egypt, reported that he had moved to the KSA *'for a new and different teaching experience and to generate more money for a better standard of living'*.

Sabir holds a BA, MA and PhD in English from his home country, Sudan. He had taught at a major university in Sudan for 12 years, before moving to Saudi Arabia through a *'personal contact'* to *'gain a new experience'* and have a *'better salary'*. He felt it was easy to get his current job and he is now a member of the editorial board of the *XXXX University Journal of Human and Administrative Sciences*, in addition to his teaching tasks.

Mobilities beyond financial gain

A number of participants did not cite financial gain as the primary reason for their relocation to Saudi Arabia, although this does not mean that financial gain did not play a role in their decisions. It was quite easy for them to be recruited into the positions they had applied for. For example, **Ahmad** learned about his current job from the internet. Alongside his teaching, he was also appointed *'Head of the Curriculum Development Committee'*. He described his experience of getting a job in the KSA as follows: *'I applied, was interviewed and then got the job'*.

Salim holds a Bachelor's degree in English Literature, a BA in English education and an MA in English Literature from a major university in Calicut, Kerala, India; he speaks three languages – English, Hindi and Malayalam. Salim had had tremendous international experience and Saudi Arabia was just another destination on his teaching journey. Prior to Saudi Arabia, he had worked in *'various countries, different curricula, [and has had] a panoramic experience with students from different parts of the world, sharing and enjoying the world of the teaching-learning process for more than one and a half decades.'* He wanted to move to the KSA because he wished

> to extend the panorama of experience in the world of teaching and learning, to extend my experience of working abroad, and to get acquainted with the current practice of language learning. (Salim)

Suhail, who holds degrees from his own country, Malaysia, and from the UK, speaks three languages – Bahasa Melayu, English and Tamil. He has an MA in Language Teaching and Management as well as a TESOL certificate. From his post as a senior lecturer at a higher education institution in Malaysia, he moved to the KSA to gain *'new experiences'* and *'see other parts of the world'*. He came across his current job through a newspaper advertisement. He felt that getting the job was not difficult at all: *'I was the first to be called for the offer of the job after the interview'*. He also held the position of Course Coordinator at his school, in addition to his teaching duties.

Bashi, who holds an MA in Linguistics and CELTA from the UK, speaks two languages – Urdu and Punjabi – in addition to English. Following his *'friends' advice'*, he left Pakistan after having taught English for specific purposes (ESP) courses and general English for more than six years and moved to the KSA in order to *'search for new experiences'*. Like his colleagues, he found it easy to get the job. However, he reported that '[it took me] *more than one year to join after my first interview was conducted. I'm still unclear about the reasons for the delay'*.

Malik, who holds an MA in English Literature and Linguistics, moved to the KSA to *'explore a new teaching and learning environment'*. He also has a certificate in ESP from the USA and had taught undergraduate students for more than 10 years in his home country, Pakistan, before moving to the KSA. He got his current job rather straightforwardly; however, it took a very long time for his employment paperwork to be processed. While teaching, he was the *'coordinator for the Personalized Learning center'* at his school.

Azhari, another multilingual teacher (English, Urdu, Punjabi and Saraiki), holds a PhD in English Literature from a Pakistani university. Like most other Pakistani TESOL teachers participating in our study, Azhari stated that *'it was not difficult'* for him to get his job in the KSA after learning about it in a local Pakistani newspaper. He had taught courses such as *'English language and literature at undergraduate, graduate and postgraduate levels'* before moving to the KSA. He described his move as:

> *A quest to teach in an international organization, explore a new learning environment and study the culture of Saudi Arabia, which is the birthplace of Islam, brought me here.* (Azhari)

Supported by professional networks and family and friend circles

As is evident from their responses, many teachers from Pakistan and India have benefited hugely from the existing and robust professional network that actively recruits and recommends other peers at home for employment opportunities in the KSA. Many of these teachers have also enjoyed the support of family members and relatives who are residing and working in parts of the Gulf region such as the United Arab Emirates (UAE), Qatar, Bahrain, the KSA and Kuwait. For example, **Aziz**, who holds a PhD in English Literature from a university in Pakistan and speaks three languages – Urdu, Punjabi and English – has over 15 years' experience of teaching English to postgraduate level students. He came across the teaching post in the KSA via *'Pakistani friends'*. He cited his primary reason for coming to the KSA as follows: *'a wish to work in a different atmosphere pushed me to work here'*. Although it was not difficult for him to get a job in the KSA, he felt that *'the recruitment process was a lengthy and tedious one and it was also disrupted because of the non-availability of work visas'*. In addition to teaching, he served as course coordinator for the program he taught at his institution. Similar to Aziz, **Salim** learned about his current job from *'friends who are working in the KSA'*. He too felt that it was never difficult to get a job in the KSA; instead, *'it was processing which took time, I suppose'*, he asserted.

Khan, who speaks English, Urdu, Punjabi, Potohari and Hindi and holds an MA in TEFL together with CELTA and DELTA, moved to the KSA owing to the availability of *'American schooling for my kids'*. Prior to the KSA, Khan had been working for several years in the UAE. He learned about his current job while participating in a *'Toastmasters public speaking contest'* at his then institution. He further stated:

> In the UAE, I was settled with my family and in-laws. I was getting a higher salary than I'm even getting now. Owing to my experience in teaching EFL and my qualifications of Diploma TEFL, CELTA and DELTA (module 2 passed), it wasn't really difficult. I was familiar with Arabic culture and language because I had worked for seven years in the UAE. (Khan)

Arshad from Pakistan has an MA in English Literature from a university in Pakistan and a Diploma in TESL from the Canadian College of Educators. He taught college students in Pakistan for several years before moving to the KSA in order explore his *'ambition of teaching at the international level'*. He got the job through personal contacts and, according to him, *'it was not really difficult'* to get a job here.

Akan, who holds a BA in English and an MA in Curriculum and Instruction from Turkish universities in addition to a DELTA from ITI Istanbul, *'taught English at a foundation university in Turkey for 13 years'* before moving to Saudi Arabia. Moving from his home country, Turkey, to the KSA helped realize his aspiration to work overseas: *'I have always wanted to teach/work abroad, and being an accredited institution, the XXX was a good place to start'*. In addition to teaching, he was also a member of the 'Curriculum Committee' and the 'Language Assessment, Testing and Development Unit' and a 'Writing Centre Tutor'. Like many of the other participants, he learned about his job from friends. Although he felt getting the job was not difficult, he considered the experience to be *'quite stressful'* because of the paperwork and because he had had to wait six months to enter the country.

Zar, who speaks five languages – English, Chinese (including six dialects), Malay (Malaysian National Language), German and French – has an MA in English, a PhD in Education Management and Leadership and a TESOL certificate. Following his friends' advice, after working in his home country of Malaysia as well as overseas in the UK, he moved to the KSA ten years ago in order to *'earn more money'*. He further shared that, *'knowing the subject well, having experience and a passion for teaching made things easy. Being known by others in the profession and knowing someone important also makes it easier'.*

Fai, who holds an MA in TESOL and Education Technology, had several years of teaching experience in Malaysia. He wanted to move to the KSA *'to gain experience and share knowledge'*. He also learned about his current job via the internet and is now Head of the Education Development Centre while performing his teaching duties. For Fai, *'it was not difficult at all'* to get his position.

Maxi, who obtained his MA in Language Studies from a university in the Philippines, shared his experience of moving to the KSA as follows:

> *the lure of the financial benefits together with the unique opportunities to explore and experience new cultures, to establish new connections, and to discover my new potential in the field of language teaching.* (Maxi)

He felt that it was easy to get the job; however, the administrative process was complicated: *'from the time I signed the job offer, it took me nine months to get here because of required documentary and government procedures'*. He also learned about his current job through the internet. In addition to his teaching duties, he was in charge of *'Quality Assurance'* and was an active member of the *'Professional Development'*, *'E-Technologies'* and *'Assessment'* committees at his institution.

Hafiz, who speaks English, Hausa, Fulah and some Arabic, and holds an MA in Applied Linguistics from his home country, Nigeria, and a DELTA certificate from the UK, moved to Saudi Arabia in order to *'acquire more experience professionally'*. He learned about his current job through friends. He also stated that getting a job in the KSA was never difficult. He shared his experience as follows:

> *I applied online and I was interviewed through the department and the RC. However, it took time to finalize the process, from April to September, I did consider it normal considering the logistics involved.* (Hafiz)

Hafiz has been appointed the Writing Centre Coordinator at his school, in addition to his teaching duties.

Unique Cases

For almost all of the participants, both native and non-native English-speaking teachers, their relocation to Saudi Arabia was largely a matter of personal choice and initiative. Nonetheless, there are some unique cases, such as that of **Salman,** presented below. His case is unique in that his relocation involved both his own desire to move and the Pakistani government's help and recommendation. Speaking four languages – Pashtu, Urdu, Balochi and English – Salman holds an MA in TESOL and a

Postgraduate Teaching Diploma in TESOL from one of the top universities in the USA. Being a former holder of the Fulbright Scholarship, Salman returned to Pakistan upon completion of his degree in the USA and found himself and his family at risk because of many escalating and complicated local issues as a result of the controversial relationship between Pakistan and the USA, and extremism among certain religious groups, among other factors. He actively sought help and advice from the Pakistani government. He stated that:

> ... as I was in trouble and the life of my family and myself were at risk after I returned from the United States, I asked the government of Pakistan to help me get out of the country and make my transition smooth. They suggested I go to Saudi Arabia which was more peaceful and had a better living environment since I could not go back to the United States – the five-year contract with Fulbright scholarship commission [meant I had] to stay outside the USA for five years. (Salman)

Although Salman personally wanted to stay on in the USA upon completion of his degree, he had to leave the USA and was not allowed to return within five years because of the conditions specified in the Fulbright Scholarship contract he had earlier signed. However, living and settling in Pakistan was not a safe option in his particular situation either. Therefore, with the Pakistani government's recommendation of Saudi Arabia as an alternative for him and his family, Salman rationalized this chance and took it. He indeed found many good reasons for the relocation. Then, after nearly 17 years teaching in Pakistan altogether – counting from before until shortly after his Fulbright Scholarship – he eventually moved to the KSA:

> The chaotic situation and unrest in Pakistan compelled me to leave the country and go to some other country where the context of teaching was relevant to my qualifications and experience, and Saudi Arabia happened to be the best choice because of the attraction of Makkah and Medina added to it. (Salman)

Another case that we could categorize as unique is that of **Ibrahim** from Sudan. While almost all of the teacher participants presented thus far acknowledge how easy and straightforward for them to get their positions in Saudi Arabia, Ibrahim had a totally different experience. Ibrahim holds an MA in TEFL as well as a TEFL Diploma from Sudan. After working for several years in Sudan, he moved to the KSA to enjoy a *'good salary and good working conditions'*. He learned about his current job from his colleagues and has now been working at XX in the KSA for the past ten years. Unlike almost all of the other participants, he described his experience applying for the job as being *'extremely and unusually difficult'*. He added, *'We sat a 2-hour exam and only four candidates (out of 300) were selected'*.

And there are cases that do not seem to make any sense in terms of paperwork. For example, **Zafar** from Pakistan, who was working in Oman while being interviewed for his current job in Saudi Arabia, was required by the Saudi side to return to his home country in Pakistan first before he was allowed to enter the KSA. This whole process made no sense to him. Zafar speaks Pashto, Urdu and English, and holds an MA in English Literature and a CELTA certificate. He had taught English in Pakistan and Oman before his current job. He was interested in Saudi Arabia because of *'economic, religious, social and family influences'*. He learned about his current job from *'friends'*, and was working as *'a foundation program coordinator'* in addition to his teaching duties when he participated in our study.

> *I was interviewed while I was working in Muscat. I didn't know if I would be offered a job here until I received an offer letter four months later. I was asked to leave that job and go back to my country of origin in order to get here. It was a painful process.* (Zafar)

Ibrahim and Zafar were perhaps the only participants that did not find it breezy and simple to get jobs in Saudi Arabia. Compared to the other participants, they seemed to have the most challenging experiences.

Unpacking Often-Hidden Layers of Factors behind International Mobilities

The above findings, although limited to the Saudi context, challenge the widely held view that native speakers of English are preferred when it comes to employment in many countries, particularly the Middle East (see, for example, Alenazi, 2014; Barnawi, 2018; Barnawi & Al-Hawsawi, 2017; Braine, 2010; Clark & Paran, 2007; Mahboob, 2010; Mahboob & Golden, 2013; Selvi, 2010). Until very recently, Moussu (2018: 4) and other scholars have consistently argued that:

> [In] many countries around the world, discrimination against non-native speakers is still present and that native and non-native speakers of English are still treated as two different species (to the point of NNESs being paid less than NESs for doing the same work, in some instances). Consequently, more research needs to be conducted in a variety of contexts (secondary education, EFL, etc.) and with new research approaches (classroom observations, quantitative methods, teaching practices, etc.) in order to better understand the challenges facing non-native speakers with regards to communication skills, individual traits (first language, personality types, etc.), pedagogical skills, teacher education curriculums, teaching opportunities, administrator and student attitudes, collaboration, self-esteem, and so forth. (Moussu, 2018: 4)

Unlike the above position shared by Moussu (2018) and other scholars (e.g. Mahboob & Golden, 2013; Selvi, 2010, 2014), the findings presented in this chapter show that NNES teachers from Asia and neighboring Arab countries have largely been accepted, welcomed and provided with good working conditions and are well paid at all the higher education institutions across Saudi Arabia where they have been employed. These teachers are valued for their qualifications (often acquired in their home countries), teaching experience and pedagogical expertise. In addition to their teaching positions, they now hold several leading positions at their respective institutions, including those of program coordinator, course coordinator and committee chairman, to name a few.

Such findings raise the question as to why and how a seemingly native-speaker-obsessed country and a very demanding English language teaching market for non-native teachers of English like Saudi Arabia has at the same time been so 'open' to non-native teachers of English and to the professional qualifications granted by other non-English-speaking countries. Given the predominant and prevalent literature on the well-documented preference for native-speaking teachers of English in general and in the Gulf region in particular, it is important to take a few steps back and engage rigorously and complexly with this question.

We have argued that there appears to be a strong sense of seemingly *local-trusting-local discourse and practice* operating on the ground in the sphere of TESOL and ELT in Saudi Arabia. This phenomenon has not been picked up and is overlooked in the existing literature. Engaging with this phenomenon offers a fresh lens through which to examine teacher identity and TESOL more broadly in the age of mobility. It has also, theoretically speaking, stretched the limits of existing frameworks for discussing, defining and conceptualizing issues of mobility in general, and of negotiation and intercultural interactions in a particular social and educational context. In other words, the local must be contextualized, understood and captured as honestly as possible instead of being forced to mimic the larger cultural politics of TESOL when it comes to native and non-native speakers of English and the like. Our data sample of 200 teacher participants, of which 79% identified themselves as non-native speakers of English, speaks convincingly of the need to move beyond taking it for granted that Saudi Arabia at both the general and specific levels submits itself to a total native-speaker mentality. The subsequent chapters continue to elaborate this argument in greater depth.

However, we also acknowledge that, by emphasizing the abovementioned important argument and finding, we do not suggest that the politics surrounding native-speakerism does not exist in Saudi Arabian TESOL or that it only exists in an insignificant manner. As a matter of fact, the remaining chapters point to many ways in which native-speakerism is played out in raciolinguistic ideologies, in varied emotion labor shouldered by different teachers, and in stereotypes and perceptions held by teachers (whether they are speakers of English as a native language, non-native language or an additional language) about certain varieties of Englishes, ethnicities and places of origin. We would like to reiterate that the data we present throughout the book are larger than the main study we conducted with the group of teachers specified above. Specifically, we also drew on data gathered in other studies on transnational mobilities of teachers/academics in global higher education that we have carried out independently and with other collaborators.

6 English, ELT and Perceptions of Peers and Students

English has now become a medium of instruction across local higher education institutions, and at the same time programs such as engineering, medicine, computer sciences, business, information technology and the like are exclusively taught in English in the Kingdom of Saudi Arabia (KSA) (Barnawi, 2018; Barnawi & Phan, 2014). This has created a huge demand for English language teachers in the Saudi market, especially for foundation year programs. English language skills account for 60–70% of these programs, in addition to academic study skills, computer literacy and basic sciences. The global trends of English language teaching (ELT) are well manifested in the structure of all Saudi foundation programs. These programs are based on the *Common European Framework of Reference for Languages: Learning, Teaching, Assessment* (Council of Europe, 2001). Through this framework, the four language skills – reading, writing, listening and speaking – are divided into a series of levels and descriptors (A1 Level, A2 Level, B1 and B2). At the same time, commercial materials including textbooks, DVDs, test banks and teacher manuals, published by Cambridge University Press, Oxford University Press, Cengage and the like, are widely in use across university foundation programs (also see Alshakhi & Phan, 2020; Shah & Elyas, 2019).

It is for these reasons that the overwhelming majority of international TESOL teachers are teaching integrated skills courses (i.e. reading, writing, speaking and listening), the aim of which is to promote fluency and accuracy among foundation program students. This is also evident in the responses we obtained from the majority of our participants; i.e. the almost exclusive majority of these teachers cited skills-based courses such as 'writing and reading', 'writing', 'reading', 'speaking' and/or 'listening and speaking'. Other teachers cited English for specific purposes courses like Writing Portfolio, Technical Communication, Technical Report Writing, Business Correspondence, Composition, Writing and Pronunciation, Reading and Writing, Technical English, Business English, Academic Writing, English for Oil and Gas and English for International Business.

There were also some teachers who cited specialized courses such as Introduction to Linguistics, History of English, English Syntax, Semantics, Pragmatics, Discourse Analysis, Second Language Acquisition, Research Methods in Linguistics, Contrastive Linguistics, Psycholinguistics and TEFL Methodology.

In this chapter, we examine in particular the teacher participants' perceptions and evaluations of English and ELT in Saudi Arabia, and their perceptions of and experiences with colleagues and students as informed, enabled, expanded, framed and hindered by their transnational mobilities and professional and educational backgrounds. As shall be seen, we have tried to offer detailed accounts of as many teacher participants as possible. From the multiple views expressed by the teachers included in the study, as is evident in the broad sample of responses shared by the participants from different nationalities, ethnicities, institutions and teaching experiences, we hope to do justice to their hugely diverse range of expertise and experiences.

Perception of the Role of English and ELT Curricula in Saudi Arabia

As the economy is expanding, the scope of language teaching is gaining more and more ground. Every sector is shifting to a compulsory trend of Anglicization to catch up with the rest of the world. (Zafar)

Within the Saudi Vision 2030 market framework, neoliberal English language education policy agendas have become more pronounced in the KSA since local higher education (HE) institutions began to internationalize their academic programs, adopt English medium of instruction policies, curricula, pedagogies and practices, franchise their academic programs and benchmark their programs with Western universities (Barnawi, 2018; Barnawi & Al-Hawsawi, 2017; Phan & Barnawi, 2015). Such 'strong desires for internationalization and Western forms of education espoused by the country have simultaneously turned the country into a breeding ground for disseminating Western TESOL products and services' (Barnawi, 2016: 89). The government's wholehearted investment in promoting mass literacy in English has attracted hundreds of TESOL teachers from Asia, Africa, the West, and from neighboring Arab countries. Despite the fact that the movements of many of these teachers have been driven by pragmatic and instrumental reasons, as discussed in the previous chapter, we argue that their critical evaluation and on-the-ground reality observations of the role of English education in the KSA need to be taken seriously by Saudi stakeholders.

What we have heard from the participants has shown that while these international TESOL teachers have acknowledged the importance of English to the economic growth of the KSA, they have also highlighted several problems associated with the current over-promotion of English language education nationwide, particularly the obvious lack of a genuine interest in improving students' learning. Evidently, according to **Chris**:

> *English is 'crucial' to the economic development of the country. However, management is more concerned with the cosmetic aspects of an institution than with the actual language learning product. This is unattractive to the average language teacher.* (**Chris**)

Similarly, **Simon**, **Aziz** and **Johnson** stated that the English language plays a vital role in the KSA today. Yet they saw that the current teaching and learning practices needed huge improvements.

The findings of our study also point to a mismatch between the endorsed importance of English and the actual condition of English curricula, teaching methodologies, learning objectives and assessment practices in many Saudi institutions. Specifically, informed by their previous teaching experiences in other contexts and by comparing the ELT situation in their current workplaces with the places where they worked before, **Ibrahim** stated that '*teachers in Saudi Arabia still need more training to get acquainted with the latest methodologies*', while for **Johnson** the current teaching methods used in KSA classrooms '*are not well adapted to the Middle East*', and hence he stressed that '*a suitable curriculum must be implemented*'.

In the same vein, other teachers expressed their views:

> *English education in the KSA needs improvement in the field of curriculum design and in creating an atmosphere where students can learn and develop critical thinking, which is crucial not only in the learning process but also in life.* (**Aziz**)

> *English teachers are still generally perceived as teachers instead of facilitators of language learning. Teachers are expected to teach instead of striving to create an interactive environment and a resource-enriched environment for students to do their learning.* (**Zar**)

> *Huge improvements need to be made. Teachers should be given the freedom to 'teach' a class rather than dictate from a book. Printing and photocopying facilities as well as online college forums should be introduced to enhance learning for our students. More strict action should be taken against students not willing to learn and failure should be taken very seriously.* (**Simon**)

Regarding students' attitudes to learning and learning objectives, some teachers also shared their observations and suggestions:

> *Students gave little importance to acquiring proficiency in English; instead, they considered it as a language to pass in the examination. Students are adamantly reluctant to practise it in their lives outside the college campus.* (**Azhari**)

The learning objectives of the syllabus are not properly aligned with the needs and levels of the learners. The expectation of the curriculum is too high for the learners. This creates a huge gap which is not easy for the teachers to bridge. (**Ahmad**)

The above responses seem to imply internal contradictions between the intended ELT curricula and the enacted curricula in the Saudi HE context. While the former are referred to as 'understandings of what is to be learnt and how', the latter are referred to as 'how these understandings are enacted (or not) in the classroom' (Graves & Garton, 2017: 443). Notably, as one of us reports (Barnawi, 2016, 2018), communicative language teaching and student-centered and critical thinking are regarded as teaching objectives in the contemporary Saudi HE curricula. Furthermore, the *Common European Framework of Reference for Languages: Learning, Teaching, Assessment* (CEFR; Council of Europe, 2001) – and its associated products, goods and services – are widely used across Saudi HE institutions. Indeed, such prescribed ELT curricula seem to restrict the freedom and autonomy of teachers and adversely affect their classroom pedagogical practices, which the participants also saw as hindering their students' progress and causing them to experience negative emotion and affect that they found it hard to voice in their workplaces.

Broadly speaking and in principle, teachers are perceived as policy actors in a given social and educational setting (Brown, 2010; Coskun, 2013; Karim *et al.*, 2019). As policy actors in the broader context of Saudi HE institutions, the above observations and suggestions from the international TESOL teachers are vital. If taken seriously, their insights could help policy makers assess the gap between policies, curricula and practices, and respond to social and market needs. Importantly, such insights could help policy makers at all levels in Saudi Arabia to address problematic issues associated with the current government's wholehearted investment in promoting mass literacy in English across Saudi HE institutions. Evidently, these international language teachers' understandings of the immediate needs of their learners (i.e. curricula, pedagogy and assessment practices) are indicative of what is actually happening in on-the-ground realities. Such realities need to be taken seriously by all stakeholders, including university administrators, with whom the teachers found themselves in an unequal power relationship, as shall be shown in greater depth in Chapter 11.

'Top-down' Policy, 'Commercialized' and 'Hegemonic' English and ELT in Saudi Higher Education

Some teachers raised concerns about the top-down policy across the board regarding curriculum, assessment, and teaching and learning objectives. They felt 'irrelevant' and that their 'expertise and prior experiences are not consulted' by any administration authority at their institutions. For example, **Sarah** reported that:

> *Saudi Arabia has to begin to evaluate and define the role of English teachers in relation to their national educational objectives for learning English. At present, some English teachers feel that their knowledge and experience is not being utilized, especially when English programs are developed without the input of teachers* (**Sarah**)

Sarah's concerns were shared by many other teachers in our study, as well as by expatriate and Saudi teachers in a study conducted by Alshakhi and Phan (2020) which we re-feature in Chapter 11. The absence of teacher input in English program and curriculum development is a serious problem in Saudi Arabia's higher education institutions.

At the same time, several teacher participants reported that they felt highly regarded in the workplace, but also acknowledged that coming from Western countries and possessing a good education and experience gave them an advantage:

> *People in my position are considered very highly (I work as a professor at one of the top universities in XXX). My colleagues are all highly educated and experienced teachers from many countries (Ireland, England, Canada, the USA, New Zealand and Korea).* (**Dan**)

Some teacher participants commented on the hegemony of English and ELT in the country, and criticized the uncritical acceptance of English products, services and goods under the current Saudi government's English education policy and practices. They also highlighted problems associated with the recruitment of ELT teachers who may have high qualifications but do not have any teacher training background. Such teachers often do not know how to teach Saudi students with limited English proficiency.

For example, **Berry**, a Canadian teacher with several years of teaching experience in the KSA, shared his observations as follows:

> *I don't like the hegemonic nature of dominant languages .... Most of my students do not grasp this truth. I also find that the students are very poorly prepared for study in English; for this I fault the high school teaching. Essentially, and this is corroborated by comments on online EFL teacher forums, Prep Year programs in the Middle East are forced to work miracles with inadequately prepared high school students. The ones who can function in English have learned the majority of it from American media sources, and not their teachers.* (**Berry**)

He further adds:

> *I have tried to press this point for the few years I have been here. In my opinion, the students do not benefit as much as they could by having teachers with an MA (or a BA), but without teacher training. Methodology trumps theory in EFL acquisition. I feel that this*

> *misalignment of teacher qualifications with student needs has a negative outcome for the students. In any event, I would prefer to see a non-native speaker of English, trained to [proper] standards ... rather than an untrained native speaker of English. I often saw this type in South Korea (we called them backpackers), and they do little good, and quite a lot of damage, owing to their inability to understand or teach their own language.* (**Berry**)

What **Berry** expresses here corresponds to critiques of many current practices that are still prevalent in ELT in many countries (Braine, 2010; Coskun, 2013; De Costa *et al.*, 2021; Lowe & Lawrence, 2018; Selvi, 2014). In particular, the commercialization of English and the ELT profession, as Ruecker and Ives (2014) note:

> marginalizes NNESTs despite relevant qualifications, thus denigrating the level of professionalism in the field. In addition, ... recruitment websites rhetorically reproduce power relations at the intersections of race and language background in a few different ways. (Ruecker & Ives, 2014: 751)

It is worth pointing out that some of the above observations shared by different international TESOL teachers working in various HE institutions in the KSA have been captured and documented in our previous work (Phan & Barnawi, 2015), entitled 'Where English, neoliberalism, desire and internationalization are alive and kicking: Higher education in Saudi Arabia today'. By using Saudi Arabia as a national example and analyzing one of its recent major government projects, Colleges of Excellence (CoE), we examined how and in what ways English, neoliberalism, desire and internationalization are expressed, enacted and pursued by different stakeholders throughout the country. We have argued that 'the Saudi government's desire to internationalize its higher education system has overlooked the many problems associated with its English-only policy, and the neoliberal shaping of social and economic pressures' (Phan & Barnawi, 2015: 545). Teaching and learning are not taken seriously by this move toward internationalization, regardless of the fancy language and discourse adopted in policy and official narratives. Saudi teachers as well as international teachers employed to teach English to help prepare Saudi students for English-medium instruction programs in these CoEs found themselves suffering, stuck in unpleasant situations. This reality is unhealthy for both teachers and students, as well as for the overall picture of ELT in the KSA.

> Largely driven by the commercialization of education and the drastic shift to English, the superficial appearance of having English-medium programs in KSA's colleges has indeed made it almost impossible to create any serious educational environment for both teachers and students. Instead, it has so far endorsed academic mediocrity and capitalism as well as the dominance of English and the legitimization of profit-driven educational entities in the country. (Phan & Barnawi, 2015: 562)

Some participants in our current study actually used to work in some of those CoEs, and they shared many concerns about *'pressures to pass students'* and *'practices that endorse plagiarism and cheating among students'*. One participant, in particular, was so disturbed by the lack of ethics in his workplace that he confronted the management team. Instead of having his concerns addressed, that teacher was threatened. He eventually left Saudi Arabia. In follow-up conversations with one of us (Phan Le Ha), he was still very irritated by the experience, yet he was relieved to be able to talk about it and to provide more background information. He said to Le-Ha:

> *I'm not the only one here. I can introduce you to many more expatriate teachers like me, who would tell you how they went through that period. But I doubt if any of them would even want to recall those days. It's so awful that we'd better forget.* (**John**)

John felt great sympathy for his students, as he reported. He felt sorry for many Saudi students whose English proficiency was very low but who still had to study content knowledge in English, pass exams in English and do presentations in English, and had to do all these under a strict timeline and between various duties.

> *They of course can't do any of those, but we're asked to pass them all. How could someone give a presentation on a subject matter entirely in English when he can barely communicate at a most basic level? I couldn't go on like that for long. I had to take a stance, and you know the consequence already.* (**John**)

Relevant accounts from other participants are presented and discussed in subsequent sections as well as in later chapters, as we delve further into unpacking critical issues in ELT in Saudi Arabia.

Experiences and Perceptions of Peer Interactions

Broadly speaking, the majority of the international TESOL teacher participants held the view that they were respected by their peers and the management at work. Nonetheless, many non-native English-speaking teachers felt that they would eventually have to confront various forms of prejudice from their peers and institutions. Hence, they used what Planken (2005) calls a 'safe space' strategy to create sociality, negotiate their identities and self-representations, and at the same time define their positions in the workplace.

In the context of negotiation and intercultural interactions between/within international TESOL teachers with mixed backgrounds as in the case of our study, the 'safe space' strategy entails *'non-native teachers avoiding native teachers and vice versa,' 'adjustments to one another based on experiences,' 'sharing of mutual respect,'* and the phenomenon of *'non-native teachers associating more with other non-native teachers'* while *'native teachers [are] hanging out together'* to present and represent themselves at work and outside campus.

Evidently, many teachers, both native and non-native English-speaking teachers, see the sharing of mutual respect among colleagues as a safe strategy for clash-free intercultural communication at work. **Aziz**, for instance, said, '*My colleagues at work come from multicultural backgrounds and we have relationships based on mutual respect*'. They also expressed appreciation of one another while implying that relationships and who you mix with are very much a case by case matter and depend on many factors.

> *In my experience, foreign English teachers are generally well regarded by people here. My colleagues are generally highly educated non-native speakers, who have achieved a near-native or fully native level of English.* (**William**)

> *Some teachers are happy and have no issues with me.* (**Adam**)

> *My colleagues at work are diverse, but I have a better relationship with those who see me as an equal. The majority have endured serious economic hardship in their youth and early adult life and this phenomenon is impacting their present behavior and how they relate to co-workers of different ethnicities and national backgrounds. In fact, teachers at the English XXX have maintained their relationships within nationality, ethnic and religious groups or cliques, reflecting the convenience of social compatibility to be enjoyed in a foreign country.* (**Chris**)

Echoing **Chris**'s observation, **Zafar,** a Pakistani teacher, did not hide the fact that he '*deliberately avoids native-English-speaking teachers and at the same time considers non-native English-speaking teachers from countries like Pakistan, Jordan, and Sudan as colleagues*'. In the case of **Mario** and **Daniel**, for example, they were working in institutions where a majority of expatriate teachers were from Western countries, and thus they mostly mingled with those colleagues:

> *My colleagues are other Westerners like myself for the most part.* (**Mario**)

> *We are afforded a high level of respect. [My colleagues] are mostly American and British.* (**Daniel**)

While the majority of the participants tended to speak positively of other colleagues, several teachers revealed their rather negative assumptions about and experiences with local colleagues and colleagues who practice Islam. For example, **Tim** said:

> *I find [them] to be generally lazy, unprofessional and arrogant. These are the three general characteristics. To put it bluntly, there are other things that seem to take precedence over teaching – recreation and religion are the general categories. Succinctly stated, the actual work experience has been rewarding – but the people with whom I have worked have posed some of the biggest challenges.* (**Tim**)

Please note that there are Europeans and Americans as well as Asians who have converted to Islam and work as teachers of English in the Middle East. Therefore, **Tim**'s observations and bad experiences referred to all those teachers, not just Saudi and other non-White, non-native teachers of English.

Dong from the Philippines, from another angle, shared his view that prejudices were adjusted as intercultural interactions began to take place within/between TESOL international teachers as well as between international teachers and students. He shared his observations as follows:

> *Most Saudi students enter college with cultural prejudices related to the quality of teaching they expect to get from their teachers of different nationalities. For instance, there is the mentality that native English speakers would teach better than non-native speakers because the former are more expert in the language. Therefore, while the native English teacher earns respect (even awe) the very day he steps into the classroom, the non-native English speaker still has to prove himself and work twice as hard. Ironically, most Saudi students carry negative preconceptions about a native Saudi teaching English. Eventually, students adjust their thinking based on the actual performance of their teachers. The same could be said of the teachers. They come to Saudi Arabia with cultural prejudices against their colleagues who come from different countries, and even against their students. These biases, however, are continually challenged and adjusted as they interact with their colleagues and understand that their personally held stereotypes about certain cultures and ethnicities will constantly be proven wrong. The XXX University [where I'm working] are comprised of teachers most of whom come from Jordan, Pakistan and the Middle Eastern region, some from North America, the UK, Africa, and a few from East and Southeast Asia.*
> (**Dong**)

Negotiations and intercultural communications are always triggered in our 'liquid individuals' – to borrow Bauman's (2004) description of contemporary individuals – in that individuals' beliefs, presentations and self-representations are constantly changing, depending on time and space. This is also exactly what Ewing (1990, cited in Dervin, 2012) argued:

> In all cultures people can be observed to project multiple, inconsistent self-representations that are context-dependent and may shift rapidly. At any particular moment, a person usually experiences his or her articulated self as a symbolic, timeless whole, but this self may quickly be displaced by another, quite different 'self', which is based on a different definition of the situation. The person will often be unaware of these shifts and inconsistencies and may experience wholeness and continuity despite their presence. (Ewing, 1990: 251)

It is, therefore, crucial to unearth these inconsistencies and contradictions in representations, and negotiation between the different forms of 'self' as well as towards the 'other', from the perspectives of what Ewing (1990: 262) called 'experiencing actors' (i.e. non-native English teachers with mixed backgrounds working in Saudi HE institutions, in the case of this study).

At the same time, the accounts presented above can be seen as combined manifestations of (linguistic) racism (De Costa, 2020; Motha, 2014), epistemological racism (Kubota, 2020), native-speakerism (Holliday, 2005), postcolonial Self and Other (Pennycook, 1998/2017; Phan, 2008) and 'unequal Englishes' reality/mentality (Tupas, 2015). These teachers adjust, behave and position themselves in relation to others according to their self-perceived identities and values as well as with regard to their perceptions of other teachers' identities and values. It is often the case that their perceived differences and similarities in terms of identities and values are influenced and shaped by linguistic, cultural, ethnic, racial and religious assumptions, prejudices and stereotypes, which determine who they side and identity with. And it is quite common that teachers who see themselves as 'non-native speakers of English' tend to come together and form a group, whereas those of 'Western' backgrounds mingle among themselves. They form 'parallel societies' (Gomes, 2022) and cultivate different experiences that are unique to their own situation, circumstance and group dynamic as well as group materiality. Nonetheless, these parallel societies of English language teachers may not be equal, because of the persistent injustices associated with the hegemony of English and preferences for native varieties of English. Such hegemony and preferences are projected in endless language and education policies and ideologies, are embedded in institutional mandates and curricula, and are coupled with the hype for English-medium instruction internationalization, to name a few (Barnawi, 2018, 2021; De Costa *et al.*, 2020, 2021; Ke, 2021; Liu & Phan, 2021; Phan, 2017; Phillipson, 2010; Sahan, 2021; Thompson *et al.*, 2022; Wang, 2019).

Recognizing and Steering Students' Attitudes and Reactions

In addition to what has been reported and discussed in the earlier sections, here we pay particular attention to the range of experiences that the teacher participants had with their Saudi students.

Through the accounts obtained from the teacher participants, we have learnt that Saudi students displayed a variety of sentiments, attitudes and reactions towards their foreign teachers. To begin with, many teachers felt that their students gave them recognition inside and outside the classroom, regardless of their background and nationality.

> *I haven't experienced any resistance on the part of my students. On the contrary, our relationship developed after their graduation. I still have communication with students I taught seven years ago.* (**Sabir**)

> *A large majority of the students are quite comfortable with non-Saudi English language teachers.* (**Bashi**)
>
> *We are always recognized. No one discourages us.* (**Kurshaid**)
>
> *My students do not really care about my nationality. What really matters to them is whether you are a good teacher or not.* (**Ahmad**)
>
> *I don't feel there is any problem in [being a foreign teacher in Saudi Arabia].* (**Ameer**)

At the same time, a number of teachers implied that this recognition was conditional, depending on factors such as the teacher's '*proper pronunciation*', on their being a '*native speaker of English*', '*being a Muslim*', '*being flexible with students*', giving students '*proper treatment*', and on the existence of '*mutual trust*' between teachers and students.

> *[Students] are generally taken in by the idea that they have to learn English and therefore enjoy meeting/talking with Western English teachers.* (**Webber**)
>
> *My students recognize the advantage of a foreign teacher, especially in the area of proper pronunciation.* (**Mario**)
>
> *I haven't experienced any resentment from students. They like the fact that I'm an American, a Muslim and a native English speaker.* (**Sarah**)
>
> *The students accord respect to a foreign teacher in the classroom by putting themselves under his authority. They trust him and believe in him. They accept what he teaches them. They follow his classroom rules and policies.* (**Alex**)
>
> *My students acknowledge the importance of having foreign teachers as they want to see changes in the quality of teaching delivery and in teaching quality.* (**Faii**)
>
> *The students give recognition to foreign teachers in the classroom by respecting and trusting them. They consider their teacher as the main anchor or facilitator of language learning.* (**Maxie**)

The participants' reported experiences with their students and the participants' perceptions of students' perceptions towards them are in line with much existing literature on students' perceptions of English language teachers (Alseweed, 2012; Benke & Medgyes, 2005; Chun, 2014; Lasagabaster & Sierra, 2002; Lee, 2020; Pae, 2016; Rao, 2009; Üstünlüoglu, 2007; Walkinshaw & Duong, 2014; Zhang & Zhang, 2021). Largely approaching students' perceptions through the native–non-native lens, these studies all show that students recognize both groups of teachers for their strengths and weaknesses, and that students do not necessarily and consistently think more highly of either group, because students' perceptions of and experiences with their teachers also depend on many factors including length of study, level of study, class and course content, study goals and priorities, English language proficiency, etc. Nonetheless, several studies such as Alseweed (2012) conducted with 169 Saudi university students, Diaz (2015) conducted with 75 French students in Brittany, Lasagabaster and Sierra (2002) conducted with 76 university students in Spain, and Tsou and Chen (2019) conducted with 20 university students in Taiwan, revealed evidence-based preferences towards native-English-speaking teachers among the student participants. These preferences are by no means fixed and do not support the native-speaker-only policy in hiring/recruitment.

Back to our study. The responses reported above demonstrate, to a large extent, that non-Saudi/foreign teachers are generally well received by their Saudi students, irrespective of whether the teacher is a native speaker or not. It is evident throughout the data that the teachers did not think that Saudi students tended to hold negative perceptions towards having *foreign*, *international* and *non-Saudi* teachers teaching them. Nonetheless, teachers from English-speaking Western countries, regardless of their ethnic and racial backgrounds, appeared to be preferred by students in some cases, and this preference corresponds to the studies conducted by Alseweed (2012), Diaz (2015), Lasagabaster and Sierra (2002) and Tsou and Chen (2019). Teachers like **Webber**, **Mario** and **Sarah** were also aware of this preference and of the advantage of being native speakers of English. They acknowledged benefiting from students' enthusiasm towards native teachers of English. Indeed, some literature explores whether being taught by native or non-native teachers of English would influence students' motivation to learn (Chun, 2014; Lee, 2020; Zhang & Zhang, 2021).

However, several teachers did point out issues regarding students' resentment and resistance in class. Such resentment and resistance did not target any particular group of teachers, but was more on a case by case basis. These teachers acknowledged that they and/or other teachers had encountered various forms of resistance from their students, including '*remaining silent*', '*avoiding speaking in English*', '*communicating in Arabic*', '*sharing their objections in straightforward way with teachers*', '*immediately reporting their dissatisfaction to the management*', and the like. The participants also admitted that they shared these concerns among one another, and therefore they were aware of what happened in other teachers' classrooms.

For example, **Chris,** mentioned that:

there is resistance to some teachers in the classroom because of their teaching style and perhaps because of the fact that some students blame teachers for their failure. (**Chris**)

What **Chris** referred to here echoes the experiences and observations of the international TESOL professionals teaching in Saudi Arabia that Alshakhi and Phan (2020) report and discuss in their study, which is reproduced in this book as Chapter 11. In many cases, teachers of English have to follow rigid syllabi and rather irrelevant and ineffective assessment practices imposed by the top management at their institutions. Teachers' inputs are generally not encouraged. Because of this, teaching and learning can be unsatisfying for both teachers and students.

Zafar saw students' resentment as a response in situations where the teacher is '*bad*':

> *It all depends on how good a teacher is. A bad fellow isn't even respected at home.* (Zafar)

Zafar did not mean 'bad' in terms of teaching quality but more in terms of a teacher's character, mannerisms, attitude and professionalism. A teacher cannot gain respect if any of these factors is problematic or questionable. And again, regardless of whether one is a native speaker, qualified, experienced or novice, bad is bad. No matter if one is in his/her home country or in a foreign country, being *bad* does travel and get noticed. Therefore, to **Zafar**, if students resent or do not cooperate with or disrespect such teachers, it is not the students' fault.

On another note, **Hafiz** referred to a prevailing phenomenon in teacher–student relationships, whereby such relationships depend to a great extent on how comfortable the students are with the language and how sensible and helpful teachers are in response.

> *Some students lack confidence in using the English language owing to their background or experience with the language. As a result, this factor tends to affect their relationship with foreign language teachers. The more comfortable the teacher can make the student in using English the better the relationship.* (**Hafiz**)

Since our study did not gather any data from Saudi students, we are unable to comment on students' perceptions of their English language teachers with their own voices or from their perspectives. Nonetheless, we are aware of Alseweed's (2012) study conducted with 169 male Saudi university students on their perceptions of 70 male native and non-native teachers coming from a wide range of countries and regions, a sample that is also reflected in our study. We take the liberty to refer to Alseweed (2012) heavily here to help put into perspective why students expressed certain views about their teachers.

In this study, drawing on both questionnaire and interview data, Alseweed (2012) shows 'a significant difference in students' perceptions of their English language teachers in favor of NESTs [native-English-speaking teachers]' and their 'positive reflection ... towards their NESTs' (Alseweed, 2012: 48). Specifically:

> 89% of the students feel more comfortable in a class taught by a NEST. In addition, 72%–83% of the students believed that a NEST is more friendly than a NNEST because he provides a relaxed learning

> environment ... [and that] 77% of the sample would have more positive attitudes toward the learning of English if they had a native English teacher. (Alseweed, 2012: 47)

While NNESTs (non-native English-speaking teachers) were seen as more suitable for language learners at a lower level because of their relatable understanding of students' learning difficulties and their shared first language (in the case of Arabic-speaking NNESTs), the majority of the Saudi students found NESTs more desirable as their language levels moved up, as the data in Alseweed (2012) indicate. This finding corroborates other studies such as Diaz (2015) and Lasagabaster and Sierra (2002).

The interview data with the Saudi students offer important insights into their significant preference for NESTs and link their preference to several factors,

> most important of which is that the Saudi students mostly like to interact with a teacher of an opposite culture. Second, the Arab student likes to communicate with a native teacher in a relaxed classroom setting without any sense of fear. Such a relaxed teaching-learning environment motivates students to speak the target language and achieve an ultimate aim of language learning. Third, the NESTs are friendly and more lenient toward students' mistakes and attendance. Fourth, very often NESTs are not particular about discipline and informality. In addition, in a class taught by NEST, students are sometimes allowed to chat, to move, to leave the class at any time without permission, and to use their native words without any blame on the part of the teacher. One student said 'I have the sense of feeling at home in a class taught by a native teacher'. Students state that such behaviors may not be accepted by a non-native teacher who may not allow students to discuss any topic irrelevant to the lesson or spend the time without focusing on the lesson. (Alseweed, 2012: 47)

> 63% of the respondents prefer the way NESTs deliver their classes and agree that NESTs would use ground-breaking teaching strategies to help students learn better. ... For this reason, 79% of the participants are in favor of the teaching strategies NESTs use as they aim toward enhancing independent learning and focus on the process more than the outcome. In addition, 65% of the participants highlight that NESTs encourage and develop students' confidence to use the language in class as well as assimilating everyday situations in class. Therefore, 72% of the sample made it clear that if they are to choose a teacher for a specific English language course, they would choose a course taught by a native English teacher. (Alseweed, 2012: 48)

Alseweed (2012) makes a clear point that the preferences and reflections shared by the student participants in his study were informed by their lived experiences, whereby they all had studied English with both NESTs and NNESTs, and thus we can infer that their preferences and reflections were neither imagined nor prejudiced but were compared and contrasted through actual interactions and encounters. Alseweed (2012) acknowledges several limitations with his study, particularly: the exclusive sample of all male students (while some other studies had both male and female students); the insufficiently long duration of study the students had with NESTs (only two semesters over 28 weeks); and that all his student participants learned English as a compulsory subject (while some other studies also included students who majored in English, for instance). Nevertheless, we find Alseweed's findings illuminating in terms of many issues that remain unsettled in TESOL, language education and applied linguistics. Indeed, issues that are centered on native and non-native teachers of English have attracted continued debates among scholars (Braine, 2010; Kubota, 2004; Llurda, 2005; Lowe & Lawrence, 2018; Mahboob, 2004; Medgyes, 1992, 2011a, 2011b; Rivers, 2017; Selvi, 2014).

The findings reported in Alseweed (2012) may appear 'upsetting' as more and more scholars in TESOL, language education and applied linguistics have been fighting against linguistic racism and other forms of injustice that are associated with stereotypes and prejudices against non-native speakers of English (see, for example, De Costa, 2020; Kubota, 2020; Motha, 2014; Park, 2018; Phillipson, 1992). Nonetheless, we should not lose sight of an important point that Alseweed (2012) also highlights:

> Although students showed marked preference for NESTs, they actually showed warmer feelings toward NNESTs. Students made it clear that they do not behave differently with both types of teachers and they focus on their strengths. (Alseweed, 2012: 50)

This highlighted point is somewhat reflected in the findings we have reported thus far. The teacher participants' recollections of their students' perceptions, attitudes and responses towards them are diverse, sweet and sour, largely for the non-native teachers. From the findings, it is clear that the responses and attitudes of Saudi students towards the international teacher participants had been expressed in various forms, including appreciation, respect, enthusiasm, acceptance, accepting the status quo, submitting to teacher figure authority, friendship, conditional recognition, and at times skepticism, resentment and resistance. Importantly, many teachers shared with us that they were able to adjust and transform their relationships with their students, believing that there would be room for negotiation. For instance, as **Adam** put it, *'negotiation between me and my students is possible'*.

Moving on, the next chapter elaborates and examines the on-the-ground realities of the participants' classroom teaching, and the ways in which they explained their pedagogical decisions and how they 'negotiated' their pedagogical practices with their students.

7 On-the-Ground Realities: From Training, Experience and Perception to Actual Classrooms

International TESOL Teachers in Saudi HE Institutions and their Classroom Pedagogical Practices

> *I am primarily a facilitator in the classroom. I do not just see myself as the sole and primary source of knowledge in the classroom. I believe that I can also learn from my students and all of us are sources of knowledge. My job is to ensure that I facilitate the smooth dissemination of knowledge and ensure that appropriate assessment procedures are maintained to ensure learning. Professionally, I describe myself as a creator of knowledge. I must conduct research and even publish it to add to the ever-growing body of literature in ELT. In society, I describe myself as a responsible citizen. As an English teacher, it is my role to uphold and respect the laws of the land and of the school where I am working.* (Ron)

In this chapter, we continue to examine various pedagogical strategies and practices advocated by the international TESOL teacher participants as they attempted to respond to their students' needs and their actual language proficiency levels in the Saudi context. While it is impossible to capture the wide range of strategies and practices shared by these teachers, the accounts we present reflect diverse beliefs, perceptions, strategies and senses of self as these teacher participants described and discussed with us their teaching philosophies, assessment and evaluation techniques and the various challenges they faced and how they understood those challenges and found ways to overcome them.

It is important to note that local Saudi higher education (HE) institutions are following global trends in the operation of their programs. This is evident in the adoption of the *Common European Framework of Reference for Languages: Learning, Teaching, Assessment* (Council of Europe, 2001) throughout their program structures as well as the heavy presence of international TESOL teachers with different epistemologies, pedagogies, ideologies and linguistic repertoires. Under these conditions, as Pennington (2014: 25) observes, 'TESOL educators can be expected to incorporate knowledge of and participation in global scapes and trends into their classroom content and methods, thereby widening their pedagogy by connecting their instructional identity to a global identity'. The global aspects of TESOL teacher identity entail knowledge of different varieties of English, and the ways in which English language is taught and valued in different contexts and settings (Fang & Widodo, 2019; Jenkins, 2012; Ke, 2021; Kırkgöz & Karakaş, 2021; Rose *et al.*, 2020). Additionally, teachers are expected to be aware of local realities, including learners' attitudes, local knowledge, local culture, the expectations of their schools, and other social and political factors (Sharkey, 2004). At any time, as demonstrated in the literature on TESOL teacher education, teachers of English these days are working under many layers of factors and are affected by ever more complicated intertwined forces at all possible levels and ideologies, including those labeled global, international, transnational, national, local, institutional, intercultural, critical, neoliberal, professional, monolingual, multilingual, collectivist and individualist (Baker, 2015; Barnawi, 2018; Barnawi & Ahmed, 2021; Phan, 2008; Polat *et al.*, 2021; Rose *et al.*, 2020; Selvi & Yazan, 2021). These characteristics and realities could frame teachers' decisions and views towards particular HE institutions in myriad ways, as the accounts presented below and in other chapters show.

Before we continue, we would again like to acknowledge that instead of aiming to create a sense of coherence across the accounts obtained from the teacher participants, we are more interested in showcasing as many accounts from the data as possible to convey the busy, crowded, diverse, colorful, rich and dynamic TESOL space in Saudi Arabia. In this space, teachers of hugely diverse backgrounds seem to teach endless classes of Saudi students in foundation programs and English for specific purposes programs across Saudi HE institutions, year after year. As shall be seen, we have included nine detailed accounts from nine teachers in this chapter, one by one. Every teacher is his own oasis and character with a life to lead, a job to perform and particular values to uphold. Hence, we have treated each account shared with us with as much care and respect as we can. We have tried not to compare teachers against one another, either.

Example 1: Alex, a Teacher from the UK – 'CLT, Pragmatism and Constructionism'

Similar to other teachers featured in this chapter and the subsequent chapters, **Alex**, a teacher from the UK with a good research background and experience in scholarly publications, used the communicative language teaching (CLT) approach to teach the students with their mixed and multi-levels of language proficiency at his school. He described his classroom pedagogical strategies as follows:

> *My pedagogical strategies are derived from the philosophy of pragmatism and constructionism. I use communicative language teaching (CLT) approaches where students are immersed in the language and are given opportunities to use it in various ways in authentic situations. In teaching mixed/multi-level students, I use personalized strategies, so the advanced students are given more challenging activities on top of the requirements of the course and the slow students are given more guided (scaffolding) activities leading them to master the intended learning outcomes of the course.* (**Alex**)

He added that:

> *In assessment, I also implement the strength-based/asset-based approach (benchmarked through the Common European Framework for References (CEFR)), in which students are identified according to their unique/distinct strengths and used as avenues to carry out appropriate and relevant formative assessment practices.* (**Alex**)

While **Alex** strongly believed that his current pedagogical strategies were '*effective in motivating students to learn English*', these practices had also created '*cultural, religious, and linguistic challenges*' in his classroom. For instance, he felt that:

> *The use of songs and some graphics/videos which are prohibited in Islam and the discussion of topics which are politically sensitive in the Kingdom also limit the linguistic and communicative experiences of the students.* (**Alex**)

Consequently, he constantly tried to address these challenges by '*creating activities that motivate learners*' as well as by '*exploring alternative activities that enhance communication skills while respecting cultural and religious sensibilities*'. He did not, however, specify exactly what these activities were.

It was through '*formative assessment*' as well as by juxtaposing the '*performance of students with the internal and external standards of the school*' that **Alex** tried to ensure the effectiveness of his pedagogical strategies and at the same time to modify them where necessary. Additionally, he listed the following assessment practices he used in order to help his students learn the language and to assess his pedagogical strategies: summative assessment like '*quizzes, projects, and major tests*', as well as formative assessment such as '*mobile apps (Kahoot, Quizlet, Padlet, and Edmodo)*'.

As **Alex** admitted, his experience of teaching English in the KSA had never been easy. It was '*challenging and rewarding*' at the same time, he believed. As he recounted:

> *It has helped me to become more flexible, patient, and understanding with different kinds/levels of learners. Somehow, it has helped me to*

become a better teacher with newer and richer insights about language teaching in unique contexts. (**Alex**)

It is for these reasons that **Alex** had constantly to adjust and readjust his *'academic standards'*, *'pedagogical approaches'*, *'assessment practices'* and *'intercultural experiences'* by *'respecting the policies and standards'* of the workplace, as well as the *'mixed backgrounds'* of his colleagues. He saw his scholarly work and research, coupled with his innovative ways of accommodating the local needs of Saudi students, as making a valuable contribution to his department.

Example 2: Bashi, a Teacher from Pakistan – 'CLT, Pair Work and Group Work'

Bashi, who holds an MA in English language from Pakistan and a CELTA from the UK, speaks three languages – English, Urdu and Punjabi. He strongly believed that 'communicative language teaching is the most effective teaching approach for Saudi classrooms'. Similar to **Alex**, he said:

> *I mainly employ the communicative approach, whereby I encourage the use of the target language in the classroom with a student-centric approach. I keep my teacher talk time controlled and only help the learners when it's necessary. I try to integrate skill practice even though sometimes learners have their skill preferences. I try to make activities fun and relate them to real-life situations, which helps to boost motivation and create interest amongst learners.* (**Bashi**)

For **Bashi**, teaching English in the Saudi context seemed to be *'a challenging experience in every way'*. For instance, although he always attempted to keep *'politics and religion out of class discussions'*, as the Saudi government is very strict about these issues, they were *'sometimes unavoidable'*. He felt that in the classroom his students often talked about cultural differences *'that sometimes inevitably led to discussions about religion'*.

Bashi also found teaching Saudi students challenging because, unlike his former students in Pakistan, *'Saudi students are not motivated to learn English, and they never arrive punctually to classes'*. Worse still, because *'mood swings are common amongst Saudi students'*, it had become challenging for him to control unpredictable issues in the classroom. As he recounted, *'a student on one particular day can be quiet and well-behaved and completely the opposite the next day'*.

It was in order to meet these challenges that he had to adjust his pedagogical strategies. These adjustments included *'becoming more tolerant'*, *'giving learners more space to express and communicate their needs'* and *'accepting the loss of some authority in classroom'* as a teacher. He acknowledged that he had to try hard to make the students learn, and keeping them busy with tasks was one strategy: *'I usually keep my class format activity-based, with learners busy in the group or individual activities assigned to them'*. Sometimes when students resisted certain classroom activities and just wanted to do things on their own, as he reported, he still forced them to '*work in pairs or groups*' and designed activities for them to compete with each other in order to assess the effectiveness of his pedagogical decisions.

Bashi also employed assessment practices such as the '*reflective journal*', '*outside the classroom activities*' and '*self-assessment*' in order to help his students acquire the language and at the same time put into practice his pedagogical strategies.

Despite all the challenging aspects of his teaching in Saudi Arabia, **Bashi** strongly believed that he was making a contribution to his school by attempting to make himself '*available for learners*', by developing himself '*professionally through training*' and by sharing his '*course reflections with the management*'. He saw himself as a dedicated teacher.

What is evident in the above cases is that **Alex** and **Bashi** are embracing mainstream ELT classroom pedagogical practices that are now the norm in every TESOL teacher training program. These pedagogical practices, with a strong focus on CLT and the student-centered approach, have been promoted as part of the 'universalized' professionalism that every ELT professional is expected to acquire and to enact in classrooms (Phan, 2014; Phan & Le, 2013).

At the same time, informed by our knowledge of the Saudi context and of the ELT situation in many HE settings throughout the country (see, for example, Alshakhi & Phan, 2020, reproduced in Chapter 11 of this volume; Barnawi, 2016, 2018; Barnawi & Phan, 2014; Phan & Barnawi, 2015), we are well aware of the difficulties faced by many international TESOL teachers in Saudi Arabia. The language of 'learner-centered education' and 'communicative language teaching' as shown in the previous examples does not register with the realities on the ground in most cases. The entry level of Saudi students into the foundation program throughout the country is generally very low. It also seems that there is little room for teachers to negotiate with students about classroom activities, although assessment activities appear negotiable. Evidently, the teachers mentioned above showed that they were aware of this tiny window as they tried to make their teaching work.

The accounts presented below continue to demonstrate the teacher participants' reflections on their teaching philosophies and beliefs as well as the challenges they faced in their teaching as they implemented and adjusted what they perceived to work with their students. Their accounts also shed light on how they managed to address such challenges.

Example 3: Chris, a Teacher from the USA – 'Peer Teaching and Direct Translation'

Chris, who holds a BA in Communications and Social Sciences from the USA and a TESL certificate from International House, Toronto, Canada, had several years of teaching experience in English for specific purposes at his college. He strongly believed that understanding Saudi students *'as a product of their society'* was a departure point for devising pedagogical practices responsive to the immediate needs of Saudi students. He commented that:

> *peer teaching is my most widely used strategy, as direct translation works extremely well among Saudi students. I utilize peer evaluation for the more proficient students and demonstration lessons to accommodate all. Pedagogical strategies for my Technical Report Writing are of my own creation.* (**Chris**)

He also reported, *'I always try to maintain a strict policy of students coming to class with writing materials, but sometimes I am powerless to force their compliance'*. Although **Chris** appeared to strongly believe in the effectiveness of his personally created pedagogies, he had experienced several unpredictable issues in his classroom, including students attending his classes *'without a pen or notebook or writing material'* and *'constantly using mobile phones.'* As a result, *'the learning process is hampered, and the focus on doing a particular task is lost'*, he reported. In situations like these, **Chris** had to change his role *'from a language facilitator to the unpleasant position of classroom disciplinarian in a high school environment'*.

Interestingly, similar to what **Bashi** revealed above about having to accommodate Saudi students' *'mood swings'*, **Chris** felt the same, as he said he had to constantly *'follow the mood of the students'* and at the same time *'strike a balance between classroom entertainment and actual language learning'* in order to make particular pedagogical decisions in his classroom. Additionally, he used various forms of formative as well as summative assessment practices in order to address the aforementioned challenges. In this *'stressful teaching environment'*, **Chris** had to learn *'not to smile in class [because] students interpret a smile as a green light to relax and socialize and therefore do nothing'*.

He also revealed, *'I have learnt nothing whatsoever from my colleagues because they are not committed to sharing their experiences'*. He hinted at a rather competitive work environment where international teachers appeared not to be supportive of one another. It was in such challenging teaching and learning conditions that **Chris** managed to persevere and learn his own way to cope. Despite many challenges, **Chris** said he believed he had succeeded. He seemed positive about the contribution he was making to his school. He commented that, *'my contributions are felt on the ESP course that I am teaching and also developing as a coordinator'*.

What **Chris** experienced is not uncommon among many international TESOL teachers, particularly those from English-speaking Western countries. They had to shoulder much emotion labor as native-English-speaking teachers, often in isolation and unrecognized, as Chapter 11 discusses.

Example 4: Akhan, a Teacher from Turkey – 'Cognitively Engaged Pedagogy'

Akhan, who holds an MA in Curriculum and Instruction as well as a DELTA from Istanbul, Turkey, had several years of teaching experience before joining his school in Saudi Arabia. In **Akhan**'s view, *'learners should be cognitively challenged and engaged whatever their purpose in learning is'*. He commented that such pedagogical strategies can be put into practice through tasks like *'peer check/peer correction'*, *'speaking/ writing activities that can help the students to personalize and tell me about themselves'* and the *'test-teach-test pattern'*. This list of pedagogical strategies advocated by **Akhan** is compatible with active learning strategies, the aim of which is to *'involve students in doing things and in thinking about the things they are doing'* (Bonwell & Eison, 1991: 120). Under these pedagogical conditions, TESOL teachers often expect that their students will actively engage with them in various classroom activities like reading, speaking, group discussions and peer/self-evaluation.

However, **Akhan** found that his students were *'content with … teacher-centered lessons'* and that they *'rarely spoke during classroom activities'*. Finding this situation challenging, he would use *'vocabulary games'* and other relevant strategies in order to engage his students actively in classroom activities. However, he continued to experience several challenges in implementing such pedagogical strategies, as he admitted.

In order to further help his students put into practice his 'cognitively engaged pedagogy,' he used assessment practices including:

> (i) *'quizzes in which I try to include as many constructed response items as possible. In this way, the students need to think more deeply about their answers'*, (ii) *'oral presentations in which they need to synthesize and evaluate what they have covered in the classroom'*, and (iii) *'a Wall Dictionary'* I asked the students to produce so that they *'can test themselves and their classmates'*. (**Akhan**)

Akhan reported that *'all these activities let the students experience peripheral learning and autonomous learning as well'*.

Teaching English in the Saudi context also helped **Akhan** reflect on his own educational experiences and preparations. As he reported:

> *When I was back in Turkey, as I could speak the same language as my students, it was easy for me to establish a good rapport with them. However, here there is the language barrier and this makes establishing a rapport a little bit challenging. Therefore, you have to be careful when using your body language and gestures.* (**Akhan**)

This response suggests that, while **Akhan** was enthusiastically implementing his *'cognitively engaged pedagogy'* in the Saudi context, he seemed also to be mindful of the risks involved in transplanting pedagogies he used in his home country, Turkey. Therefore, he had had to make several adjustments to teach in the Saudi context. These adjustments entailed the following:

> *I speak a lot more naturally since the Saudi students' level of English is a lot better than those I taught back in Turkey.*
>
> *I am stricter, although I am friendly, than when I was in Turkey. Here, the students are very careful about the teacher's compliance with the rules and regulations.* (**Akhan**)

Akhan reported that he also relied on the quality of the '*written forms*' produced by his students together with their '*oral production*' as the basis for his decision to pursue his pedagogical strategies in the classroom. In fact, he justified his pedagogical decisions as follows:

> *Their level of motivation and engagement in the classroom is also another thing that helps me decide to continue to do things in the way I have been doing or change them.* (**Akhan**)

He seemed to have a strong belief in the effectiveness of his pedagogical strategies; as a result, he evaluated his pedagogical decisions according to the following culture of teaching:

> *If such decisions help the learners achieve the lesson objectives, this means that they are successful. However, if they do not pave the way for the attainment of the lesson objective, even if the students seem engaged and motivated thanks to my pedagogical decisions, they fail.* (**Akhan**)

Akhan listed the following three contributions which he believed he had made to his institution:

> *Through my teaching practice, I believe I have been teaching very professionally and conscientiously since I came here, both in the classrooms and in the Writing Centre. By preparing tests in the Unit, and taking part in Curriculum Review.* (**Akhan**)

Through the data we collected with **Akhan**, we felt the confidence as well as the wisdom of a highly experienced teacher. **Akhan** spoke with authority and a strong sense of reflection. Unlike almost all the other teacher participants who often raised concerns about Saudi students' low English language proficiency, **Akhan** actually praised his Saudi students' English level, something he had not experienced with his students in Turkey. Because of this, he saw himself as wanting to make his teaching more challenging in order to keep up with the students' language needs. Nonetheless, we felt from the data that **Akhan** did not seem to have been able to establish a good rapport with his students, and because of this his students' learning did not appear to go well, despite the effort and careful thought he had put into his teaching and assessment preparations. He attributed this problem to the language barrier and the fact that his students were more content with teacher-centered teaching and resisted his learner-centered approach. Although he did not want to identify with teacher-centered teaching, he felt forced to implement it to accommodate the students' preference. **Akhan** was not alone in this regard, as the subsequent accounts continue to show.

Example 5: Ahmad, a Teacher from Sudan – 'Meaningful Learning Will Never Be Achieved with this Type of Learner'

Ahmad, who holds an MA in Applied Linguistics and a TEFL degree from universities in Sudan, had taught English language in Qatar for several years before joining his current school in Saudi Arabia. A *'learner-centered approach'* formed the core of his teaching philosophy as well as pedagogical strategies in real-life classrooms.

Ahmad, although he strongly believed in the effectiveness of the 'learner-centered approach' in real-life classrooms, commented that his students were *'neither motivated nor eager to learn'* the language in the classroom. Thus, he concluded, *'meaningful learning will never be achieved with this type of learner'*. Consequently, he referred to vague pedagogical strategies that he used to enforce what he considered *'active learning'*, such as:

> *I try a variety of methods to create an environment which promotes learners' autonomy. I help my students to control their own learning and actively contribute to the learning process.* (**Ahmad**)

Elsewhere, he also adopted 'an eclectic teaching approach' in his classrooms:

> *I also use mixed methodologies to best meet students' needs and a variety of strategies which are appropriate to the learning context where the individual differences between students are highly considered.* (**Ahmad**)

In this context, **Ahmad** attempted to make different pedagogical decisions in his actual classroom teaching so as to accommodate the needs of his students and at the same time to validate these pedagogical strategies through a variety of assessment practices (formative and summative).

Ahmad felt that his current teaching experience in the Saudi context helped him reflect on his own educational experience and preparations in many ways.

> *My teaching experience in the Saudi context has provided me with the skills and the new techniques with which I can motivate learners who are not eager to study and learn. It has also given me the opportunity to deal with the most recent technological teaching aids.* (**Ahmad**)

We got a clear sense from **Ahmad** of his frustration with the fact that his students were not motivated to learn. He tended to blame the students while defending the learner-centered approach that he considered core to his teaching principles. The accounts from **Akhan** presented earlier and from **Ahmad** again confirm the global spread of this teaching approach and the tendency to shift the blame onto students when the approach fails to take effect.

The learner-centered approach, a key principle of CLT, has gained increasing acceptance from the TESOL profession in recent years, and many TESOL teachers have implemented it in an almost celebratory way in their language classrooms. As Phan (2014) argues:

> [these concepts] in many ways embody values proved to contradict and assumed to be superior to 'teacher as authority' or 'teacher-centric teaching.' These principles can be at odds with ... how they do their everyday teaching as well as can obstruct teachers in certain principles of teaching that are not effective in real-life classrooms ... (Phan, 2014: 396)

This argument suggests that we should be aware of the fact that teachers who fixate on the superiority of the communicative-oriented learner-centered approach tend to treat students' silence as 'an inferior and undesirable state' (Phan, 2014: 395). Phan further argues that this mindset could enable 'another form of oppression to both teachers and students, whose positions are defined in expert terms rather than in their own chosen terms' (Phan, 2014: 395).

Example 6: Arshad, a Teacher from Pakistan – 'There is no Single, Universal Approach that Suits All Situations'

Arshad, from Pakistan, who holds an MA in English Language and a Diploma in TESL from a Canadian institution, taught an integrated English skills course in a foundation program at a Saudi comprehensive university. He made it clear that *'there is no single, universal approach that suits all situations'*. Therefore:

> *I use differentiation in my teaching style. I devote extra care to the low ability students and design extra activities for the challenging students. Different strategies used in different combinations with different groupings of students will improve learning outcomes.* (**Arshad**)

Nevertheless, he admitted that *'lack of motivation on the part of some students is the biggest issue'* he faced in his institution, despite using *'different strategies to inspire and motivate students'*. He went on to say:

> *I use my flexible, intuitive, and creative style to accommodate my students in the classroom. I believe that there is a major relationship between student learning and the teacher's flexibility, creativity, and adaptability.* (**Arshad**)

He often evaluated his pedagogical decisions through constantly developing new strategies, and defining and reinterpreting them. He later described the assessment practices he would employ in his classrooms in order to help his students learn the language and to realize his pedagogy as follows:

> *I use diagnostic assessment at the beginning of any lesson to assess the skills, abilities, interests, experiences, levels of achievement or difficulties of an individual student or a whole class. I use summative assessment to make judgments about student achievement in the learning process and measure the level of achievement of learning outcomes. I use formative assessment to monitor students' ongoing progress and to provide immediate and meaningful feedback.* (**Arshad**)

Arshad explicitly expressed that as a non-native English-speaking teacher he felt that having an opportunity to teach in the KSA had helped him '*grow professionally*'. He further revealed:

> *[Teaching here helps me] develop competence to cope with classroom situations and remove social or psychological barriers. I seek my students' feedback from time to time; this helps me to revise my teaching strategies. When teaching, I always make attempts to customize myself with the Saudi culture, and this customization makes me more acceptable in the classroom.* (**Arshad**)

Arshad felt that he was contributing to his school in different ways, such as '*classroom instruction*', '*advising/supervision/mentoring of students*', '*coordination of courses*' and '*doing research on teaching*'.

Throughout the data collection process, although **Arshad** saw the '*lack of motivation on the part of some students as being the biggest issue*' in his teaching, he did not blame the students for the challenges that came his way. Instead, he emphasized his ability to make a difference to students' learning via his flexibility, adaptability and creativity. He showed clear evidence of not being swayed by the communicative-oriented learner-centered approach, although he implied that he was aware of the pressure to apply it with students, as all other teachers seemed to do so.

Example 7: Aris, a Teacher from the Philippines – 'To Teach is to Help, Support and Uplift the Lives of the Students'

Aris held similar views to **Arshad**, in that he was clear that '*there is no single effective strategy or method of a teacher who has the heart and passion to teach*'. Instead, he felt that a teacher must have a strong understanding of his students. This is because '*to teach is to help, support and uplift the lives of the students. It is therefore supporting their learning*', as he stated.

Like most other teachers who shared their stories with us, for **Aris**, religion was one of the unpredictable issues that most often arose in his real-life classrooms in the KSA. Religion appeared to play a significant role in **Aris**'s experience working in the country. He revealed that he constantly struggled with the fact that he had to silence his religious practice, ignore it and pretend that it did not matter so as to protect himself and accommodate his students' learning and their religion. In addition, he reported that *'cultural differences, the community and colleagues' behavior and attitudes'* were major concerns for him while working in Saudi Arabia. In this context, it was through continuous self-reflection that he managed to address such challenges. He told us that:

> *The moment I face my students, I always remind myself that I am one of them. This means I show respect to my students with the same amount of respect I give to myself, my family and to the people in the community.* (**Aris**)

Aris constantly reminded himself of the importance of giving in and serving others as a **Chris**tian. Although never expressing it explicitly and openly to anyone, he brought to his teaching a strong sense of caring and giving, influenced by his faith. Indeed, scholars like Baurain (2007, 2015), Wong *et al.* (2013) and Wong and Mahboob (2018) have discussed at great length the intimate relationship between religion and (English language) teaching. What **Aris** practiced in his teaching and the values he projected and upheld are highly relevant to what is examined in this body of work. Nonetheless, the emotions he had to manage and navigate must not be taken for granted, particularly when he felt he had to silence his religion in Saudi Arabia where Islam is the only religion allowed. He had to censor himself, but his commitment to caring, giving and serving with regard to his students was so strong that he felt rewarded and thankful to his religion.

In the classroom, **Aris** used *'negotiating strategies'* to ensure that his classroom pedagogies were effective and at the same time *'cater[ed] to students' varying needs'*. He employed various assessment practices in order to help his students acquire the necessary linguistic competency. These assessment practices included *'assessment of learning – quiz, progress tests and oral examinations'* and *'assessment for learning – a formative type of assessment (talking to the students about what they can and cannot do in the classroom)'*. He said, *'I always give chances and opportunities to my students where they can also evaluate their own performance, such as student conferences, feedback sessions, etc'*.

Similar to **Arshad** from Pakistan, referring to himself as *'a non-native English-speaking teacher from the Philippines'*, **Aris** said that teaching EFL in Saudi Arabia meant *'a lot'* to him. It helped him reflect on his own educational experiences, qualifications and preparations. He reported that:

> *[It] is a kind of reflection where I can also assess my teaching competence and motivate myself to perform tasks needed in the academic environment. Understanding [my students] means understanding my role and duties as a teacher in an EFL environment, for teaching is a process: involving students in the teaching-learning situation.* (**Aris**)

Aris also commented that his current pedagogical practices were assets to the college where he was working. He emphasized that his college benefited from his *'opinions, suggestions and contributions, especially in the development of the students'*. Notably, his beliefs about putting himself in the shoes of his students, together with being reflective in his pedagogical strategies, served as the guiding principles for his decision making and action.

We felt a sense of warmth and compassion from **Aris**, someone who was very conscientious, down to earth and committed to his students' learning. His account indicates the willingness of a teacher who was religious but managed to put aside his religion to show respect to the host country while still being able to incorporate his religious values of care and service in teaching.

Example 8: Zafar, a Teacher from Pakistan – 'I Work with a Sense of Empathy'

Alongside sharing with **Aris** a strong sense of care, **Zafar** stated that empathy was his guiding light in teaching. **Zafar** holds an MA in English Language and Literature from Pakistan as well as a CELTA from the UK, and speaks three languages – Pashto, Urdu and English. His several years of teaching English in Pakistan, Oman and now in a Saudi HE institution had led him to reflect on his own experiences as language teacher. From these reflections, he described the pedagogical strategies he used in Saudi classrooms as follows:

> *Since English is my second language, I work with a sense of empathy while working with my students. I believe I have been through all the stages which my students face in the classroom every day. At times, each student needs an individual approach that is decided in the given circumstances. I have been working with pairs, teams and class-as-one-group depending on the task and the nature of individual students.* (**Zafar**)

These beliefs about teaching held by **Zafar** are in line with Richards and Lockhart's (1996: 30) argument that 'all teachers were once students and their beliefs about teaching are often a reflection of how they themselves were taught'. **Zafar** believed his pedagogical strategies were effective; as a result, he never encountered any unpredictable issues in his classrooms. Instead, he said:

> *The only thing that sometimes frustrates me is that weaker and relatively stronger students don't like to sit together. Initially I force them to pair up, and with the passage of time, they do it willingly when they find their partners dependable and human.* (**Zafar**)

The ways he placed students in groups were based on a variety of factors, including *'students' spoken fluency'*, *'students' writing assignments'* and '*progress tests*'. He could sometimes evaluate his classroom pedagogical decisions based on '*a student's immediate response*' in some activities.

Formative assessment appeared to be commonly used among the international teachers, including **Zafar**.

> *Formative assessment seems to be working for me as it does for other teachers, since this practice takes the fear of grade achievement off the minds of my students. Writing is the most difficult skill to learn and to assess. But I usually start with familiar topics and scaffolding the ideas. Initially, I am least bothered about the accuracy of my students' writing. After they achieve their fluency, I start working on their accuracy.* (**Zafar**)

Notably, the everyday classroom teaching in Saudi Arabia helped **Zafar** appreciate his own educational experiences and preparations. As he recounted, '*as a trained CELTA teacher, I have been teaching what I had been trained for. Every new day gives me a fresh challenge that I love to work on*'.

It was clearly evident that many international teachers including **Zafar**, **Aris** and **Arshad** had developed a great deal of self-esteem and confidence as non-native English-speaking teachers, when they had the opportunity to teach English in Saudi Arabia, known for its preference for native teachers of English (Alshammari, 2020). These teachers all felt that they had been making valuable contributions to their schools as well as gaining experience and expertise that could be applicable anywhere. As **Zafar** said:

> *After teaching English language to students in GC [Gulf Cooperation] countries for more than ten years, I claim to have confidence that can help me teach students of any background. I believe I can help other teachers understand the classroom dynamics in this part of the world. Currently, I work as Program Coordinator at the Foundation Level. I work as a bridge between the teachers and the management. I help the management to execute the policies to improve the teaching and learning environment.* (**Zafar**)

Among all the teacher participants, **Zafar** is perhaps the one displaying the highest level of confidence. He was very clear about how he taught, what he did and how he worked with students to bring about the best outcome. Empathy was the way to go for **Zafar**. He was also appreciative of his workplace and the opportunities given to him in Saudi Arabia. The experience accumulated in this country after more than 10 years had prepared him for any teaching challenge, as he further confirmed.

On-the-Ground Realities Challenging Dominant Normative ELT Pedagogies

It is fairly consistent in all the accounts that the teachers tended to embrace mainstream ELT classroom pedagogical principles and practices that have become the norm in many TESOL teacher training and TESOL professional development programs around the world (Bolitho & Rossner, 2020; Polat *et al.*, 2021; Rose *et al.*, 2020). These pedagogical practices, with a strong focus on CLT and the student-centered approach, have been promoted as part of the 'universalized' professionalism that every ELT professional is expected to acquire and to enact in classrooms, as discussed in Phan and Le (2013) and Phan (2014). As is evident in all the accounts presented in this chapter, the participants appeared to endorse 'communicative language teaching' as the way to go, and accordingly employed the respective 'correct' vocabularies to refer to their roles and the ways they conducted classes and performed assessment.

All the international teachers acknowledged that culture, religion and Saudi students were major factors influencing their pedagogies, classroom decisions and how they presented themselves in class. The findings indicate that many international TESOL teachers are alternating 'between different perspectives' and being 'conscious of their evaluations of difference' (Byram *et al.*, 2001: 5). The findings also show that intercultural communication and negotiations are ongoing processes in that international TESOL teachers in Saudi Arabia have been devising different strategies to 'communicate effectively and appropriately across cultural differences based on particular knowledge, skills and attitudes' (Poole, 2019: 60). The intercultural negotiations can be conceptualized as 'critical interculturality' and 'a never-ending process' (Li & Dervin, 2018: 13). Seen in this manner, 'individuals do not approach every interaction as a new encounter but rather, on the level of lived experience, draw upon frames of reference (experiences and identities) in order to (re)negotiate the familiar, new and unexpected' (Poole, 2019: 61).

The classroom pedagogical practices advocated by the international TESOL teachers, coupled with the ways in which they responded to unpredictable issues (e.g. cultural, religious, pedagogical or linguistic) in real-life classrooms and the evidence they drew on in order to justify their classroom pedagogical practices, reflect varying degrees of criticality. By criticality we are here referring to 'the embodied intellectual, disposition and attitudinal attributes of "being critical"' (Kuske, 2015: 284). Specifically, while some teachers showed sound criticality in their responses, others reported that they were attempting to manage their classroom pedagogies, taking into consideration cultural-specific values and/or opening spaces for alternative practices. Although they may appear to have been strongly influenced by the normative discourse of CLT and the learner-centered approach in ELT, they all came up with specific ways of teaching and responding to their students' actual abilities and needs. Those teachers with much teaching experience in other EFL contexts also appear to have been more authoritative in sharing their views and justifying their pedagogical choices.

In the subsequent chapters, we continue to show how different international TESOL teachers may think, see, read, believe, act, react and value, as well as negotiate their classroom pedagogical practices in their respective classrooms. We also discuss the ways in which they respond to unpredictable issues in their classrooms and programs in Saudi Arabia.

8 Every Teacher is Different, Every Classroom Has its Own Dynamic

In this chapter, we showcase more in-depth data collected from semester-long classroom observations with six international TESOL teachers. These teachers allowed us to observe their teaching as often as we could afford to. They were teaching English to male Saudi students at different Saudi institutions. Each teacher brought with him unique expertise, experience, background, beliefs and pedagogical orientation. Informed by our earlier work (Barnawi & Phan, 2014: 269), the classroom observations were mainly on '(1) the pedagogical strategies employed by each teacher to meet his students' needs, and (2) the underlying principles behind those strategies'.

We resist the temptation to frame these teachers' teaching and on-the-ground situations into 'manageable research variables'; instead, we let the data speak for themselves while presenting minimal interpretations. As Halkes and Oslon (1984) argued several decades ago:

> Looking from a teacher-thinking perspective at teaching and learning, one is not so much striving for the disclosure of the effective teacher, but for the explanation and understanding of teaching processes as they are. After all, it is the teacher's subjective school-related knowledge which determines for the most part what happens in the classroom; whether the teacher can articulate his/her knowledge or not. Instead of reducing the complexity of teacher-learning situations into a few manageable research variables, one tries to find out how teachers cope with these complexities. (Halkes & Oslon, 1984: 1)

In an attempt to capture these teachers' pedagogical strategies, we have borrowed their own descriptions and labeling of their teaching, such as 'mixed methods' (**Maxi**), 'communicative approach' (**John**), 'Saudified teaching strategies' (**Hafiz**), 'new teaching strategies every day' (**Adam**), 'product-oriented approach to writing' (**Khan**) and 'authenticizing teaching approach' (**Peter**). The different strategies/approaches reflect 'the complexity of the teaching beliefs that informed their everyday teaching practices' (Barnawi & Phan, 2014: 268). We argue that these different pedagogical perspectives or beliefs brought to the Saudi context by international TESOL teachers should not be construed as necessarily mutually exclusive. Instead, they should be considered as complementary constructs that represent the wider realities of the field of English language teaching (ELT) in general and ELT within the Saudi higher education (HE) context in particular.

Echoing Canagarajah's (2002: 142) study, we find that our teacher participants' pedagogical strategies 'do not constitute a method but function as a heuristic to develop an appropriate pedagogy from the bottom up' in order to accommodate the specific educational and linguistic needs of their respective Saudi students. We also take into account the fact that 'classroom realities often do not correspond to any recognizable method; in other words, a teacher might commence his class with a specific method in mind, but then might be influenced by classroom contingencies to alter his strategies as he goes on' (Barnawi & Phan, 2014: 269; Kumaravadivelu, 2003).

Visiting the Classrooms of Six International TESOL Teachers

Hafiz: Saudified teaching strategies

Hafiz, who holds an MA in English from a university in Nigeria and a CELTA from International House, London, teaches a four-credit course called English 001 to foundation program students at a comprehensive university in Saudi Arabia. Specifically, the course is designed for first-term students preparing for specialized undergraduate studies within the university where the medium of instruction is English. An integrated approach to teaching the four basic skills – reading, writing, listening and speaking – is used on the course, and at the same time close attention is paid to fluency and accuracy. Upon successful completion of this course, the students move to English 002 level, another skills-based course, before they go on to their specialized programs. At the beginning of the term, **Hafiz** discussed the entire syllabus with his students in order to familiarize them with course expectations.

> *Notably, he often greets the class by saying 'Salamu Allikum Warahmutillah' and uses some Arabic words to introduce himself, his nationality and his religion to the students. The main classroom pedagogical strategies employed by* **Hafiz** *can be briefly described as explicit instruction followed by questioning techniques as well as group and pair work. He would often start his class by asking questions about a previous lesson and at the same time check the student's homework. He would then list new vocabulary on the board and read it aloud several times. He would also explicitly demonstrate rules of English grammar (e.g. simple past, present simple tenses etc.), using examples from the book. After that, he would invite individual students to read the examples he had given them aloud and give some examples of their own. For instance, he*

would explain the rule of the past simple tense on the board, provide several examples and then ask the students to give examples. After that, he would ask the students to work in groups or pairs to complete some exercises from the book. While this was happening, he would go around the class and offer support to some students and encourage others to participate more, using expressions such as 'very good', 'mashallah' and 'yes, correct'. He would also warn those who refused to participate by saying 'you have to work with us if you want to pass the course', 'be serious please' and 'be careful'. (Classroom observation notes)

Hafiz justified his rather straightforward and explicit teaching techniques as follows:

> *I think the students are familiar with such teaching methods from their high schools. Thus, I have to use some Saudified teaching strategies. It is also culturally appropriate to use stick and carrot techniques here. This way I can control the classroom very well.* (**Hafiz**, Interview).

During the classroom observation sessions, it was clear that even when some students were unwilling to take part in group activities or pair work, **Hafiz** still tried his best to have them participate. In a follow-up interview, he revealed, '*I know sometimes my students are reluctant to participate in class. These strategies work best for them when I repeatedly employ them in class. I can see them positively responding to my strategies*' (**Hafiz**, Interview).

Guided by his Saudified teaching strategies, **Hafiz** negotiated a favorable ground for language instruction with his students. He often started his class by saying 'Salamu Allikum Warahmutillah' and at the same time used Arabic to introduce himself, his nationality and his religion to the students. This strategy is what Kramsch (2009) referred to as 'symbolic competence'. That is:

> the ability to understand the symbolic value of symbolic form and the different cultural memories evoked by different symbolic systems, to draw on the semiotic diversity afforded by multiple languages to reframe ways of seeing familiar events, create alternative realities and find an appropriate subject position between languages. (Kramsch, 2009)

Through what was observed during the classroom observations sessions with Hafiz, it was evident that he was proactive in making an effort to relate to his students and to build a rapport with them. That he shared their religion and understood Arabic also gave him some advantage. He felt that his so-called '*Saudified teaching strategies*' could help to create a meaningful learning environment for the Saudi students. In a way, **Hafiz** found a '*comfort zone*' with Saudi students via religion and Arabic. We did not see Arabic being used in his classes except for the greetings at the beginning of each lesson; nonetheless the fact that he knew Arabic might have made the students relate to him more easily. He could be both friendly and strict with them, and they seemed to accept this.

On another note, **Hafiz** could fall into a category of international TESOL teachers who tend to look deliberately for a 'comfort zone' in Saudi Arabia, as raised by some teacher participants. These teachers often avoid confronting cultural conflicts and pedagogical challenges. They tend to go with the flow and do little to teach anything beyond the basic language skills.

John: Communicative, communicative, communicative approach

John, a Canadian teacher with a MA (TESOL) degree, teaches a Basic English course at a vocational training institution in Saudi Arabia. The main aim of the course is to enhance students' basic skills in reading and writing.

John would always ask his students to work in pairs and/or small groups. He would then ask them to answer questions or complete a set of activities in class. While the students were working on the assigned tasks, he would walk around the class providing feedback and sometimes participating in the group discussions. After that, he would ask one student from each group to write the correct answers on the board and at the same time invite the class to ask more questions. (Classroom observation notes)

He argued that, '*through such teaching strategies students should be able to share their answers and learn from each other*' (**John**, Interview). He also commented that, '*through writing my students will become better thinkers*'.

He also does a lot of demonstrations in order to break the ice and make his students feel comfortable in class. Notably, he often does not give direct feedback to his students, nor does he answer their questions directly. Instead, he encourages the students to guess the correct answers by themselves. If they cannot guess the correct answer, he will keep explaining, repeating and demonstrating the same questions in different ways. At the end of each class, he asks a group of students to ask questions and the other students to respond to their questions. (Classroom observation notes)

John pointed out that, through this type of interactive task, '*more learning will take place*', students would be '*engaged in relevant dialogue*' and '*the classroom will turn into an enjoyable place where students can practice what they have learned immediately*' (**John,** Interview).

John's classroom practices were guided by the principles of the communicative language teaching (CLT) approach. Specifically, student–student collaboration through pair work and group work, elicitation, re-casting questions and similar practices were the salient features of his classrooms. According to Dobao (2012: 40), 'pair and small group activities constitute one of the most common practices in communicative second language (L2) classrooms, theoretically supported by both psycholinguistic and sociocultural perspectives on L2 acquisition'. Through collaborations and interactions with their peers, students become able to construct knowledge and use the language for a wide range of functions, including questioning, negotiating and other forms of meaning-making.

It could be argued that the principles of the communicative approach used by **John** and most other teachers featured in this book are indicative of their pedagogical beliefs, 'and [their] specific educational and teaching experiences, including those in teacher education programs' (Pennington, 2014: 17). These pedagogical beliefs and experiences often affect 'the teacher's choices as to classroom roles and instructional emphases in content and methods' (Pennington, 2014: 17). These beliefs about teaching are also in line with Richards and Lockhart (1996), who observed that teachers were often influenced by the ways they themselves were taught during their own education.

Khan and his eight-year-long effective approach to teaching writing

Khan, who holds an MA in English from a university in Pakistan, was teaching English for academic purposes specializing in English communication at a Saudi engineering college. The course focuses solely on communication for the workplace. Students on this course are required to write inquiry, order, claim and adjustment letters, take an active part in group discussions and debates, and deliver effective oral presentations. The English proficiency levels of the students on this English course range from B1 to B2, according to the *Common European Framework of Reference for Languages: Learning, Teaching, Assessment* (Council of Europe, 2001).

> ***Khan** uses a wide variety of teaching strategies to help his students master workplace communication skills. His teaching strategies can be summarized as follows: he often begins his class by talking about the value of English language learning for young Saudis. He then uses several examples to persuade his students. After that he asks each student to write a short essay on the importance of English for their future career and then these essays are discussed in small groups*. (Classroom observation notes)

As **Khan** explained later in a follow-up interview: '*... in these warm up activities, I am able to build up a rapport and motivate my students to take their learning seriously*' (**Khan**, Interview).

> *Throughout the course, he would constantly ask the students to read samples of texts (e.g. inquiry, order, claim and adjustment letters) from the book and then answer comprehension questions based on the texts. He would then ask each student to write, for example, an inquiry letter using the examples in the book. After that he gave each student a*

'self-editing' checklist to help him revise his paper. In the self-editing checklist task, students can revise their papers on the basis of rhetorical organization, sentence structure, layout, transition signals, and the common expressions discussed in the book. **Khan** would then distribute a 'peer editing' checklist to the class and invite the students to work in pairs and discuss their papers with each other. While this was happening, he would walk around the class and encourage the students to start their discussions by providing three compliments and then sharing their suggestions with their peers. (Classroom observation notes)

Khan seemed confident that his teaching strategies could help his students produce a good piece of writing. As such, in the classroom he often provided a wide range of bottom-up approach activities as well as language usages such as moving 'from sentence to paragraph and text level' (Tribble, 1997: 84). This approach to teaching writing seems, as Pincas (1962: 185) put it, 'mindless, repetitive and anti-intellectual'; it encourages students simply to mimic a model text from the course and hinders their creativity and self-voicing in writing. Nonetheless, **Khan** had a different view.

Specifically, **Khan** seemed to hold a strong belief about the value of this classroom pedagogical practice. He justified his teaching approach as follows:

I have been using this approach for the past eight years and it is working perfectly with my students. This approach helps my students to discover their own grammatical mistakes and also imitate from the models given to them in class. At the end, I collect their papers and give my final judgment. (**Khan**, Interview).

Khan appeared to be fully convinced of the effectiveness of his pedagogical strategies, even after the interviewer (Barnawi) drew his attention to the fact that issues of 'self-discovery', 'individual needs' and expressions of individual ideas were overlooked. He said simply, *'my students are doing great in their final exams, so why should I change my approach if it is working effectively?'* (**Khan**, Interview).

To be fair, Saudi institutions as well as Saudi students pay much attention to exam results as the results determine whether the students will be 'qualified' to move on to the next proficiency level. Without having completed their compulsory language courses in the foundation program, they cannot proceed to their chosen majors. Likewise, students need high exam results if they want to undertake certain majors as these majors are highly competitive. In other words, their English exam results play an important role in their educational trajectories at university and what may follow afterwards. It seems there is little room for *self-discovery* and *individual needs* when these desirable constructs may be at odds with the pressure to pass exams and to score highly, among both teachers and students. **Khan** was well aware of this reality and demonstrated his commitment to helping his students achieve the results they aimed for. He saw himself as performing at his best and that there was nothing wrong with his teaching. He did not hide the fact that he was not a fan of the CLT bandwagon, something *'everyone talks about but most of the time does not work in reality'*, based on his experience and observations.

Khan displayed a strong sense of care towards his students' success and their future orientations. He wanted to encourage and inspire them to take responsibility as young Saudis and to do so with knowledge and pride, as the classroom observations with him indicated. He wanted to instill moral values in these young men's future outlooks. This reminds us of the Western-trained Vietnamese teachers of English in Phan's (2008) study who regarded teaching as being about both knowledge and character building. They also saw themselves as moral guides, as role models who often incorporated the teaching of values, ethics and civic responsibilities into their English language lessons. Phan (2008) argues strongly for the role of teacher as moral guide in understanding teacher identity and identification in specific local and professional contexts, as globalization, mobility and hybridity continue to impact ELT in profound ways. Indeed, scholars like Baurain (2004), Johnston (2003) and Morgan (2004) have discussed the close relationships of values and ELT. That **Khan** often talked to his students about the many promising roles young Saudis would play in today's society, in order to emphasize the importance of English language learning for young Saudis and how English would be useful for their future, ties in closely with this understanding of teaching and values.

Maxi and his mixed-methods approach

Maxi, who holds an MA in Language Studies for Teachers as well as an Educational Management degree from a university in the Philippines, teaches a reading comprehension course at a comprehensive university in Saudi Arabia. The aim of the course is to help first-year university students to improve their English reading skills. It focuses on active reading, critical thinking, evaluating written texts and making inferences and decisions.

> *Throughout the course of the term,* **Maxi** uses a variety of methods to improve the students' comprehension skills (e.g. skimming for main ideas, scanning for details, summarizing and discussing what they have read with direct reference to the text), English vocabularies (e.g. using the context to identify the meaning of words, and identifying unfamiliar words) and reading speed (e.g. reading aloud). Prior to the beginning of each class, **Maxi** would distribute reading hand-outs to the class and ask the students to read them at home. He would then ask each student to identify: (i) three things he liked about the text with justifications, (ii) three things he did not like in the text with justifications, and (iii) four to six new words and transition signals. (Classroom observation notes)

He felt that these strategies would *'help students make sense of their reading by evaluating the texts, sharing their opinions and exploring new words'* (**Maxi**, Interview).

> *Building on the students' prior understanding of the required texts, he would ask them to share their reading responses in pairs and small groups. After that, he would ask different students to read the text aloud in class. While different students were reading aloud, he would stop them from time to time to correct any pronunciation problems or intonation patterns, using expressions such as 'read it in an understandable way', 'very good' or 'this is not clear'. He also asks some vocabulary and spelling questions when the student finishes reading. After that he asks the class to answer the comprehension questions in small groups and awards points to those who finish the task first. These strategies have created a lot of competition in the class and at the same time have made his students engage in group discussions and debates. While the students are engaged in the assigned tasks, he goes round the class and provides correct answers to the comprehension questions.* (Classroom observation notes)

Maxi stated that:

> *my methods and strategies were mainly based on the communicative language teaching approach, [and the] active learning and learner-oriented approaches. Asking the students to read aloud and engage in group discussions will give them the opportunity to practice the language in authentic ways, I believe.* (**Maxi**)

Nonetheless, **Maxi** emphasized the importance of employing a variety of strategies and methods in teaching, arguing that his *'mixed method strategies can help each individual to benefit from the course since there is no one-size-fits-all strategy in language teaching'* (**Maxi**, Interview). He further claimed that he was utilizing *'mixed methods'* to improve his students' comprehension skills (e.g. skimming for main ideas, scanning for details, summarizing and discussing what they have read with direct reference to the text), their English vocabulary (e.g. using context to identify the meaning of words and to identify unfamiliar words) and their reading speed (e.g. reading aloud).

> *The most prominent feature of* **Maxi***'s pedagogical strategies is that he is attempting to adopt CLT and TBL approaches that require students to work in pairs and/or small groups in order to practice the language and at the same time accomplish various tasks centered on language elements.* (Classroom observation notes)

In further correspondence with **Maxi**, we learnt that although he emphasized CLT as his core approach, he tended to lean towards what he called *'adjusted strategies'* in his teaching. He listed the following keywords to refer to the range of options that he could navigate across: *'communicative language teaching'*, *'active-learning'*, the *'learner-oriented* *approach*', '*Cooperative Language Learning*', '*Whole Language*', '*Content-based Instruction*' and '*Task-based Language Teaching approaches*'. He stated that he drew on all of these in order to serve his Saudi EFL students in the best way he could. While he employed '*cooperative and collaborative learning*' to manage his mixed and multilevel students in the classroom, he also introduced '*life-like*' and different '*task-based activities*' to motivate his students and keep them engaged. All these were evident in the classroom observations Barnawi had with **Maxi**.

Maxi referred to the '*performance of students in class*' and their '*communicative competence and linguistic outputs*' to assess the effectiveness of his pedagogical initiatives and decisions in the classroom. He also reported that he paid attention to assessment tools to make them compatible with his classroom pedagogical practices: '*when I design my own assessment tools, I make sure they are authentic, learner-appropriate, and culturally sensitive*'. Indeed, **Maxi** felt that his current teaching experience in the Saudi context had helped him reflect on his own '*educational experiences and preparations from both a linguistic and a cultural point of view*'.

Because of '*enormous differences*' between the Philippines and Saudi Arabia as far as ELT orientation was concerned, he said:

> I find my teaching career in the KSA more challenging but rewarding. My unique experiences have bequeathed me new teaching principles and helped me validate some linguistic theories. (**Maxi**)

Maxi used linguistic and sociocultural adjustments in his classroom in order to accommodate the language conditions of his students. He would often '*simplify the language he uses in class*', '*avoid complex sentences*' and '*use facial and body gestures to aid verbal language*'.

He strongly felt that his current teaching practices and '*adjustment strategies*' were making a positive contribution to his school '*in such a way that they help [him] reach the learners linguistically, socially and culturally*'. Additionally, he believed that his current pedagogical strategies (e.g. the communicative approach and task-based learning) had made his teaching '*more effective, enjoyable and transformative*'.

Although during the classroom observations, Barnawi did not detect any challenging moments involving religious or cultural difference, in further communication with **Maxi** we learnt that cultural and religious issues were the two unpredictable challenges that constantly occurred in his real-life classrooms. He told us that he employed two strategies to address such challenges: (i) he spent time '*explaining the inappropriate materials presented in the textbooks*', as well as '*getting students to work in pairs and small groups to talk about the materials: for instance, the unfamiliar jobs, routines, festivals, food and places*'; (ii) he would '*leave out the inappropriate activities and topics in the lesson and find alternatives to* *them'*. Socioculturally speaking, he described the adjustment he had to make as follows:

> *I have adjusted the way I deal with people (e.g. social graces, grooming, etc.), as locals have their own specific ways. I also became a bit more flexible when it comes to time management, as some students have different concepts and '[a different approach to the] management of time'. They have all the reasons for coming to class late. Lastly, I have to be extra careful and sensitive with some topics/lessons that may offend students' religious sensibilities.* (**Maxi**)

Maxi was very passionate when sharing with us his teaching experience and his reflections on working in Saudi Arabia. He made extra effort when working with and helping students, and it was evident from the classroom observations that his students were not only able to participate in class but also showed a keen interest in learning the language and performing various integrated tasks. **Maxi** was particularly cautious about crossing the line when it came to cultural and religious matters. He made a conscious effort not to be on the wrong side of the students' beliefs and judgements. **Maxi** is not alone in this, as almost every other teacher we talked to highlighted this very matter. We could tell that he was popular among the students and they were very respectful and cooperative. That **Maxi** does not know Arabic, is not a Muslim and is a non-native English-speaking teacher (NNEST)did not seem to interfere with his students' learning and progress. Everything seemed to work fine in his English-only class. This finding seems to challenge much existing literature on NNESTs which uniformly affirms that their shared language background with students is an ultimate strength and advantage over native-English-speaking teachers (NESTs). Such an assigned NNEST–NEST dichotomous framework clearly does not apply in **Maxi**'s case.

Peter: 'Authenticizing teaching approach – learn to speak like native speakers in academic, business and social life'

Peter, who holds a BA in English Language from a university in the UK, was teaching an English communication course at a Saudi technical college. This course covers different aspects of oral communication skills, including group discussions, debates and presentations. It helps students to develop their public speaking skills as well as their knowledge of different parts/functions of speech. At the beginning of the course, **Peter** informed the students that his responsibility on the course was to help them *'learn to speak like native speakers in academic, business and social life'*.

> *Peter's classroom pedagogical practices during the 14-week course can be summarized as follows: he would start his class by showing various video presentations given by native speakers to the students. He would then stop the video presentation from time to time to ask comprehension questions. While the students were answering the questions, he would*

correct their pronunciation and other grammatical mistakes. **Peter** places a great deal of emphasis on improving students' pronunciation. In fact, he always tells his students: 'Your speaking needs to be understandable to native speakers of English'. After that he divides the class into small groups and gives them instructions for classroom debates. While the students are engaged in small group debates, he walks around and provides feedback on correct modes of expression, grammar and pronunciation. Next, he invites some students to give individual presentations in front of the class and at the same time asks other students to ask questions and/or provide suggestions on pronunciation. At the end of each class, he nominates what he calls 'the best speaker' in the class. It was clear that these teaching strategies had caused a situation of hypercorrection among the class, in that the students tended to focus a great deal on intonation, grammar and gestures, while overlooking the elements of ideas, voice and criticality in speaking. (Classroom observation notes)

Peter, in a follow-up interview, revealed that the strategies he used would *'enhance students' interpersonal skills as well as [encouraging] team-building and group problem solving'* (**Peter**, Interview).

Through excessive use of video presentations given by native speakers to the students and an overemphasis on pronunciation, **Peter** seemed to be trying to increase the students' awareness of the importance of accurate pronunciation in communication. Indeed, as Saito and Lyster (2012: 630) argue, pronunciation recasts 'can be quite salient to learners when their targets are L2 pronunciation errors, because inaccurate pronunciation has more potential to seriously interfere with understanding.' In the light of much existing literature, **Peter**'s decontextualized classroom pedagogical practices are more likely to hinder language acquisition among Saudi students. In his teaching, **Peter** seemed to be treating the target language and its culture as 'static and uniform'; hence, students are urged to 'assimilate into the monolingual' culture (Kubota, 2004; Kumaravadivelu, 2001). These scholars and others such as Piller (2016) and Sung (2020) have warned against the promotion of monolingualism and normativism, by which EFL students in their learning of English are forced to master standardized English and norms as opposed to non-native and non-standard varieties of English which include other dialects. Thus, teaching strategies like that implemented by **Peter** can create unequal power relations within/between students and teachers (De Costa, 2020).

Nevertheless, from the classroom observations with **Peter**'s class, the students seemed engaged and motivated to learn. They did not appear resentful about the native-speaker model that **Peter** insisted on. If anything, they participated eagerly and showed a sense of excitement as they could speak English like native speakers or at least that they were being trained for this. The data obtained from **Peter** confirmed Alseweed's (2012) findings in that the majority of the 169 Saudi male students included in his study were fond of native teachers and overwhelmingly praised them for their teaching and abilities to create an enjoyable classroom atmosphere.

Alseweed (2012) also reported that these Saudi students were largely interested in learning about native-English-speaking countries, peoples, societies and cultures. What was observed in **Peter**'s class and the findings presented in Alseweed (2012), on the one hand, imply that the native-speaker model was rather well received by students in actual classrooms. On the other hand, both these accounts counter the established literature on the association of native speakers and native-speakerism with monolingualism and on the inherent unequal power relationship between non-native speakers and native speakers if the native-speaker model is perpetuated and presented as a teaching goal.

Adam: New teaching strategies every day

Adam, from the USA, who held a BA in Sociology and Education and a TESOL certificate from institutions in his home country, was teaching an integrated-skill course for first-term students at a Saudi university. The aim of this integrated-skill course is to improve the students' four language skills – reading, writing, listening and speaking – as well as their grammar and vocabulary. The course has a wide range of learning materials such as images, videos and posters. For this competency-based course, **Adam** used themes and topics from real life.

> *Adam, from the very start of the term, would create his teaching strategies based on the students' immediate needs throughout the course. He therefore was not using any fixed specific pedagogical strategies to help his students acquire communicative and linguistic competency. Instead, throughout the course of the term, he was constantly negotiating and renegotiating his pedagogical strategies with the students. For instance, in one lesson he would explain the difference between the present perfect tense and the present continuous through games and group activities. He would then revise the same lesson in the subsequent class using a teacher-centered approach – explaining the rules governing the two tenses on the board for around 20 minutes. After that, he would give the students several examples from the book and at the same time ask some of the students to give their own examples of the different uses of the two tenses. At the end of the class, he would ask the students to form small groups and produce examples showing the different uses of and rules governing the two tenses. In the following lesson, he would prepare the group for the subject of a new lesson (e.g. using the simple past tense) and give the students clear instructions. While the students were working in pairs and small groups, he would walk around the class and offer advice and at the same time answer any language-related questions.* (Classroom observation notes)

Adam justified his pedagogical practices as follows:

> *I know I am using new teaching strategies every day because the way my students are learning is unpredictable to me. So, I have to change my teaching style every day according to the reaction of the class. Sometimes they are not willing to participate so I have to control the class by explaining everything in detail. And sometimes they are willing to*

participate so I have to give them a space to create their own learning environment. In this way, I do not often experience problems with Saudi students. (**Adam**, Interview).

He further revealed that, '*I am new to the system so I have to invent my own teaching philosophy to survive and keep the students engaged all the time. Otherwise, they will complain to the management*' (**Adam**, Interview). In this context, it could be said that Adam was attempting to devise strategies responsive to everyday teaching realities. It is undeniable that Adam was very dedicated and committed to helping his students.

Being new to the system, **Adam** did not yet have much to reflect on. He focused more on making sure he conformed and put as much effort as possible into his teaching and adjusting his class activities and ways of conducting teaching according to the students' responses and projected energy levels. His students appeared to enjoy learning with him and benefited from the wide range of strategies that he invented on the go. He did not seem to be dictated by any dominant teaching principles or dogmas. Again, what we observed from **Adam** confirms Alseweed's (2012) findings that the Saudi student participants, in comparing their experiences when studying with both native and non-native teachers, largely praised native teachers for their creativity and extraordinary teaching methods that could stimulate their learning. By making this point we do not mean to offer any misleading or biased views regarding native and non-native teachers of English. Chapter 11 offers more nuanced accounts and reflections from four native teachers of English, and in that chapter we show that the on-the-ground realities can be very unpleasant and exhausting for these teachers.

The Absence of Global Englishes, English as a Lingua Franca and Translanguaging Pedagogies

An important point we would like to highlight is that, in all the accounts presented above as well as the accounts featured in Chapters 6 and 7, there seems to be no sign of what Kuske (2015: 286) refers to as 'the hybridity and indeterminate character of transcultural English use, as instantiated in the fluid, negotiating-centric communicative practices that multilinguals freely adopt despite the prescriptive dictates of authoritative texts and institutions'. Scholarship on Global Englishes and English as lingua franca pedagogies (De Costa *et al*., 2020; Fang & Baker, 2018; Fang & Widodo, 2019; Irham *et al*., 2021; J. Jenkins, 2006, 2012; Matsuda, 2017; Sung, 2020) did not seem to play a role in these participants' pedagogies and practices. Neither did they seem concerned about the multilingual turn in language teaching (Conteh & Meier, 2014) and about translanguaging and the like (Canagarajah, 2011a, 2011b; García & Lin, 2017). The English that each teacher speaks seemed to have been the only language in class, and students' linguistic resources did not seem to play a role, either. We are not suggesting that these teachers' ways of teaching were not effective or beneficial to students. We are surprised by the gap between these teachers' actual classroom teaching and the growing body of progressive scholarship in TESOL, language education and applied linguistics.

Different Classroom Pedagogical Perspectives as Complementary Angles

The snapshots of the classroom observation sessions presented above also show that all the observed teachers had found Saudi Arabia a contesting space for negotiating their various classroom pedagogical practices, assumptions and social-cultural knowledge base. For instance, while **Peter**, a native speaker of English, took advantage of his *native linguistic capital* in the classroom, **Hafiz**, a non-native speaker, capitalized on his *symbolic competency* as a Nigerian Muslim with a basic understanding of the Arabic language. At the same time, while **Maxi** from the Philippines was attempting to reject the embedded 'marginality' of method as a colonial concept (Canagarajah, 1999; Kumaravadivelu, 2003) and was exploring, through a mixed-methods approach, alternative practices, **Khan** from Pakistan felt that product-based instruction could optimally accommodate the immediate needs of Saudi students. **Adam** from the USA, by contrast, was very skeptical about following any existing pedagogical strategies. Thus, he was endlessly exploring new teaching strategies to ensure he could help his Saudi students learn.

Notably, these teachers' justifications of their chosen pedagogies as well as the different levels of on-the-ground negotiations demonstrated by each teacher in his respective classroom reflect the complexity as well as the disparity of the 'knowledge bases' of international TESOL teachers working in Saudi Arabia. They were all experienced teachers with relevant expertise and training. Despite the dominance of certain ELT norms and discourses in teaching that we have discussed in the previous chapters, these teachers expressed strong positions as to why they taught in certain ways. We argue that the complexities, diversity and disparity of the knowledge, expertise and training bases displayed by these international TESOL teachers are indications of ELT as a dynamic field. Those working in this field are individuals with different histories and evolving identities that we cannot simply categorize into any generalized groups. Neither can they be framed in any rigid and biased way. They all make up the fields of TESOL and ELT, in their own ways. As Pennington (2014) argues:

> Each of the different practice-centered and contextual frames can be considered to represent different facets of teacher identity in TESOL which together make up a composite identity of the TESOL educator and define how an individual who works in the TESOL field conceptualizes and performs 'being a teacher'. (Pennington, 2014: 72)

Starting to Bring Some Dots Together

Bringing Chapters 6, 7 and 8 together, we hope that by now readers have already gotten a clear sense of the crowded and busy TESOL market in Saudi Arabia as well as the range of expertise, knowledge and experience international TESOL teachers enjoy and project. What is evident in the accounts presented across these chapters is that the teachers were highly aware of their pedagogical choices as well as perceptive of the dynamic of their classrooms and the workplace in some cases. They appeared confident about their teaching approaches but were realistic about whether such approaches were effective. They seemed observant and responsive to their students' needs and attitudes. They also showed willingness in adapting their teaching to specific situations and even switching their teaching styles and principles almost completely once they had learnt about their students' habits, proficiency levels and learning needs. The range of perspectives, examples, techniques, strategies and teaching principles/philosophies/values they referred to and explained placed them on a par with any TESOL teachers considered experienced, professional, dedicated, knowledgeable, down-to-earth and aware.

As a matter of fact, international TESOL teachers with mixed backgrounds working in the Saudi HE institutions enjoy different historic-ontological and epistemological conceptualizations of English education stemming from their former TESOL training in their home countries and/or overseas, and from their prior work experience. At the same time, the Saudi context has its own expectations, values, cultural traditions and norms pertaining to English language teaching and learning. In this context, it is important to pay attention to the ways in which those international TESOL teachers talk about their teaching, conceptualize their pedagogies, reflect on their teaching and classroom dynamic, and devise 'context-sensitive and institution-specific classroom pedagogies' (Barnawi & Phan, 2014: 264) and the underlying rationales.

One phenomenon that stands out is what we called **the emulation of dominant normative ELT pedagogies and the leaning towards English-only pedagogies** found in much of the data. Mainstream conceptions of English language teaching and learning were well pronounced in the responses of the majority of the native- as well as the non-native-speaker teachers we surveyed. These teachers cited the '*communicative language teaching approach*', '*task-based language teaching*' and '*active learning*' as the guiding principles for their classroom teaching and assessment. Taking classrooms as a site of advocacy for their ontological and epistemological understanding of English language teaching and learning, the overwhelming majority of native and non-native English-speaking teachers described their roles in the classroom and in the profession as '*facilitator*', '*coach*', '*mentor*', '*leader*', someone who is '*willing to take risks*', '*role model*', '*creator of a productive classroom environment*' and '*contributor*' to the learning processes (e.g. Barnawi, 2016; Canagarajah, 2002;

Kumaravadivelu, 2006; Phan, 2014; Phillipson, 1992). Such responses, indeed, echo their TESOL training 'heritage, literacy resources, and culturally-situated ways of knowing and being' (Kuske, 2015: 286), while confirming their identification with an industry that has been driven by enthusiastic submission to communicative approaches at all levels of policy, training and classroom practice (Bax, 2003; Pham, 2004; Vu & Phan, 2020). These responses also show that the teachers were well aware of the demand to make Saudi learners able to *communicate* in English – the very demand behind the aggressive promotion and embrace of English and ELT in Saudi Arabia. The employment of foreign teachers to teach English in the country has come with this expectation.

The view of the teacher as a 'facilitator', a 'coach', a 'mentor' and a 'leader' stems from the concept of learner-centered education (see, for example, Phan, 2014, for detailed discussion), which encourages learners to take control of their own learning in the classroom. It is important to acknowledge that we are not condemning the learner-centered approach and its associated discourses, such as the teacher as a facilitator, coach and/or mentor in TESOL classrooms. Instead, we are concerned about the ways in which these discourses are projected in many non-English-speaking countries, including Saudi Arabia. As Phan (2014) argues, in many cases, the learner-centered approach and its associated discourses are presented 'in absolute terms' in policy and teacher training vocabularies, implying the absolute need for them to be adopted to replace '[other] pedagogies and practices, some of which are actually working well in the immediate context' (Phan, 2014: 393). At a practical level, however, teachers often experience 'a mismatch between what actually happens and the optimal desire conveyed in public discourse and policy [and in training programs]' (Phan, 2014).

Another important phenomenon we would like to put forth is that, when facing realities that are far from those predominantly presented in the CELTA short courses and even in the TESOL degree teacher training courses they have taken, many teachers start to question the relevance and appropriacy of their training. Theoretical constructs underlying CLT as well as many tips, activities, designs, formats and strategies provided to them through their training do not work. Hence, these teachers start to approach these idealized and promoted teaching canons with doubts. They, instead, look for other ways that may work, including *'drilling and grammar-translation'* and *'direct translation'* methods and the *'teacher-centered approach,'* which have been fiercely condemned in their training and by them and their peers. We refer to this phenomenon as **resisting the emulation of dominant normative ELT pedagogies and exploring alternative practices.**

It is important to note that the above phenomena happen simultaneously. And this is when reflective teaching happens, in all different forms and shapes. Indeed, how each teacher deals with each specific teaching situation varies. Likewise, the degrees to which they reflect on their teaching and adjustments and new discoveries also differ. Each of the specific accounts we have presented, in various ways, embraces the abovementioned phenomena, although we acknowledge that all the teachers expressed a sense of criticality of the situation they found themselves in, whether critical of their own teaching approaches and beliefs, classroom activities, institutional mandates or the ways in which they interacted with students and handled difficult situations.

While some teachers whose accounts were featured in the previous chapter felt that they brought with them their prior knowledge and training and pedagogic experiences to inform their teaching in Saudi Arabia, our classroom observations and further data collected with the teachers in Chapter 8 point to the becoming aspect of teacher identity and professional growth (Phan, 2008; Varghese *et al.*, 2005; Yuan & Lee, 2021). Saudi Arabia offers a challenging yet fertile space for international TESOL teachers to transform pedagogically and cultivate a sense of teacher self, which is unique because of its very specific sociocultural and religious conditions, as discussed in the first several chapters.

Indeed, what happens on the ground contributed significantly to these teachers' professional identity, an identity in the making, as they revealed. Importantly, from all the data collected we have gotten an impression that teaching Saudi students is overarchingly difficult; hence, those teachers who have remained in Saudi Arabia for at least a few years have tended to develop an overt sense of confidence – *'if you can deal with Saudi students, you can deal with just any students'*. We have found this phenomenon quite unique when we locate it in the existing literature.

Moving on, the subsequent two chapters (Chapters 9 and 10) focus on TESOL international teachers' experiences beyond the classroom, particularly with regard to their perceptions of their status and experiences, and their interactions with colleagues, administrators and the outside society more broadly. In these chapters, race, ethnicity, language, religion and lived experience play out in various ways, all of which combined present persisting challenges to language education, TESOL, applied linguistics and the collective efforts to combat inequalities in the age of mobility, transnationality and superdiversity.

9 Examining the (Im)mobility of African American Muslim TESOL Teachers in Saudi Arabia

Sulaiman Jenkins[1]

Preface

This chapter engages in greater depth with a new line of scholarship surrounding raciolinguistics, as briefly introduced in the first chapters of the book. This focus is inspired by our encounter with our guest author, Dr Sulaiman Jenkins, an African American scholar affiliated to the Fahd University of Petroleum and Minerals in Saudi Arabia.

In studying international TESOL teachers in the Kingdom of Saudi Arabia (KSA), we have had the opportunity to meet and learn from some participants who also do research on international TESOL teachers teaching in the KSA. Dr Sulaiman Jenkins is one of them. Specifically, he is interested in the transnational experiences of African American Muslim TESOL teachers who have moved to the Gulf region in order to pursue a teaching career. Raciolinguistics is the main conceptual lens through which he approaches and makes sense of such experiences. Seeing himself as one of them, Dr Jenkins has acknowledged that his research, to a great extent, has had to do with his own identity formation and identification on the move.

In talking to us, Dr Jenkins referred back to his article,[2] originally published in 2019 in a Special Issue of *Transitions: Journal of Transient Migration* on the mobilities, immobilities and inequalities embedded in and arising from ELT and English-medium instruction globally that both of us (Phan Le Ha and Osman Barnawi, together with Dat Bao) guest edited. Both before and after the publication of his article, we (Phan Le Ha and Osman Barnawi) had elaborate conversations with him on the many issues he examines in his line of research on African Americans in general and on African American Muslim TESOL teachers in particular, which has helped us obtain nuanced understandings of the complexities accompanying the intersections of race, religion, ethnicity, language and identity in the larger context of contested mobility, neoliberalism, transnationalism and intense polarization between groups. Some of these complexities are portrayed and discussed in the next chapter.

Dr Jenkins has also kindly agreed for his 2019 article to be republished here in our book, as it connects strongly with some of the issues identified and discussed in the next chapter which provides a snapshot of old and new politics on race (Black/African), religion (Muslim), and language (Englishes/Arabic), ethnicity and country of origin. We are aware of the originality and novelty of the new scholarly inquiry in raciolinguistics that Dr Jenkins has been engaged with and helped build further, and we are, hence, keen to highlight Dr Jenkins's research in our book, as a token of appreciation and recognition of the importance of deepening and expanding critical issues underlying transnational (im)mobility of Black native-English-speaking Muslim TESOL teachers.

The remainder of this chapter is taken from Dr Jenkins's 2019 article, with minor updates here and there. Specifically, through the lens of raciolinguistics, Jenkins's nascent study examines the mobility/immobility of two African American Muslim TESOL teachers (AAMTTs) working in the Saudi Arabian higher education (HE) context. The data were collected through interviews and autobiographies in order to examine the participants' lived experiences and their stories. It also explores the paradoxes, tensions and duplicities in treatment experienced by these two TESOL teachers while teaching English as a foreign language (EFL) in Saudi Arabia. These teachers moved to the Gulf region with diverse forms of cultural, symbolic, linguistic, economic and social capital, including being 'native speakers' with an excellent command of the English language, identifying (and being identified) with the culture of hip-hop and Hollywood (which is replete with famous African Americans), and representing American ideals of individualism, freedom of expression, open-mindedness and upward mobility. Conversely, navigating through Saudi Arabia, these AAMTTs have also experienced marginalization by consistent questioning of their national origins, failure to secure employment or being flatly rejected due to color, and skepticism from students and administrators about their level of linguistic competence, accent, rhetoric and accuracy in delivering English lessons. Likewise, as subscribers to the Islamic faith, their lofty expectations of what life would be like in the Gulf have been further complicated by experiences of direct and indirect racism (a direct contradiction of Islamic teachings of universal inclusion), and they have also striven to learn the Arabic language in order to gain religious and social capital while simultaneously fending off perceptions that Arabic speakers cannot be 'native speakers' of English.

Therapeutically, the researcher [Sulaiman Jenkins] reflects on his own experiences with transnationalism as well as in relation to the experiences of these two TESOL teachers and their struggles with constantly re-conceptualizing identity and self as new challenges present themselves in Saudi Arabia. The paradox of possessing the cultural tools for mobility while also having features that hinder mobility is explored and the researcher discusses the strategies ultimately adopted and employed to navigate living in the Gulf.

Foregrounding the Charge

Through resistance, oppressed and disenfranchised people have had to develop strategies, explicit and implicit, to overcome unjust and unfair burdens placed on them by society. And as James Baldwin states, although 'not everything that is faced can be changed', it is necessary to take the initial strides to confront the issue(s) in order to initiate a cycle of change; without confrontation, the cycle can never begin. Thus, one of the issues that has yet to be critically examined in academic discourse in applied linguistics is the plight of African American TESOL teachers (AATT) working as 'transmigrants' in different capacities overseas. Still yet, AATT who also identify as Muslims (African American Muslim TESOL teachers [AAMTTs]), the subjects of this study, will represent a unique, fresh and novel perspective to academic discourse in the relatively new field of raciolinguistics.

With regard to the teaching of English, there has been a growing global need by various nations to equip citizens with the linguistic tools necessary to develop and advance, leading to an explosion in the demand for English language teachers abroad. The Middle East has been one such region advertising this tremendous need. In turn, that has led to the migration of countless AAMTTs overseas, and to Saudi Arabia in particular, seeking to both earn a better living and nurture their spirituality in a more Islamic friendly environment. In the age of mobility – mobility of people, capital, goods, knowledge, ideas, ideologies, culture, knowledge and language – issues surrounding AAMTTs working overseas remain underexplored, and thus this piece seeks to highlight some of the salient racial identity, mobility and transnationalism issues that potentially affect hundreds of AAMTT professionals. Through the lens of raciolinguistics, this study engages with discussions of the intricate relationship between race and identity, and transnationalism and mobility in the age of neoliberalism.

Early AAM Identity through Historical Lenses of Forced (Trans)migration

This section provides a brief history of the plight of African American Muslims (AAMs) in the United States beginning from forced migration in Africa to their settling down in the 'New World'. The purpose is to contextualize the emergence of the AAM identity that the participants identify with. The section begins with presenting a framework built on current discussions on forced transnationalism, forced migration and mobility in order to synergize between AAMs' historical narrative and current transnationalism and mobility literature.

Forced migration and transnationalism for early Africans in America

Transnational mobility is an important cog because 'opportunities for mobility [...] both generate and frame the experience of transnationalism' (De Fina, 2013: 509). The prospect of mobility presents opportunities for the transnationalization process, and it is deeply connected to individual agency and the reconfiguration of identity once an individual decides to move beyond his or her natural borders. Thus, mobility is intimately connected with identity as individuals seek to redefine themselves by 'new transnational identities [...] characterized by the use and appropriation of cultural resources [...] [and] coming to terms with the contradictions created by the need to navigate traditional boundaries' (De Fina, 2013: 511). In order to understand the dynamic of identity and mobility we must first establish that mobility, beyond the mere literal geographic meaning of 'human population movements', must be understood as the metaphorical movement both socially 'between economic sectors, income levels, and social classes' and culturally by 'the processes of acculturation, integration, and [...] assimilation' (Carlin *et al.*, 2014: 5). This dichotomous layer to mobility allows me [Sulaiman Jenkins] to examine transnational phenomena not just by the conditions that necessitate physical movement of individuals but also sociocultural and economic factors that, through mobility, drive individuals to seek to cross borders seeking out new identities.

That said, in the case of AAMs in America, transnationalism or transnational mobility was never an 'opportunity' that was sought out, individual agency never a factor neither in choosing to relocate from one's homeland nor in choosing to reconfigure one's identity. Early Africans were simply forcibly sold into slavery and brought to America as 'coerced transmigrants'. One driving force behind transmigration can be currently understood as a 'reflection of demographic shifts in labour markets embedded in the changing composition of capital accumulation' (Piper & Withers, 2018: 558); and the forced transmigration of early Africans was in response to colonial powers seeking 'manpower' to exploit newly discovered lands for maximum economic benefit.

In one of the world's most tragic recorded cases of mass forced migration and forced transnationalism, as many as '12 million [African] slaves were forcibly taken to the Americas', '[coercively displacing] some 50 different ethnic and linguistic groups' all across North and South America as well as the Caribbean (PBS, 2013). Forced transnationalism can be understood as 'transnationalism [which] is an involuntary experience defined by economic and social hardships that are endured in the absence of meaningful alternatives' (Piper & Withers, 2018: 563). In the case of early Africans in America, their 'involuntary experiences' were the result of being sold into bondage with no 'meaningful alternatives'.

When transmigrants are immersed in a new and foreign society, they are often forced to rethink and restructure their identities. Identity is a complex phenomenon which can be best described as 'how a person understands his or her relationship to the world, how that relationship is constructed across time and space, and how the person understands possibilities for the future' (Norton, 2013, cited in Preece, 2016: 5). The process of restructuring and reconfiguration, negotiating and renegotiating, operates on a continuum, with transmigrants determining to what degree they will assimilate the new culture (King & Ganuza, 2005). The next section details how early forced transmigrant Africans restructure their identities to become African American (AA), reconciling between old identities and new concepts in new environments. It also examines how a particular group of AA slaves maintained transnational ties to their religious Islamic roots and how such transnational ascription contributed to upward mobility in early White America.

Birth of the AA identity

Early Africans, hailing from various African countries such as Senegal, Ivory Coast and Ghana, would need to undergo the extraordinary task of redefining themselves as they 'resettled' themselves in the New World. There was a tremendous need to assume a new collective identity as many Africans were not only separated from fellow countrymen when they arrived in the Americas, but families would also be separated, and these forced separations often led to Africans working together as slaves on the same plantations but being incapable of communicating or identifying with each other. Thus, early Africans would need to quickly reconcile what it meant to be both 'African' and 'American', creating a shared identity for survival.

The reconciliation and restructuring of an 'African in America identity' took dramatic form in the late 1700s. Literate slaves versed in American revolutionary literature began to embrace the 'Enlightenment language of liberty and rights' and petition to be given their inalienable rights as they argued that slavery and Enlightenment thought were incompatible (Mandall, 2016). For some historians, these petitions represented the

> earliest expression of African American identity [...] a people who identified as Africans and Americans and who held strong trans-Atlantic connections transcending nation and liberal individualism, and who, at the outset of the war, embraced Enlightenment ideals, sentimentalism, and Protestant notions of virtue. (Mandall, 2016: n.p.)

Thus, early Africans understood that restructuring and redefining their identities in the new America, even if that meant adopting values and worldviews different from their origins, would be essential to their survival.

The American Revolution, according to Daniel Mandall (2016: n.p.), presented the perfect opportunity for such restructuring. He states:

> These petitions formed, or at least represented, what quickly became the dualistic nature of African American identity, drawing on both their quasi-racial origins and their participation in the American Revolution. These documents not only indicate that an African American identity emerged during the Revolution, but also highlight the essential links between their embrace of the Revolution and rapid adoption of an African identity. African American petitioners used the upheaval, rich language, and political and intellectual opportunities of the Revolution to develop, claim, and promote an idealized vision of their past, and to join that memory to Enlightenment concepts of natural rights and human equality. In this fashion, Revolutionary rhetoric and memories – African and American – became vital aspects of Black identity. (Mandall, 2016: n.p.)

Thus, the historical narrative of slavery, the language of resistance inherent in American revolutionary doctrine, the language of equality, and the language of human rights became the cornerstones in forming AA identity, and from this vantage point early AAs were able to successfully negotiate and restructure what it meant to be of African descent in an American society.

Transnationalism of early AAMs within the framework of mobility

Not only was there the need among early Africans in America to form a new identity, but some Africans actively sought to maintain transnational ties to their origins, salvaging prior identities whose connections transcended time and geographical boundaries. One such group of African immigrants were African Muslims, and there is tremendous evidence that although Africans were scrambling to form a new identity in the New World, African Muslims' identities essentially remained stable and even flourished (in some cases being praised by early American White leadership). In this excerpt by Muhammad, well known American politicians extolled the praises of early African Muslims in America:

> Many of America's earliest presidents, beginning with George Washington, the father of our country, engaged Muslims directly on some of the most critical issues of the day, from paramount détentes to commerce relations to abolishing slavery and more. Washington once personally wrote to the ruler of Morocco, '[W]hile I remain head of this nation I shall not cease to promote every measure that may contribute to the friendship and harmony which so happily subsist between your Empire and this Republic'. (Muhammad, 2013: 4, emphasis added)

This account highlights not only the presence of early African Muslims in America but also the prestige that many of them enjoyed as they made invaluable economic, political and moral contributions to a burgeoning American society. What is interesting to note from the excerpt is that not only was the AAM identity born as a result of forced transmigrants wishing to maintain their transnational religious ties but, as evidenced by the quote, AAM identity was also distinct and recognizable, affording AAMs various opportunities for political and societal mobility.

AAMs today

Islam is the fastest growing religion in the world and it continues to occupy an important place in AA culture and society, mainly because it connects AAs with a truly global network, and it represents an alternative identity for Black people who live in a highly racialized society. There are droves of entertainers, celebrities and other high-profile individuals currently entering the fold of Islam. Most notably, Mutah Napoleon Beale, a retired rapper formerly known as 'Napoleon' with the Outlawz group with Tupac Shakur, is the single most identifiable Muslim personality who spends a significant amount of time using his celebrity status to explain the simple tenets of the faith. Historically, prominent figures like Muhammad Ali, Kareem Abdul-Jabbar, Malcolm X, Mike Tyson, Jermaine and Janet Jackson (among others) have served as flagships for raising the profile of Black American Muslims domestically and abroad as well as raising awareness of the Islamic faith among AAs (Porter, 2016). And 'African Americans make up some 40 per cent of the total Muslim population of the United States today' (Pluralism Project, n.d.: n.p.). For many, Islam for Black Americans continues to represent an alternative identity which is not mainstream White America and yields tangible positive results on Black communities (e.g. giving to charity, promoting brotherhood that decreases gang violence, etc.).

Identity and migration of AAMTTs to Saudi Arabia

AAMTTs create multiple identities and those identities are intentional ascriptions and 'membership [to] particular groups' (Preece, 2016: 6), be it 'African American' or 'Muslim'. However, such identity ascription is not confined to a particular location (i.e. America). Because of globalization and the cross-pollination of nations as a result of the unprecedented ability to experience other cultures and cultural models, notions that identities are limited by 'boundedness and stability cannot account for language variation and identity formation among mobile individuals and communities' (De Fina, 2016: 167). Thus, identity cannot be viewed as a stagnant phenomenon but one that is fluid and capable of being reimagined depending on environmental circumstances. That is, as the increase of opportunities for transnational mobility necessitates being exposed to different cultures and world-views across different spaces, the individual in a post-structuralist world has the ability to reposition himself or herself based on the environment that surrounds him: 'understanding [...] identity/ies as a fluid network of subject positions' (Baxter, 2016: 38). Although AAMTTs may have an identity in the US, such identity also allows for transnational mobility to other countries where English language teaching expertise is sought out; and thus AAMTTs have the unique ability to pursue financial opportunities afforded to them by virtue of their mobile abilities. The Kingdom of Saudi Arabia presents one such opportunity for AAMTTs and is the prime location of interest for the purposes of this study.

To clarify, with Saudi Arabia being one of the largest recruiters of English language teachers, such demand creates a valuable opportunity for AAMTTs, who through virtue of being US passport holders utilize mobility (due to being 'native speakers' of a dominant world language) to work overseas and capitalize on more financially beneficial teaching opportunities. Yet, merely describing this transaction as a neoliberal pursuit of better living conditions would completely ignore other important influences on the decision to migrate. Identification of AAMTTs with Islam also inherently creates an opportunity and space in which many AAMTTs long to travel to Saudi Arabia, the destination of two of the most significant religious sites (Mecca and Medina). It represents an opportunity to practice religious tenets in complete freedom and comfort, gain valuable linguistic and cultural artifacts (i.e. Arabic and Arab culture), as well as have the chance to redefine what it means to be an AAM in a Muslim majority country.

Racism in TESOL and Raciolinguistic Ideologies in the Age of Increased Neoliberal Mobility

Racism in TESOL

TESOL, the acronym for teaching English to speakers of other languages, is concerned with teaching the English language for various instrumental functions across the globe. What one would assume would be a politically sanitized educational enterprise is in fact laden with subtle and even institutionally racist and discriminatory practices. Ryuko Kubota, a renowned scholar on race matters, introduced critical concepts and theories of race, ethnicity and culture that have become central to the teaching of English (in Kubota & Lin, 2006), as it is our 'responsibility to examine how racism or any other injustices influence [our field's) knowledge and practice' (Kubota, 2002: 86). One such injustice is the systemic, institutionalized racist ideologies or practices used to essentialize 'the Other'. Although English language speakers represent a diverse spectrum of ethnicities and nationalities, textbooks and curricula, Kubota argues, continue to perpetuate the image of 'authentic' English speakers as 'White', thus 'constructing the norm with regard to what is legitimate linguistic and cultural knowledge' (Kubota & Lin, 2006: 479). Teachers who do not 'fit' this prototype (i.e. non-Whites) are often viewed as inferior.

The (mis)representation of 'authentic' English speakers in textbooks also contributes to real-life employment practices that seek to dictate normative standards of 'good' teachers by using the native speaker–non-native speaker dichotomy. Institutes and companies purposely discriminate against those whom they deem to not be original speakers of the language (i.e. White) (Jenkins, 2017) or discriminate against original speakers of the language who happen to be Black: 'position[ing] African Americans as afterthoughts and white Americans as the normative center' (Owens, 2017: 35). Thus, issues of race and the racialization of English teachers and critical discussions thereof create uncomfortable spaces in the field of applied linguistics. It is imperative that 'critical scholarship [...] [condemns overt] [...] bigotry and pure race ideologies [...] [as well as] [...] more subtle institutionalized inequalities and injustices that affect teaching and learning' (Kubota, 2002: 86). This study, hence, seeks to address how two AAM teachers perceive themselves as essentialized 'Others' working in a market underpinned by subtle racist and discriminatory practices in Saudi Arabia, as the findings revealed.

Raciolinguistic ideologies in TESOL

Raciolinguistics, a new branch of applied linguistics attributed to Nelson Flores' and Jonathan Rosa's timely discussions on the intersectionalities of racism and linguistics (Flores & Nelson, 2015), seeks to examine the delicate relationship between language, identity and race. It can be defined as 'a new field [...] dedicated to bringing to bear the diverse methods of linguistic analysis to ask and answer critical questions about the relations between language, race, and power across diverse ethnoracial contexts and societies' (Alim, 2016: 3). Not only does raciolinguistics seek to 'focus [...] on both the central role that language plays in racialization and on the enduring relevance of race and racism in the lives of People of Color' (Alim, 2016: 4), but it is also fundamentally concerned with how individuals navigate in 'hyperracialized' contexts in which race and racism continue to pervade many facets of People of Color's lives.

Also critical to a working definition of raciolinguistics is our need to contextualize it within the framework of globalization and mobility. Globalization has contributed to 'the enhancement and intensification of global flows not only of people, but also of artefacts, cultural products and practices' (De Fina, 2016: 166). It has 'lowered resource constraints on mobility', 'strengthened migrant networks and transnational ties by making it easier to stay in touch with family and friends, to remit money, and to travel back and forth between destination and origin countries' and 'increased people's capabilities and aspirations to migrate' (Czaika & Haas, 2014: 284–285). And while this model of a post-structuralist globalized world is supposed to facilitate much easier movement (physically) and flow of ideas and cultural artifacts (metaphorically), there are raciolinguistic ideologies that stymie such free movement for certain groups of people. That is, the race, language and identity of some people inhibit opportunities for them at a time in human history when opportunities created from a globalized, interconnected world have increased dramatically.

Thus, despite the dawn of an age of increased (neoliberal) mobility, raciolinguistic ideologies have the power to mitigate the mobility of peoples when either their 'social or cultural capital' (Bourdieu, 1986: n.p.) is viewed through structurally (e.g. socially constructed racial hierarchies) or institutionally (e.g. language policies determined by departments of education) racialized lenses. To illustrate, Flores and Rosa (2015) argue against a focus on linguistic 'appropriateness' when legitimizing which variety of English was acceptable or not in academic settings. Certain English language varieties, such as African American English(es), considered as 'legitimate variet[ies]', are deemed 'deficient' due to their lack of conforming to Standard English. They argue that such a perspective is rooted in raciolinguistic ideology, which seeks to 'produce racialized speaking subjects who are constructed as linguistically deviant even when engaging in linguistic practices positioned as normative or innovative when produced by privileged white subjects' and that such 'subtractive approaches to language diversity are stigmatizing and contribute to the reproduction of educational inequality' (Flores & Rosa, 2015: 150). Later on in their treatise of abandoning appropriateness in language education, they describe instances in which raciolinguistic ideologies inhibit racialized minorities' access to social capital and social standing because their language varieties are always stigmatized and never accepted in the mainstream. Likewise, they show how raciolinguistic ideologies perpetuate a 'racial status quo' in which Whites are in the very positions of power to deem what is acceptable English and what isn't, thus delegitimizing Others' lived experiences (Flores & Rosa, 2015). Thus, the intersectionality between globalization, raciolinguistic ideology and neoliberal mobility will present an important framework through which AAMTTs' transnational experiences are analyzed. The study informing this chapter is one case in point.

Methodological Notes

Drawing on qualitative data collected from semi-structured interviews and critical autobiographical reflection (CAR), the study addresses the following research questions:

- What do AAMTTs perceive as valuable artifacts for their mobility in Saudi Arabia?

- How do AAMTTs identify themselves in transnational spaces?
- What is the view of AAMTTs of themselves in TESOL in Saudi Arabia?

The researcher adopts a quasi-CAR approach because 'the use of reflective, autobiographical narratives allows the researcher to draw from questions that examine life experiences to analyze the self within the lens of criticality' (Walker, 2017: 1900). The researcher specifies the 'quasi' nature of this reflection because it is not truly autobiographical in the sense that the researcher is analyzing his own life: rather, the researcher examines himself through the lenses of his participants working vicariously through them to make sense of their transnational experiences from his standpoint of researcher positionality. In this way, the researcher 'identif[ies] with [his] participants, both as educators and as individuals, ground[ing] [his] work and in some ways mak[ing] their worlds and experiences an extension of [his] own' (Aneja, 2016: 578). This approach is necessary in a study of racialized inquiry because 'by connecting personal life stories with inquiry, autobiographical research has the potential to transform the learning, values, and identities of individuals, institutions, and greater society' (Walker, 2017: 1905).

It is also important to acknowledge that although the researcher's positionality is one of identification with his subjects from professional and personal levels, a critical measure had to be adopted so as to ensure the objectivity of the study. Thus, the researcher elected to share the transcripts of the interviews with the participants, soliciting assurance of interpretive accuracy from them, and constantly reengaging this process to ensure meaning from the transcripts was not lost, changed or distorted in any way. Such a stringent exercise was necessary given the positionality of the researcher.

The researcher used semi-structured interviews to collect the data from the two teachers. Both Tyrone and Jerome (pseudonyms to protect their identities) are US nationals and identified as being of Black ethnicity. Both participants had been living in Saudi Arabia for more than 13 years and were teaching English at public Saudi universities at the time of the data collection. Both participants also had brief stints in other Arab Muslim countries before coming to Saudi Arabia (Tyrone in Egypt, and Jerome in the UAE). Tyrone is a fluent Arabic speaker and has earned a BA degree in Islamic Studies in addition to his original BA degree from the United States. Jerome classified himself as a high beginner Arabic speaker.

The interview prompts were based on the overall research questions set forth earlier. The researcher generated 12 questions that addressed three primary domains: mobility, transnationalism and identity in TESOL. Questions were designed so that they were easily discernible, and during the interview the participants were encouraged to add pertinent information they felt relevant to the conversation, even if said response was not directly answering the particular interview question that was asked. This was done to maintain the natural flow of the interview as well as to prevent 'the interviews [from] appearing stilted and formal' (Choak, 2012: 92).

This nascent study is significant on several horizons. First, heretofore a narrative of AAMs and their transnational experiences teaching English in Saudi Arabia does not exist in the applied linguistics literature. Such a rich intersectionality between cultures, geographical spaces, languages and identities provides a very fresh and uniquely underrepresented voice in ELT literature and will provide greater insight into this particular strain of raciolinguistics. It is also significant in that it can be linked in myriad ways to the original diasporic movement of Africans to the Americas during the slave trade, and a comparative analysis of this sort allows for future studies of emergent commonalities between the two events.

The Desire to Restructure a New Identity in an Islamically Friendly Environment

Both participants, Tyrone and Jerome, were asked how their religious affiliation (Islam) and ethnicity (Black) influenced their decision to leave the US and come to Saudi Arabia to teach English. Both remarked that from a religious standpoint they wanted to live in an *'Islamically friendly environment'*, *'adopt the language and culture (Arabic)'* and *'to become spiritually enlightened'*. When prompted about any ethnic influence on their decision, Tyrone immediately remarked that becoming a Muslim was a way to escape the prescriptive categorization of him as a *'Black man'* in America. Jerome acknowledged that although ethnicity was not a primary consideration in his decision to leave the United States, his time in Saudi Arabia had retrospectively magnified what he perceived to be a life of living under a *'racial filter'* back in the United States, something he said was/is not the case in Saudi Arabia:

> *So when I accepted Islam, I wanted to lift my [...] that European influence as much as I could [...] It gave me an identity other than European also one that I chose, not one that was forced upon me and my ancestors.* (Tyrone)

> *But obviously people do make snap judgments; that's part of human nature, but you don't feel like you're being prejudged and some negative connotation comes along just because of your skin color as opposed to the states where you constantly feel the need to validate your presence to be worthy of being wherever you are.* (Jerome)

Tyrone spoke of the desire to escape an identity he called *'forced upon [him]'*. Embracing Islam and moving to a Muslim country would afford him the opportunity to reconfigure his identity in a way that was fitting to his perception of self. This motivation for migration complicates those who adopt prescriptive approaches to why people migrate and who remove individual agency (De Fina, 2016). Clearly, Tyrone made a conscious decision to migrate, not due to poverty or a precarious political environment, but rather to his own desire to *'reinvent'* his identity. Jerome also articulated that transnational migration presented an opportunity for him to escape the racialized lenses of American society (hyperracialization) and enjoy a normal life in a less racialized society that had welcomed him because of his religious affiliation.

Possession and Attainment of Valuable Cultural Artifacts

Tyrone and Jerome were asked if they felt that coming from the US, they owned valuable cultural artifacts from which the locals could benefit. Tyrone acknowledged that the country could benefit from his native-English-speaking teaching experience and that they could benefit from learning traditional American ideals, such as organization and efficiency. Jerome felt that being American could help provide a more complete understanding of American culture, providing an authentic version that locals, and particularly young Muslims, would not be exposed to otherwise during this age of globalization:

> *So one of the things we can do is share bits and pieces of our culture with more nuance so that the younger generations and even the Muslims we come and contact gain a more complete understanding of the good and evils of the globalization that's taking place.* (Jerome)

So for Jerome, his Americanness coupled with his Muslim faith positions him as a gatekeeper for young Muslims and Muslims in general by explaining firsthand what aspects of American culture should be internalized and welcomed and what aspects may pose conflicts with Islamic values. Interestingly, both Tyrone and Jerome only identified these as general American cultural artifacts that could be beneficial and they said they could not identify any cultural artifacts from Black American culture that would be of any benefit for the local Saudi population.

When asked about gaining any cultural artifacts from Saudi Arabia that would prove beneficial at home, both participants immediately indicated that learning the Arabic language and religious knowledge would be a tremendous resource for Black Muslims in the US. Such artifacts allow for the teaching of important Islamic principles and help Black Muslims to understand and implement their faith in more comprehensive ways.

A Subtle Struggle to Be an AA in the Middle East

When asked about their overall experience in Saudi Arabia as Americans, both Tyrone and Jerome remarked that their experiences as

Americans were overall very positive. They said they felt *'entitlement'* in society and were at the top of a *'highly stratified'* society because they were American citizens. Saudi Arabia is a society 'characterized by a high degree of cultural homogeneity and by an equally high degree of social stratification' (Metz, 1993: 62). It is structured by a tribal system with certain prominence given to particular tribes above others. The most prominent of them is the Al-Saud tribe which currently governs the entire country. On the expatriate front, it is often believed that Western expatriates (i.e. the US, the UK, Europe, Canada, etc.) enjoy greater prestige and better financial packages than expatriates from other non-Saudi Arab countries (i.e. Egypt, Sudan, Morocco, etc.) and other South Asian countries (i.e. Bangladesh, Pakistan, India, etc.), the bulk of whom form the workforce for menial and physical labor jobs in Saudi Arabia. Although Tyrone and Jerome extolled the praises of living in Saudi as Americans, such pronouncements of gratitude and positivity were short-lived once the participants were asked to describe their experience as *Black* Americans.

Both Tyrone and Jerome acknowledged that although they were treated well because they were Americans, it was clear that Black Americans would not enjoy the same prestige or entitlement that White Americans would enjoy. This was due to an overwhelming perception in Saudi Arabia that Americans are usually not Black:

> *[…] you have people who will literally try to change your nationality for you because they aren't comfortable and you don't fit in their box […] I've had multiple conversations where I've had to explain about our history […] for 300 years I have no idea where my ancestors are from. […] I wouldn't say it's been negative, but it's been challenging.* (Jerome)

> *Being an American allows me to have privileges, higher status than someone of a non-Western nationality. But at the same time, being Black in the workplace I'm not at the top of the totem pole because I'm not White and not non-Muslim.* (Tyrone)

Both make a clear distinction between being *American* and being *Black American* although Tyrone would go on to emphasize that the brotherhood of Islam, which does not favor any Muslim above another due to race, ethnicity, social status or otherwise, mitigated such experiences. This presents a salient point of tension. Tyrone came to Saudi with the express intention of reconfiguring an identity through his own agency, one that would emulate Islamic ideals and be as non-European as possible. Yet, in his transnational space he recognized that the identity (AAM) he ascribed to would always be considered inferior to the very identity (White European) he wished to escape association with back in his home country. For Jerome, he stated that he consistently felt uneasy in the US having to constantly *'validate his presence'*, yet in Saudi Arabia he continued to need to validate his identity when locals questioned the authenticity of his ascription to being American. For them, he was African, not American, and he affirmed he was neither African nor American, but AA. Such tensions in transnational spaces speak to these transnationals who have the mobility tools yet also possess characteristics that inhibit a more complete and fuller range of mobility in a foreign society.

There is also a tension regarding religious significance. Both Tyrone and Jerome mentioned that spiritual growth and advancement and living in Islamically friendly environments were important considerations in their move to Saudi Arabia, yet the questioning of their identity by fellow Muslim 'brothers' who purport to follow the Islamic faith presents a tension when Islam, Muslims and Islamic society should essentially be colorblind.

Another side of this religious tension is the speaking of Arabic. Although both Tyrone and Jerome acknowledged earlier that learning Arabic was a very valuable cultural artifact to attain, not just to obtain greater religious understanding but also to communicate with the locals, they stated that speaking it at times became an indicator of Otherness, or immediately brought their identities into question:

> [...] a negative aspect is when you speak people realize you're not from part of this world [...] dialect [...] classical Arabic. They don't speak classical Arabic. They speak slang. (Tyrone)

> If you speak the language fluently then maybe they might assume that you aren't who you say you are [...] because they don't expect someone from the West to be able to speak Arabic fluently. But then again even if you don't know Arabic, sometimes you're told that you're not from the West just because of your appearance [...]. (Jerome)

In Tyrone's response, we see that using the language indicates that he is not from Saudi Arabia, which may cause one to never feel like he or she truly belongs. Thus, this very reality complicates his initial hope to become a part of the society, when learning '*to adopt the culture and language*' was only to be considered an outsider when he made the effort. Jerome's response is indicative of a more troublesome issue in that language use negates nationality. That is, for many locals, speaking Arabic *and* being Black combined is a definitive way to convey that you are not American. This is based on the logic that Americans don't speak Arabic and most Americans are White. Such tensions are fascinating examples of how the same cultural artifacts [speaking Arabic and being Black] can be both a means of mobility and at the same time a cause for immobility and a hindrance.

Being a Black American Muslim TESOL Teacher

When Tyrone and Jerome were asked about being a Black American teacher or Black American Muslim teacher abroad, the responses were overwhelmingly negative. Both Tyrone and Jerome acknowledged that Black teachers are considered inferior compared to White teachers. This was due to the general perception held by administrators and not necessarily because of students. This perception suggests that the ELT market maintains a dichotomy of native 'White' speakers of English and others who do not fit such a prototype (Kubota & Lin, 2006). Tyrone and Jerome also mentioned that Blacks did not equate with '*authentic Americans*', while White teachers were automatically equated with '*original Americans*'. It was a must for them to '*establish competence*' in order to dispel any suspicion that they were not originally American teachers.

> *I think we're perceived as not being as good as White ESL teachers. We're perceived as being inferior [...] because that's what the media promotes and I think that's a perception that they have because of their convictions about the West. They feel that White is superior [...] they don't look at us as being original. They might see us as being immigrants or from different parts of Africa [...] but once that's established that you're an American native speaker in the end that's what actually protects us.* (Tyrone)

> *[African Americans are perceived] as Others. I mean because what I've learned and experienced is that generally the perception is that someone who's Caucasian there is more authentic as an American teacher [...] so I think we have to prove ourselves more and prove our competence and ability to teach [...].* (Jerome)

Another negative layer was added when Jerome mentioned that being Muslim sometimes might call an AAMTT's integrity into question as administrators might feel that the sole purpose for teaching in Saudi Arabia would be religious, not professional, motivations:

> *Again, the idea that I have is that we're only here because of the religious aspect and so even if you have the credentials and experience and qualifications that sort of trumps your ability to do your job well and to teach [...] but the two are not contradictory in any way. I mean the two ideas are both compatible. I can want to be here and I can be credentialed and also competent but that's the perception I think they have of African American Muslims.* (Jerome)

Jerome would go on to mention that he had personally heard of many anecdotes in which administrators or recruiters would explicitly prefer Whites or non-Muslims to hire because their intentions for coming to Saudi Arabia would most likely be professional and not necessarily religious. Although both of these teachers voiced unpleasant social and institutional constructions of Black American Muslim identity, they remarked that did not feel this had any immediate impact on the day-to-day teaching and learning of English, nor did it disrupt the student–teacher dynamic in any way.

Sulaiman Jenkins: Researcher Positionality

The researcher's positionality is important to revisit here as 'positionality is [...] determined by where one stands in relation to "the other"' (Merriam *et al.*, 2001: 411). My position as an insider (as opposed to an outsider), sharing the same culture and having had similar transnational experiences as the participants formed a strong bond from the onset of the study. Because of this, they felt completely open and honest to share whatever experiences they had in order to contribute positively to the data value of this study. Utilizing CAR, the researcher concurs with many of the participants' experiences because the researcher lived through many similar instances. Thus, feelings of being marginalized based simply on race and religious ascription are feelings I have certainly experienced.

However, the researcher has occupied more administrative roles in his career as an English teacher in Saudi Arabia than the two participants and that has a critical influence on experience. Thus, the researcher occupied two positionalities within the study: one of interpretive inquiry in which he sought to 'understand the purpose and meaning of [the] social actors and [their] social actions' (Lin, 2015: 25), and the other a critical positionality in which he interpreted the participants' responses from the perspective of an administrator, with the hopes of '[empowering] [...] subordinated groups in society through demystifying educational institutions, practices, and policies that produce and reproduce the domination of certain groups' (Lin, 2015: 26). As a teacher/administrator, and one is a position of authority, there is a certain level of acknowledgement by other authorities of power of one's expertise and competence which has no bearing on skin color, nationality or 'native speakerness'. That is to say, from the researcher's point of view, any negative perceptions or assumptions about AAMTTs were easily overcome by demonstrating high levels of competency from the onset of any course. As such, the participants' perspectives might have been enriched had they had access to different experiences and roles in more administrative and authoritative positions. These tensions of roles would be an interesting area for further inquiry.

I personally enjoyed conducting the study as I could intimately relate on various levels to what the participants were describing and thus this study served as a therapeutic reflection on my own transnational experience.

Concluding Remarks

This study examined the plight of two AAMTTs and their transnational experiences abroad in a country considered to be the heart of Islam, Saudi Arabia. While both participants have overwhelmingly positive expectations of gaining valuable cultural artifacts from the host culture, they could not help but realize the tensions involved in identity and mobility when matters of race, religion and competence were brought into the picture.

The forced transmigration of early Africans compelled them to negotiate between assuming a new identity in early America, accepting cultural artifacts of a new culture, or maintaining transnational religious ties to the lands they came from. Based on the findings of this study, AAMTTs are caught in a conundrum: while they possess artifacts that grant them access to high levels of mobility within the Arab world (based on their nationality status as 'native speakers' and 'American'), they also feel restricted in terms of being racially (and religiously) marginalized.

The were some limitations to this study. The number of participants, gender, varying years of experience, location in Saudi Arabia, and government versus private employment are factors that could have all yielded very different results and thus these are key areas of interest for future studies.

As far as implications are concerned, this nascent study was conducted to serve as an impetus for further research. With such scarcity in the literature on this important issue of mobility for AAMTTs, it is crucial to provide a platform where ELT professionals find their voices and experiences having been studied formally in academic journals. It is hoped that the results of this study will serve as a catalyst for others including AAMTTs to pursue further avenues of important inquiry related to transnationalism and mobility, especially as they relate to the dynamic of working from positions of authority and influence.

Afterthoughts (by Phan Le Ha and Osman Z. Barnawi)

In his study featured above, Jenkins (2019) shows that not all so-called native teachers from the West/America are looked up to or receive the privilege often attributed to them. Instead, he shows that race plays a vital role in their identity positioning, professional status and overall experience in Saudi Arabia. That these teachers are African Americans who speak both English and Arabic does not seem to give them more advantages, largely because the ways they identify themselves in their profession and in everyday life do not match the public imagination of them. That they are 'Black', can speak Arabic (and are Muslim) makes them appear *less authentic* as native-English-speaking Americans. Jenkins' (2019) study continues to confirm and strengthen the well-established literature on racial discrimination and racism in TESOL that authors like Kubota (2020) and Motha (2014) have examined over the years. Indeed, these issues have not disappeared or been weakened in the context of globalization, neoliberalism, multiculturalism, multinationalism and mobility as the field of TESOL continues to expand and thrive with the progress of scholarship. These issues are, on the contrary, still alive, active and mutate in many different forms and intensities in TESOL and in the life and work of teachers of English around the world, as we are going to show in the next chapter with close-up accounts from several other international TESOL teachers teaching in different Saudi institutions.

Notes

(1) King Fahd University of Petroleum and Minerals, Saudi Arabia.
(2) Jenkins (2019). See https://doi.org/10.1386/tjtm_00005_1

10 Unpacking Hardly-Ever-Revealed Emotions, Pains and Complexities

The mobility of international TESOL teachers with different backgrounds and nationalities across Saudi higher education (HE) institutions entails mobility of knowledge, ideas, pedagogies and other sociocultural and linguistic resources. These international teachers employ various negotiating strategies in order to respond to the demands, needs and expectations of their students, peers, institutions and the profession. While this is all happening, unique stories, pains, gains and other uncertainties experienced by some individuals distinguished by race, religion, skin color, nationality, language, work politics and professional perspectives are often sidelined within the broader discourses of TESOL teacher mobility and teacher identity.

In this chapter, we discuss three hardly-ever-revealed accounts by **Montreal, Benjamin** and **Othello.** These accounts show that many deeply rooted perceptions and discourses associated with native speakers of English (Westerners), race (Black) and religion (Islam) continue to travel, invade different professional TESOL/ELT spaces and haunt teachers themselves. Many international TESOL professionals in Saudi Arabia are still trapped by these perceptions and discourses, as victims, offenders, or both.

We acknowledge that we are not going to focus on just one particular race or ethnicity, but instead we are determined to bring together a range of narratives that we could extract from the pool of data we have collected.

Montreal: Mobility of 'Black Pains' and 'Depressive Symptoms'

> But as the sociologist Glenn Bracey wrote, 'Out of the ashes of white denigration, we gave birth to ourselves.' For as much as white people tried to pretend, Black people were not chattel. And so the process of seasoning, instead of erasing identity, served an opposite purpose: In the void, we forged a new culture all our own.

Today, our very manner of speaking recalls the Creole languages that enslaved people innovated in order to communicate both with Africans speaking various dialects and the English-speaking people who enslaved them. Our style of dress, the extra flair, stems back to the desires of enslaved people – shorn of all individuality – to exert their own identity. Enslaved people would wear their hat in a jaunty manner or knot their head scarves intricately. Today's avant-garde nature of Black hairstyles and fashion displays a vibrant reflection of enslaved people's determination to feel fully human through self-expression. The improvisational quality of Black art and music comes from a culture that because of constant disruption could not cling to convention. Black naming practices, so often impugned by mainstream society, are themselves an act of resistance. Our last names belong to the white people who once owned us. That is why the insistence of many Black Americans, particularly those most marginalized, to give our children names that we create, that are neither European nor from Africa, a place we have never been, is an act of self-determination. (*The New York Times Magazine*[1])

The above painful statements, taken from Nikole Hannah-Jones's (2019) work, 'Our democracy's founding ideals were false when they were written. Black Americans have fought to make them true', show complex forms of pain (e.g. psychological, emotional, cultural, self-identity, etc.) that Black Americans have been experiencing in their everyday realities, be they public or private, institutional or educational realities. Indeed, the complex forms of pain faced by Black Americans in the US HE system have been widely examined and documented in the professional literature (see, for example, Bristol & Mentor, 2018; Carter-Andrews *et al.*, 2016; Jenkins, 2019). Nevertheless, the mobility of such pains (be they real or imagined) is still under theorization. Simply put, the ways in which Black American TESOL teachers bring such pains with them outside the US HE realm are still being explored.

The account below shared by **Montreal** – an African American TESOL teacher with an MA in English Education from the US working in a Saudi HE institution – shows what we call the mobility of 'Black pains' and 'depressive symptoms.'

> ... I just completed my probationary period and things are cool. I have a meeting tomorrow morning with the head of curriculum coordinator to discuss planning for the basic program for next year. It's nice to be appreciated for what one can bring to the table, rather than having to follow the lead of people who either don't know what they are doing or just don't care .... During the first term I taught reading and writing courses. At the beginning of the second term I started out teaching reading and writing again but the coordinator of the basic program insisted that we should develop curriculum for the writing component of the basic program together. We started with a bang but things slowed to a halt by the fourth week of instruction. This is because the coordinator of reading course also wanted me to cover classes, proctor exams, sit on some committees

and at the same time take care of the new English graded reader programs. I've been stiffened by having two Arab [Jordanian] coordinators over me who have very little insight about curriculum and instruction in English language teaching, so we haven't accomplished much. This is my first year and I have been mistreated by these two unqualified Jordanian coordinators. Malcom (pseudonym) joined this college long before me. Why can't they dare to give him such clerical tasks? I am telling you, this negative attitude toward Black people needs to be changed here. If Malcom is a white British, I am also an American, and I know my right. I am not somebody's property here. They can fire me if they want to. (Montreal)

The above narrative shared by **Montreal** suggests that his school trusted in his qualifications (i.e. an MA in English Education from the USA) and classroom pedagogical practices. That is, like other international TESOL teachers working across Saudi HE institutions, he had successfully completed his '*probationary period and things are cool.*' It also shows that he was willing to intellectually contribute to the development of his school. Yet, he felt that he did not have the same privilege that his White peers and/or non-Western colleagues had. This is because he is '*BLACK,*' as he believed. '*I am not new to this game. I am already sick and tired of it in my country.*' In this context, **Montreal** was bringing racially complicated pains, memories and historic symptoms of oppression to his new academic workplace (i.e. Saudi Arabia).

In addition to the above, **Montreal** reported that he had been sympathetic to Black Saudi students, assuming that they had been discriminated against and silenced in school. Worse, conflicting responses from students as well as colleagues to his pedagogical practices further made him believe that he had been personally targeted.

… sometimes I use hip-hop language in classroom to motivate my students. I can see positive responses from my students, particularly Black dudes. And they do not complain. So why the upper management is always asking me to use Standard English. We have some Asian and Arab teachers here with heavy accents and bad grammar. And, nobody is picking on them. Well, I should not be surprised. I must say anti-Blackness is a universal phenomenon anyway. (Montreal)

This incident points to painful experiences and encounters that **Montreal** had undergone as he was living his professional and racial identities. He was deeply troubled by the described unfair treatment from the administrators, and thus saw them as ganging up on him. **Montreal**'s account somewhat resembles the accounts of **Tyrone** and **Jerome** discussed in the previous chapter, whereby hip-hop language – African Americans' pride – was downplayed as a marker of linguistic incompetence and lower-tiered English. We will encounter this same issue as we introduce **Dave** later in this chapter.

Back to **Montreal**, the way he told his experiences as shown above also embeds his own projection of *'Asian and Arab teachers'*, whom he referred to as having *'heavy accents and bad grammar'*. Perhaps what seemed to bother him more was his observation that these teachers were not *'picked on'* by the administrators, and as such he alluded to his being Black as the sole reason behind such mistreatment. He hinted that the administrators' unfair treatment of him caused his bitterness towards other colleagues with whom he did not necessarily have problems. As we shall show in Chapter 11, the emotion labor shouldered by many teachers has indeed resulted from administrators and institutional policies and practices that pit teachers against one another instead of working together.

At the same time, **Montreal**'s identification with Black Saudi students echoes Aker's (2016) argument that because Black teachers and Black students have many things in common including 'experiences with marginalization' (Aker, 2016: 2), it is possible that some Black teachers may be able to provide academic support to Black students. Nonetheless, the diverse forms of capital including cultural, linguistic, emotional and social capital **Montreal** brought to his school/department were not recognized. This corroborates what Sulaiman Jenkins discusses in Chapter 9. As Jenkins notes, African Americans bring with them to Saudi Arabia diverse forms of unique excellence and assets but do not often receive sufficient recognition, and in many ways tend to be undermined and discriminated against by various stakeholders as well as by the society more broadly. These teachers, like **Montreal**, on navigating through Saudi Arabia, have been the target of marginalization by virtue of their skin color, by being consistently questioned about their national origins, and by extra layers of difficulty in securing employment. What is more, these teachers have also been marginalized by repeated skepticism from students and administrators who question their linguistic competence, accent, rhetoric and accuracy in delivering English lessons.

Montreal, in actuality, felt *'oppressed'* and *'discriminated'* against for his entire period working in Saudi Arabia. For him, being Black seemed to be the one defining element based on which his workplace and non-Black others projected him and constructed his identity. He saw his entire stay in Saudi Arabia being *'a journey of struggle and pain'*, whereby he developed a strong bond with Black Saudi students, seeing them as experiencing the same pain as him and as the target of discrimination from non-Black Saudis and non-Saudis as well. He expressed a perception that all African American TESOL teachers teaching in Saudi Arabia as well as all Black Saudis were on one side, sharing the same pain.

We by no means disregard the experience and perspective that **Montreal** shared with us. We could sense a great deal of pain and heaviness in his voice, facial expressions and body language as he was retelling what he had undergone and observed. That he felt deeply connected to Black Saudi students gave him a worthwhile justification to continue to stay and work in Saudi Arabia. He felt responsible for them and wanted to help lighten their pain caused by subtle and overt discrimination from their society and other groups in the population. Indeed, **Montreal** is not alone in feeling discriminated against, as is evident in the accounts from Tyrone and Jerome discussed in the previous chapter. Nonetheless, the on-the-ground realities appear to be far more complex than any mere polarized constructs, be they race, gender, ethnicity, language, religion, worldview, etc.

In our interviews with other African American TESOL teachers, we learnt from them that they did not necessarily agree with **Montreal**'s projection of discrimination on the basis of race and Blackness. They acknowledged that there were African American teachers as well as Black teachers from the Caribbean who tended to '*exaggerate tensions and [were] quick to accuse others of being racist whenever issues and problems arose at work or outside work*'. They also noted that African Americans in particular tended to be '*aggressive against others*' as they '*exercise their rights as Americans over others*' and '*shout, scream, and make demand without reflecting on their own behaviors*'. These behaviors tended to cause tensions at work and often forced administrators to take disciplinary action. And as a result, many Black teachers did not want to be associated with such behaviors, as these participants further confirmed. These participants tended to distance themselves from those '*loud*', '*aggressive*', '*dramatic*' and '*calculating*' Black teachers in general, as they put it. Although they were aware of the preference and fondness among Saudis towards Americans in the country, they did not want to be viewed as '*the entitled American*' and/or '*the whining Black*'.

A teacher whom we call **Dave** offered a nuanced comment on the above phenomenon:

> *There are many benefits from this country [Saudi Arabia]. If everything was so terrible, I don't think many of us still want to come or could stay long. Words travel. Racism travels. And so do benefits. Everyone comes to this region with a baggage and assumptions and personal calculations, and African American teachers like us are not the exception. If anything, I find many Black Saudis here leading a life of luxury and opportunities, so it's way too simplistic to say that Blacks suffer from racism and discrimination in this country. Poor Saudis are here too, and they're not Black. Migrant workers are here too, and they're not Black.*
> (**Dave**, from the USA)

Dave and several other teachers observed that once African American teachers let the racism tag obsess them, they could become '*blinded*' and then '*separated themselves from other teachers and students*' in their professional and after-work interactions. This led to some of them being '*harsh on Saudi students*' who would then complain to their department administrators. Once complaints had been made, administrators were under pressure to investigate, and in some cases, '*ugly actions could be* *taken*' that would further escalate the already-existing tensions between some African American teachers and their colleagues, the administrators and the students. Another problem that **Dave** pointed out was that some of these teachers, because of their perception of racism and discrimination, lost interest in teaching; consequently, they tended to under-perform in class. This very problem could easily be picked up on by the students, who would then lodge complaints and demand that they were replaced by better teachers. So, this is '*a vicious circle*', as **Dave** put it.

Dave's insight confirms Jenkins' reflection as an African American TESOL professional who has held several administrative roles in Saudi institutions. Having experienced many unpleasant encounters in his own life and work as an African American individual, in his administrative roles Jenkins reveals that he pays much attention to teachers' competence and their tenacity in delivering what the workplace expects from them. Jenkins says that administrators are under pressure to make things work, given the hugely diverse backgrounds of their teaching staff. Barnawi can relate to this perspective, as he has also held varied administrative roles in his college. It is '*[a]lways a headache to manage conflicting interests and problems at work*', as he has revealed many times.

In the next section, we present and discuss the account of a teacher from the Caribbean whose narratives bring more food for thought into the already complex picture of race, language, ethnicity, religion and native-speakerism.

Othello: 'The Extra Mutawa[2] and Me'

Othello is a Black Jamaican teacher with a BA in Education and a certificate in Teaching English as a Second Language (TESL). He had worked at a Saudi HE institution for nearly 13 years as a teacher as well as being the coordinator for a course in business communication. He felt that Saudi students were always eager to learn from him and respectful of his teaching. **Othello** loved the Saudi culture and wanted to learn more about it. Workwise, he did not mind paying out of his own pocket to take part in events that would enrich his expertise and work performance such as conferences like TESOL Arabia or local professional development activities. These events and activities helped him learn '*suitable classroom strategies for Arab students*'. Yet, he believed that he had been the target of a particular group of teachers and/or specific teachers in his workplace, whom he referred to as '*extra Mutawa*'. These people, he reported, were '*contaminating the place and destroying the future of Saudis*'.

> I am telling you this place is a heaven. Nobody in this world could give you free house, medical insurance, tickets and 70 days paid annual leave just for teaching English language. I taught in New York and Saint Lucia as well. I never had such benefits before. I am telling you I love this place,

and I always respect Saudis. My only problem is those extra Mutawa who are taking the advantage of this place. You know whom I am referring to right! I mean those conservative Muslims teachers from India, Pakistan, Jordan and Africa are literally destroying the place with their poor English. (Othello)

On the one hand, there seemed to be a geographic divide that was running deep among the international TESOL teachers in **Othello**'s workplace: those from the Caribbean and the rest. **Othello** felt that there was also a religious dichotomy separating him from other international TESOL teachers in his institution: '*conservative Muslims*' and others. On the other hand, it was important to note that the segregation **Othello** referred to was taking place among expatriate teachers rather than between Saudis and foreign teachers. Within this expatriate community, alongside geographic and religious divides, there is another one that involves language and speaker identity. This divide is embedded in perceptions of English and what variety of English one speaks, which runs in parallel with projections of who speaks what English: '*conservative Muslims teachers from India, Pakistan, Jordan and Africa are literally destroying the place with their poor English*'.

Coming from Jamaica, **Othello** was proud of his identity and Jamaican English, a recognized variety of English (Sand, 2013; Schneider, 2020). Nonetheless, while American English was highly regarded, Jamaican English was seen as an '*inappropriate*' or a '*substandard*' language and was thus *marginalized* in his school in Saudi Arabia, as he reported. Such sentiments and social categorizations reported by **Othello** are common in contemporary HE settings where international TESOL teachers with different backgrounds and nationalities are working together (see, for example, Hicks, 2013; Kubota & Lin, 2006; Margić & Širola, 2014; Nagatomo, 2015; Phan, 2017). As Park (2013) notes:

> Issues of marginalization are rampant in the lives of individuals who are of a certain gender, race, ethnicity, language, and class as a result of how society constructs and privileges certain identities and discourses in the dominant culture at the same time, disenfranchises individuals in accessing various equitable opportunities. (Park, 2013: 110)

Scholarship on perceptions of and attitudes towards language and different language varieties including varieties of English, such as Hsu (2019), Margić and Širola (2014) and Sung (2015), show that people's perceptions and attitudes are often informed by certain worldviews, exposures, experiences and discourses, and also project their views and associated images about those who speak a particular language and/or variety of language. For example, in their study about attitudes held by Croatian university students majoring in teaching English as a foreign language (TEFL) on different varieties of English, Margić and Širola (2014) have found that the students associated Jamaican English and Irish English with fun and having fun, while referring to British English as a means to show off. These attitudes and perceptions further perpetuate stereotypes and/or create new stereotypes about social statuses and identities of those who speak these varieties of English.

As for **Othello**, he was labeled *'crazy or a Jamaican gangster'* because he used Jamaican English or creole expressions to joke with his students or communicate with colleagues from the same cultural background. He felt that he had been professionally disrespected because of his ethnicity, accent, and the specific English he spoke and drew on to teach and interact with others. Likewise, his appreciation for and awareness of different varies of Englishes, which should be applauded in the light of much scholarship on World Englishes and English as a foreign language (EFL) cited throughout the book, got picked on as a weakness and an indication of inferiority. He revealed:

> I use creole language to communicate with Amir [pseudonym] during office hours because he is from Barbados. I sometime crack jokes with my students using Jamaican English or expressions. This does not mean that I am crazy or I am a Jamaican gangster as those extra Mutawa describe. I am proud to be Jamaican, and there is nothing wrong if my students learn about varieties of English including Jamaican English. (Othello)

Importantly, **Othello** revealed that nobody but *'those extra Mutawa'* took issue with his Jamaican and creole English. He felt that their act of picking on him helped mask their own vulnerability about themselves and their submission towards native varieties of English like American English. He saw *'those extra Mutawa'* as having an identity crisis.

> Why can't they pick on American English? Some Jordanians here I cannot even understand their English because they are struggling to speak with American accents. They have identity issues here and I never commented on such issues. I do not want to disrespect my coworkers. (Othello)

It looks like **Othello**'s colleagues tended to view one's linguistic competence and academic performance in relation to particular 'standards of English language education' (Holliday, 2008: 119). While **Othello** acknowledged being comfortable about who he was (a Jamaican Black qualified TESOL teacher who was able to bring to his teaching the real world of diverse accents and Englishes), he felt sorry for the other teachers who seemed to look up to American English as the way to go. For him, those teachers had *'no legitimacy, linguistically, pedagogically and professionally, to disregard'* him.

That **Othello** is a non-Muslim Black Jamaican also tended to make him a target for attack by the *'extra Mutawa'* in his workplace. He felt that his genuine interest in wanting to learn more about Saudi society often got treated as a disrespect for Islam by those *'extra Mutawa'*, as he further revealed:

> When I ask questions about local culture, traditions, and Islamic values it does not mean that I disrespect Muslims. I wanted to learn more about Saudis, and act in a professional way. But those extra Mutawa are very sensitive, and always twist my words and expressions to put me in trouble with the upper management. This is how they want to survive here anyway. You know they would never have such type of jobs in their countries. (Othello)

For **Othello**, discussions about local culture, traditions and Islamic values should be seen as opportunities for professional growth, and a means to establish a healthy relationship with colleagues at work. Yet, he felt that his good intentions were often politicized by his peers in order to put his job at risk.

> I moved here to enjoy my professional career. But the politic of the place sometimes consumes the energy of my brain. Thank God that I will be retiring in 2 years from now. So I really do not have to deal with those extra Mutawa. Again, I always consider myself a professional teacher. (Othello)

It is important to note that, from **Othello**'s perspective, he was not bullied by any other international or local Saudi teachers, except for the '*extra Mutawa*' he mentioned. He seemed to be the exclusive target for them, because of where he comes from and his nationality (Jamaican), his accent (Jamaican English), the English(es) he speaks (creole English), his non-Muslim background, and his interest in learning about Islam and Saudi Arabia's culture and society, which he saw as a genuine intention to establish rapport with Muslim colleagues and students and to pay respect to the country that had treated him very generously. He wondered why no other teachers but the '*extra Mutawa*' had a problem with him being who he was.

In today's world, a teacher like **Othello** should have been in great demand because he possessed and projected all the desirable attributes that progressive scholarship promotes in TESOL teachers: qualified and experienced; aware of different varieties of English and active in incorporating these varieties for pedagogical and intercultural purposes; enthusiastic about cultural difference and local society; mindful of religious difference; not submitting to native-speakerism; keen to create a conducive learning environment for students; and committed to professional growth. It seems that there is a total disconnect between aspirational scholarship and the on-the-ground realities of many teachers who believe their professionalism and capabilities are often undermined by stereotypes and attitudes surrounding race, ethnicity, language, religion and work politics.

Othello's speculation and confusion about the ways he was treated have made us (Phan Le Ha and Barnawi) reflect further on many existing double-standard practices in TESOL, language education and applied linguistics. For example, the normalization of the neoliberal approach in identification is prevalent. Indeed, it is common to see biodata like that below from professionals and scholars in many disciplines including TESOL who, on the one hand, may produce scholarship that is highly critical of the cultural politics of English/ELT and of growing neoliberalism in ELT, English and the like but, on the other hand, are maximizing their credentials and association with the English-speaking West in order to draw the world's attention to and recognition of their profile: *'I am from ..., a scholar committed to social justice and interested in the intersectionality of ... I obtained an MA and PhD from a top-tiered American university whose English program is ranked among the best in the world. My scholarship has been published in tier-1 academic journals ...'.* We find this double-standard practice inherent in the very center of our profession and penetrating every level of it. We believe many readers can relate to this.

Othello's account is symbolically powerful in many ways, we must admit. We cannot help but reflect on it. To delve into more nuances and challenges in workplaces in which international TESOL teachers in Saudi Arabia have found themselves, the next section presents a White native speaker's detailed account, through which we further discuss issues of race, ethnicity, Englishes, native-speakerism and the dynamics of multi relations influencing professional experiences and perceptions of international TESOL teachers in this very complex place/space.

Benjamin: A Qualified, Experienced White British Teacher, His 'Horror Story' and the 'Anti-Western' Gang

'If you Google "teaching English in Saudi Arabia," you will surely find many "horror stories"', many of our participants and colleagues in Saudi Arabia have told us. And one such horror story we were directed to was one from a British teacher whom we refer to as **Benjamin**.

Benjamin is a native speaker of English with relevant qualifications and desirable cultural and symbolic capital as often highlighted in the existing literature, such as a British accent, White, male, experienced, multilingual (Appleby, 2013; Kubota, 2018; Nonaka, 2018; Park, 2013; Rivers, 2017). He worked at a Saudi HE institution for almost eight years as a teacher as well as program coordinator. Yet, he felt that the sudden replacement of Western teachers with non-native speakers and Western Muslim converts of different backgrounds and nationalities had brought about job insecurity, uncertainties and decline in quality and standards, as well as reflecting strong anti-Western sentiments in his workplace. Thus, he felt he had no choice but to resign from his position and leave Saudi Arabia.

Benjamin posted a long open letter on Dave's ESL Café in 2006[3] called *'Avoid Yanbu Industrial College and Saudi Arabia in General.'* We learnt from his letter that **Benjamin** was a qualified and experienced native-English-speaking teacher from Britain who decided to go public about his highly problematic workplace after his resignation and departure from Saudi Arabia. He was of the view that posting the letter on this forum was the only way for his story to be known, and for other teachers to be aware of the work politics at Yanbu Industrial College where he used to work and of teaching English in Saudi Arabia more generally. His letter soon went viral among the expatriate community and beyond. Many Saudi colleagues were/are also aware of this letter and the many accusations included in it. '*This one was scandalous*', as one colleague put it.

In the letter, we learnt that **Benjamin** felt marginalized by and concerned about the anti-Westerner sentiment in his former workplace. For example, there was '*the Deputy Managing Director (DMD) ... who has always been unsympathetic to the western teachers*'. This DMD even threatened to replace them: '*I'm going to replace all of you with Sudanese teachers*'.

> I was at YIC for 8 years as a teacher and coordinator, and have seen the place become more and more unfriendly to westerners. During my time, there were three heads of department. The first two were fired or replaced: a Palestinian/American ('The DMD has asked me to tell him every personal detail about the teachers to use against them and I have refused to do that.') and a competent Irishman, who understood westerners because he was one. (Benjamin)

In addition to this DMD:

> now there is a Libyan-born Canadian as Head of the English Department (HOD) [at Yanbu Industrial College YIC] ('I've been told to clean up the department.' i.e. get rid of westerners he doesn't like and deplete the department of its native speakers, some at YIC years before he set foot in Saudi Arabia.) (Benjamin)

Benjamin found himself resentful of the changes that were taking place at YIC, particularly when the familiar discourses, knowledge and pedagogical practices of native speakers of English had been replaced by the DMD and the newly appointed HoD who was a Libyan-born Canadian.

> The HOD replaced a 10-year-veteran of the department who actually improved the department by personally training teachers in the new electronic marking system as well as suggesting needed improvements in examinations. Contrast this with the HOD who, after 3 years, still remains ignorant of the workings of the electronic marking system and leaves that as well as the writing of exams totally to the coordinators. (Benjamin)

Interestingly, while **Benjamin** included the '*Palestinian/American*' former *HOD* in his workplace in the circle of Westerners, implying that this

Palestinian-American was one of them, he did not consider the new *Libyan-born Canadian HOD* as such, but instead as one of the Others who were anti-Westerners. So, what made the *Libyan-born Canadian* not a Westerner in **Benjamin**'s view?

> So why does the HOD not get along with many of the westerners on his staff? First, living in Qadaffi's Libya with a constant diet of anti-western propaganda is going to bend your mind from the start. ... As well, Saudis at YIC I have spoken with who know the HOD say that despite his having Canadian citizenship and giving his permanent residence as Ottawa, he is vehemently anti-western. (Benjamin)

Ideologically, **Benjamin** saw the HOD as being influenced by his home country's history of anti-Western sentiment. Holding Canadian citizenship did not necessarily change this HOD's deeply ingrained anti-Western mindset. Then, professionally, **Benjamin** described the HOD as follows:

> Next, the HOD lacks the people skills necessary for his position. ... Does he also find the westerners a problem for the same reason he doesn't issue any memos to the staff? Simple inadequacy and fear that his own lack of competence with the English language will be found out. In a department of high powered, professional English teachers, can a man who writes 'fill up this form' really have any place in the lead. Certainly not. The HOD warmed an office chair in the administration building at YIC long enough to become on good terms with the directors. He knew nothing about the English Department. In other words, he had no basis for gaining the respect of long-serving western teachers. Therefore, he formed strong alliances with the few teachers who did defer to him, mainly western Muslims who, like himself, had just arrived. (Benjamin)

Here we see another set of dichotomies being drawn: Westerners versus Western Muslims, and '*high powered, professional*' English teachers like **Benjamin** and other non-Muslim Westerners versus '*inadequate*' professionals like the HOD and his Western Muslim allies. The former had been in the workplace and ruled it for many years, but they found themselves threatened and put down by the new HOD and his allies, who were making many replacements and changes that **Benjamin** found ill-informed professionally and pedagogically.

In addition, what was going on in **Benjamin**'s workplace appeared to be very toxic, according to what he wrote. Categories such as race, ethnicity, religion, nationality and language had been used by the new HoD and his allies to divide, punish and spy on Western teachers. He also stated that the Department did not have this problem prior to the appointment of the current Head and the Western Muslim converts. A series of toxic actions and behaviors became dominant, none of which served teaching and learning, as seen in **Benjamin**'s detailed examples given in the letter. All in all, the workplace was no longer the place **Benjamin** wanted to be in and to devote himself to, and he resigned.

He also felt that anyone against the changes or thinking differently from the HoD was being punished. This was an undesirable situation for the workplace, for teachers and students, as **Benjamin** revealed in the long letter.

> And as his relationships with the teachers who didn't respect him worsened, [the new HOD] began to take his revenge. During the HOD's brief headship, at a time when institutions in Saudi Arabia including YIC are crying out for native speakers, nearly 10 western teachers, extremely professional native speakers, one of them at YIC for more than 10 years, were either fired, quit or simply ran away. It takes the Royal Commission months to complete the paperwork to bring a teacher to YIC. The HOD can alienate and get rid of that teacher in a matter of minutes. Just how useful then is this man to the Royal Commission?
>
> Two teachers, an outspoken Australian and New Zealander, who the HOD particularly abhorred, were given just days to leave the country. ('Sorry I have to divide up the contact hours of the two teachers who "left".') When they were forced out, the HOD, now extremely paranoid of his western staff, partitioned off the room where we chatted, took out the seating and put his good friend, an American Muslim on the other side of the partition to listen and report to him what was said. You could actually see this teacher rush to the HOD's office when he overheard something particularly interesting. Spying on teachers and even students is common in Libyan universities where the HOD claims to have been a department head.
>
> And the HOD wasn't satisfied with causing western teachers to lose their livelihood, he had to bad-mouth them behind their backs as well. He ran around the staffroom announcing that this teacher was 'crazy' or that teacher needed 'psychiatric help' in an effort to see which teachers supported his antics and which didn't.
>
> On one occasion, the HOD ordered me into his office to tell me how he was going to ruthlessly break up, this 'group' of westerners conspiring against him. There was, in fact, no group, only individual teachers who were not giving this proud but incompetent and inexperienced head of department the deference he felt was owed to him. (Benjamin)

Ridiculing and insulting teachers as well as creating a work culture whereby spying on one another and even on students became the new norm had destroyed work morale and ethics, as **Benjamin** revealed.

At the same time, **Benjamin** was particularly concerned about '*non-native speakers*' appointed to take charge of positions and responsibilities that used to be exclusively under the control of Western native-English-speaking non-Muslim professionals. As seen in the specific examples in the letter, the non-native speakers he referred to did not seem to have any understanding of the workplace and were clueless about what was available to accommodate students' examination activities. Neither did they have a good command of English. They then also relied on native speakers to check, correct and verify examination papers. This new reality made

Benjamin feel that the workplace was declining in quality. He felt the anti-Western sentiments and the resultant actions only caused the workplace to go downhill. This problem bothered **Benjamin** a great deal.

> Disliked western coordinators who were skilled at writing examinations were gradually replaced by non-native speakers, who did not have the English competence to write examinations but were trusted by the HOD. Therefore, you have the ludicrous situation of a coordinator with a shaky grasp of English ordering a native speaker to write an examination, then editing that examination to include grammatically incorrect alterations. Or a similar coordinator will have a native speaker do an examination marking key because the coordinator is not sure of the answers himself. I speak from first-hand experience here. And, HOD, it isn't possible to have a class of 28 students do a listening examination in a language laboratory with only 12 working booths no matter how proud you are of your out-of-touch examination schedule or how unwilling your newly appointed sycophantic coordinators are to acquaint you with reality. The department has become more and more third-world and unprofessional under the HOD. (Benjamin)

Maybe because **Benjamin** was so engaged in his own frustration, anger and disappointment, in his letter he used words and terms that embodied widely condemned stereotypes, prejudices and biases. Admittedly, it is very tempting to criticize him for his publicly expressed anti-non-native speaker attitudes, and his overt preference towards native speakers. We, however, would like to put his criticisms of the workplace in perspective, as we did not talk to him directly and what was conveyed in a written letter might easily be misread if we were rushing to use any normative ideological framework to make sense of it.

First, **Benjamin**'s letter reminds us of the well-established scholarship on Whiteness and its manifestations in all shapes and forms, although we acknowledge that we do not know if **Benjamin** is White as he did not say anything about his race in the letter. Park (2013) and Kubota and Lin (2006), for example, have long argued that 'whiteness exerts its power as an invisible and unmarked norm against which all Others are racially and culturally defined, marked, and made inferior' (Kubota & Lin, 2006: 474). Intentionally or unintentionally, **Benjamin** exerted a strong sense of superiority as a (White) native speaker of English, and appeared to judge other teachers along this line. For **Benjamin**, the credibility and legitimacy of his Libyan-born Canadian HoD could only be verified by *'western, high powered, professional English teachers'* like himself. Being approved of by this particular group of teachers appeared to be the only way for the HoD to gain respect and prove his linguistic as well as interpersonal competency. Therefore, that the HoD was able to gain respect and support from any other teachers in the department such as *'western Muslims'* or *'non-native speakers'*, as **Benjamin** mentioned, was not regarded as being credible and trustworthy by **Benjamin** and those who thought like him.

Next, **Benjamin** also seemed to miss the opportunity to reflect on different varieties of English and English as an international language as well as the ways in which native speakers of English are perceived in different social and educational contexts and settings. For him, it seemed, there were only two types of English: one by native speakers and the other by non-native speakers. To be fair to **Benjamin**, he did not discriminate against the idea of native speakers having to be Westerners, loosely defined in terms of race and ethnicity – i.e. British, American, Irish or Australian Caucasians. For him, native speakers could be those of multi-ethnicities such as Palestinian-Americans, as long as they were somehow included in the circle of Westerners.

Another argument we can put forth is that what was mentioned in **Benjamin**'s open letter confirms that the mobility of international TESOL teachers could bring about ideological tensions within/between teachers, and even turn native-speaker privilege into what we call '*a perceived victim*'. Perceived marginalization of native speakers of English occurs when native-speaker privilege is challenged by the heavy presence of international TESOL teachers, with different backgrounds and nationalities, in a given social and educational context. **Benjamin** felt that his identity as a British native speaker of English with relevant qualifications and years of experience had been deliberately targeted. This experience seemed unique, hard to believe and unexpected for **Benjamin**, given the dominant discourses of White and native-speaker privilege pervasive in the field of TESOL and reported to be the case in Saudi Arabia, as evident in Alenazi's (2014) study with 56 Saudi recruiters for ELT jobs, and in Abdul Qadeer's (2019) anecdotes gathered from teachers and recruiters for Saudi institutions.

Benjamin also seemed to place more credibility and legitimacy on himself as a native speaker of English, whose linguistic and cultural capital was seen as his privilege. Yet, **Benjamin** seemed to perceive himself as a marginalized victim vis-à-vis other international TESOL teachers, because of what he described as '*a general anti-Western-teachers sentiment*' among the management and some other international teachers, mostly Western Muslim converts. In his view, the new Head of the English Department, a Libyan-born Canadian, was '*incompetent*', whose mission was to get rid of Western teachers. **Benjamin** and some other native-speaker teachers were openly against this move.

Moving on with his letter, **Benjamin**'s account also points to another problem inherent in the recruitment policy and practice of many Saudi institutions, particularly in relation to '*Western Muslim converts*'. It seems that there must have been prejudices against non-Saudi Muslim teachers including '*Western Muslim converts*' in Saudi Arabia. According to the teachers in Jenkins (2019) and some participants we have interviewed, Saudi institutions generally did not/do not like to recruit TESOL teachers from Muslim backgrounds for fear that those teachers may want to use the teaching venue as an excuse to come to Saudi Arabia for religious purposes. Saudi institutions, as a result, were not in favor of or were even against hiring such teachers. Nonetheless, the terrorist attacking Westerners in Yanbu in May 2004[4] made it very difficult for Saudi institutions to hire non-Muslim Western English language teachers. This greatly changed recruitment policies and practices; as a result, Western Muslim converts were employed in higher numbers.

> Since, the terrorist attack on Yanbu, YIC has only been able to hire one or two new non-Muslim western teacher[s], so its policy of not hiring western Muslim converts, especially the kind who dress in short Saudi thobes ('If it's too long, Satan can grab hold of it and drag me down to hell.') has been waived. So if an obese British white man wants to grow a bushy red beard and prance around in Saudi national dress and doesn't mind the behind-the-back ridicule and laughs of derision from students, so be it. (Benjamin)

Benjamin described these *western Muslim converts* in a very negative and condescending manner but with evidence, as seen below:

> However, these new teachers can be unfriendly to non-Muslim staff. And if they are reported for infractions: rudeness to fellow teachers, lateness to class, not handing in marks to inputters and coordinators, they simply label the complainant 'a well-known hater of Islam and Muslims'. Such labels are a rallying cry for help from other Muslims. 'I am hated not because I am despicable but because I am a Muslim like you. HELP!!!' No. The simple truth that you must one day face is that you are despised for ... yourself. No matter. The bogus defense is readily accepted by the HOD if it suits his purposes and unprofessional behavior swept under the carpet. ... Muslims have told me such fabrications are even used by one Muslim against another: 'I am being reported by X (not because I am incompetent and unprofessional) but because I am a more devout Muslim than X'. (Benjamin)

The fact that his department started to recruit Western Muslim converts became a point of concern for **Benjamin** and other teachers, including Muslim Saudis and other Muslim teachers. For whatever reason, those Western Muslim convert teachers also became allies with the new HoD, and this very situation heightened the problem in **Benjamin**'s workplace.

Like the concept of native speaker of English, Muslim has become a contested notion in the domain of ELT in Saudi Arabia. Muslim was a tag that teachers could use against one another, both within the religion and between religions. It can be a marker of exclusion, and can be abused and exploited in many different ways including in relation to race and ethnicity, as shown in **Benjamin**'s narrative above and in the case of **Othello** discussed in the previous section.

Putting It Together

We have provided detailed analysis and discussion the previous sections, so in this concluding part we only highlight several points and arguments we consider important.

The above accounts from **Montreal**, **Othello** and **Benjamin** – three individuals virtually distinguished by race, religion, skin color, nationality and professional perspectives – invite us to rescale our lenses and reread the contemporary scholarship of TESOL teacher mobility. Our open approach to examining, analyzing and interpreting these accounts has helped us capture different forms of mobility that need further scholarly attention. These include mobility of 'Black pain', 'depressive symptoms', 'mobility of perceived native-speaker privilege', 'mobility of varieties of Englishes' and the like (be they real or imagined). We, thus, argue that such phenomena need to be critically unpacked, analyzed and framed in order to gain complex understandings of international TESOL mobility and realize socially unjust relations in the domains of TESOL and ELT.

In the same vein, as we have shown throughout the chapter, religion is often used by different parties as a convenient proxy for power gain, for getting away with complaints, for getting others into trouble, for professional and personal competition, for dealing with professional jealousies, and for self-worth legitimization. Saudi Arabia, as a TESOL/ELT/EFL site, offers another layer of complexity in which religion, race, nationality and native-speakerism are often manipulated, politicized, utilized, appropriated and abused by multiple actors.

We acknowledge that writing this chapter is particularly mentally challenging for us, because of the emotional weight we felt obliged to carry as we engaged with the various unpleasant experiences, rage, anger, anxiety, helplessness and mistreatment projected in the teachers' accounts presented thus far. At the same time, we are convinced of the need to interrogate difficult questions and controversial topics and issues in our fields if we are genuine about addressing them and pushing for well-informed understandings that would then help bring us together instead of further polarizing groups and sub-groups fixated by labels.

To put this spirit in perspective, the next chapter brings to the fore another set of difficult conversations involving the emotion labor experienced by White native-English-speaking teachers in Saudi HE institutions. Their narratives reveal often-hidden nuances, particularly those surrounding the socially, socioculturally, pedagogically and linguistically ascribed advantages and privileges as White native speakers of English working in an EFL context.

Notes

(1) See https://www.nytimes.com/interactive/2019/08/14/magazine/black-history-american-democracy.html (accessed on 3 October 2020).
(2) 'Mutawa' refers to the cultural police or very conservative Muslims.
(3) See https://forums.eslcafe.com/job/viewtopic.php?t=40250 (accessed on 3 October 2020).
(4) See https://www.nytimes.com/2004/05/02/world/five-foreigners-killed-in-attack-at-saudi-office.html

11 A Much-Needed Conversation with Native-English-Speaking Caucasian Teachers: Emotion Labor and Affect in Transnational Encounters

Abdullah Alshakhi[1] and Phan Le Ha

Preface

The many complex issues discussed in the book point to an important aspect of TESOL teacher (transnational) mobility, that is, teachers' management and navigation of their emotion and affect at work, as we have briefly established in the previous chapters. As a matter of fact, one of us (Phan Le Ha) has been writing on emotion and affect, and her most recent article (co-authored with Abdullah Alshakhi, a Saudi colleague from King Abdulaziz University), published in the September 2020 issue of *Research in Comparative and International Education*[2] is on the emotion labor of Western-trained TESOL professionals teaching in Saudi Arabian higher education. This article unearths many often-hidden complex realities at work experienced but rarely talked about in the scholarly literature. For this reason, we have decided to reproduce the article in this book in order to help readers see a fuller picture of international TESOL teachers in Saudi Arabia – a land of promise yet a challenging, daunting and draining work environment at the same time. The nuanced insights put forth in this article have forced us to revisit many normative assumptions and even considered 'settled' views about native-English-speaking teachers found in much existing work. We have also added new references and inserted extra data and discussion here and there to the original article as we have reproduced it in this book.

Specifically, informed by an ethnographic qualitative research study conducted with expatriate teachers of English in Saudi Arabia, we (Alshakhi and Phan) examine *emotion(al) labor* in the context of transnational mobilities with regard to sociocultural and institutional tensions. Engaged with wide-ranging interdisciplinary literature on emotion and affect (see Chapter 3 for details), we discuss the place of transnational emotion(al) labor in four inter-related manifestations: (a) struggles and efforts to interact and communicate with students; (b) internalization and resentment of privilege and deficiency underlying discourses of native speakers; (c) responses to challenges from social, religious and cultural difference; and (d) prolonged endurance, frustration, helplessness and resistance to prescribed curriculum, testing, and top-down policy and practice.

As transnational scholars teaching and researching writing ourselves, we also bring into the article/chapter our own reflections, particularly those from Abdullah, a Western-trained Saudi transnational scholar currently teaching English in Saudi Arabia. His own emotion labor plays an important role in how he relates to the experiences of the teacher participants. We have incorporated his reflections in this article/chapter to shed light on how research studies of this nature could inspire dialogues with the self and conversations among researchers for support and solidarity beyond constructed boundaries of race, language, religion, ethnicity and nationality.

Let's start.

> For me, teaching and assessing writing requires a decent knowledge about the local culture and students' interests. As a Western-trained Muslim teaching assistant in the US [during my PhD], I found it very challenging to discuss what I consider sensitive or taboo topics such as sexuality. I could not prevent it, and I could not discuss it because I had not thought I will ever discuss it with my students. How could I grade it and how could I improve a written argument on a topic I always avoided? My vision for my US students was different from the program vision and the students' vision. I found it difficult to compromise my own beliefs while in a more open culture like the US. My dilemma was the same as the Western transnational teachers in Saudi Arabia. The only difference, an essential one, is that they deal with a very conservative context and I dealt with a more open one. (Abdullah, Reflection 3)

For decades, the global drive towards English has enabled English language teachers at all levels to move around the globe for employment purposes. Likewise, the growing demand for English globally has created opportunities for many English-speaking individuals to work as teachers of English in almost every country and territory. These teachers are indeed at the forefront of transnational mobilities. They also contribute to the growth of teaching English to speakers of other languages (TESOL). Existing scholarly inquiries centered on these transnational/international TESOL teachers/professionals include their (transnational) identity formation, their attitudes and experiences teaching English transnationally/internationally, their professional growth and pedagogical innovation, and their negotiations of teaching pedagogy and (inter)cultural issues and linguistic capabilities (for instance, Bright & Phan, 2011; S. Jenkins, 2019; Kostogriz & Bonar, 2019; Petrol, 2009; Poole, 2019; Rose *et al.*, 2020; Stanley, 2013; Stewart, 2020). The surveyed literature has also raised many concerns surrounding the continued endorsement of Western superiority in English language education and other ethical issues involving race, ethnicity, gender, religion and ideology, as well as risks and precarities associated with short-term employment contracts and TESOL teachers' lack of appropriate teaching qualifications and experience.

A high percentage of the thousands of English as a foreign language (EFL) teachers working in Saudi Arabia are from overseas and of hugely diverse cultural, social, ethnic, academic, linguistic and professional backgrounds (cf. Mahboob & Elyas, 2014; Phan & Barnawi, this volume; Shah & Elyas, 2019). They have moved to Saudi Arabia for many different reasons, including competitive salaries and benefits, religious pursuits, personal reasons, career moves, or unemployment back home (see Chapters 4 and 5 in this volume for specific examples). While many of them appear unqualified, many others have extensive international teaching experience (S. Jenkins, 2019; Phan & Barnawi, this volume). The growing demand for international TESOL professionals corresponds to Saudi Arabia's boost for more English at all levels of schooling and for the expansion of English-medium instruction courses and programs at the university level. Saudi Arabia's Vision 2030, introduced in 2016 to diversify the country's economy and to aspire to be at the forefront of modernization and technology advancement, is believed to have made the country even more aggressive in embracing English and English language education.

The strong presence of native-English-speaking teachers in Saudi Arabia as well as advertisements for English language teaching jobs that target and favor native-English-speaking Westerners have contributed to rather negative views towards this teacher population (Barnawi & Phan, 2014; Mahboob & Elyas, 2014; Phan & Barnawi, 2015; Zhang, 2004). These teachers are often criticized for generating problems in Saudi EFL classrooms and are largely projected as being unqualified, inexperienced, incapable, monolingual, money-driven and unresponsive to Saudi students' needs. However, this proposition needs to be challenged, as we have done in the present study and as informed by the findings of a large-scale study (presented in this book) conducted by Phan Le Ha and Osman Barnawi with more than 200 international teachers in Saudi Arabia. These expatriate teachers go through multiple layers of difficulties, some of which come from their institutions and the wider social and cultural factors that often depict them as a uniform group of foreigners who enjoy privileges and are ignorant of the society and religion. Their struggles, difficulties, emotions and attempts to communicate their emotions have, hence, been overlooked.

This chapter brings into the existing literature a different angle for viewing transnational language teacher mobilities, that is, emotion(al) labor and affect in the workplace. Drawing on a qualitative research study that examines classroom and assessment experiences of transnational/international TESOL teachers at a university in Saudi Arabia, we show these teachers' complex transnational emotion(al) labor and their affective displays. They engaged in complex interactions with themselves, their professional training and experience, their students and the institutions where they worked, and the broader cultural, social and religious surroundings of Saudi Arabia. These teachers also expressed explicit appreciation of being invited to participate in our study, seeing their participation as a way to communicate their emotional capital and emotion(al) labor. Such interactions and expressions, conveyed in various forms and intensities, are manifestations of emotion(al) labor and affect shouldered by English language teachers in transnational contexts, which remains under-researched and therefore demands more scholarly investigation.

We approached the study design, data collection, and data analysis and interpretation from a critical ethnographic vantage point (Creswell, 2014; Stanley, 2013). Critical ethnography has been employed to examine the teaching and learning of language in diverse cultures and to study teacher and learner identity; it has helped researchers understand the cognitive, sociocultural and critical perspectives of language teaching and learning in more depth and with more nuance. We have approached this methodology, keenly aware of the power dynamics and of *ideology and power as lived and felt* (Phan & Bao, 2019) that the surveyed literature on emotion and affect pinpoints (see Chapter 3 for details). This approach also corresponds well with our discussion of emotion, affect and emotion(al) labor, particularly the relationality of emotion, power, discourse, representation, practice, negotiation, and sociocultural and sociopolitical contexts.

We recognize the importance of differentiating our participants' emotions from our own emotions and from our responses to and interpretations of emotions (Prior, 2019). Hence, together with presenting the data collected with the participants, we also include in this article/chapter our own reflections during the data collection. In particular, Abdullah Alshakhi, who directly collected the data for this study, has reflected on his past experience as an international teaching assistant teaching in a writing composition program in a US university while pursuing his PhD. Abdullah has also reflected on his current academic position as an assistant professor teaching writing and composition at his Saudi university. Abdullah's transnational experiences and exposures enable him to relate to the participants' responses and varied emotions. The communications Abdullah had with the participants came from an interactive and engaged perspective as Abdullah sought to situate their experiences, pedagogies and ideologies about teaching and assessment in Saudi EFL classrooms. For example, he felt he understood their anxiety when their teaching and performance were constantly observed and evaluated by their Saudi students, peers and institution, precisely because while teaching in the USA his teaching was also evaluated by his students and by the Writing Program Administrator who observed his classes and then provided him with feedback. Abdullah, in those days, felt threatened by these evaluation acts because he was the only non-US international teacher in the writing program. He acknowledged being worried about being judged because of his Saudi accent and limited knowledge of American society and culture. Abdullah's reflections and emotion(al) labor offer us critical and reflexive lenses to engage with nuanced emotion(al) labor experienced by international native-speaking TESOL teachers in EFL contexts. This very dimension of transnational academic mobility remains un(der)explored.

The English Language Program, Writing Assessment at Mannar University and the Teachers

Our participants teach English writing in the foundation program at Mannar University in Saudi Arabia. There are two English learning tracks in the program: the academic track and a general track that students have to take and pass before they can start their majors at the university. Both tracks have four levels that follow the *Common European Framework of Reference for Languages: Learning, Teaching, Assessment* (CEFR; Council of Europe, 2001) descriptors. Those levels are A1, A2, B1 and B2. Writing instruction is integrated into the other language skills – listening, speaking and reading – and no separate, stand-alone writing classes are offered. Simply put, each unit includes a writing lesson that addresses different topics varying from basic writing issues to more complicated genres depending on the course level.

All teachers, Saudi and non-Saudi, have to follow the same prescribed writing curriculum, pacing guide and assessment tools that are all aligned with the CEFR and designed by the English language program at Mannar. The *Reading, Writing, and Critical Thinking* book in the *Unlock* textbook series by Cambridge University Press is mandated for the English academic track. The main writing assessment tools used are time-driven exam systems used for the purpose of preventing memorizing and plagiarism. The university also mandates cross-grading for writing exams. Therefore, teachers are neither allowed to grade their own students' exam papers nor invigilate exam sessions. All teachers must exchange their students' exam papers with another section teacher. After that, they receive their students' exam papers graded based on an analytic rubric and then they have to discuss with each of their own students the feedback on their exam papers that have been graded by another teacher. If any room exists for these teachers to implement their own writing assessment tools, they might apply their assessment techniques to in-class activities during writing instruction. However, teachers cannot assign any grades to their students' writing pieces because those grades are not counted towards their final grade. For our study, we only focused on teachers who teach in the academic track, whereby more writing instruction and more writing assessment are required. In the academic track, students take two exams: a mid-term module writing exam and a final module exam.

Four international non-Muslim Caucasian native-English-speaking TESOL professionals at Mannar University were deliberately chosen as participants: Ian, Jonathan, John and Shaun (pseudonyms). All of them were born, raised and educated in their native countries, Australia, England, the US and Ireland, respectively. They were chosen because they each had been teaching writing at Mannar University for more than three years, and thus would be able to reflect on their accumulated experience. They were also committed to the intensive data collection required by this study. We provide a brief synopsis of each teacher's profile below.

Ian is in his early 40s, from Australia. He had been working in Saudi Arabia for about five years. Before coming to Saudi Arabia, he had taught in Korea for several years and before that in Australia for five years. For most of his English teaching career, Ian taught international students from different backgrounds and from different ethnicities. As a matter of fact, he had the opportunity to teach some ESL Saudi students in a language institute in Melbourne.

Ian has a Bachelor's degree in journalism and a Master's degree in Teaching English as a Second Language (TESL) from Australia. He was teaching at Mannar University in the men's campus at the time of the data collection. He taught in the general track and in the academic track where English is taught with an integrated approach. However, in the last two years he had only been teaching in the academic track. Ian also worked part time in the university's writing center for a semester.

Jonathan from England is in his mid-40s. He holds a BA degree in English and a Certificate of English Language Teaching to Adults (CELTA certificate). He had been teaching English as a second and a foreign language for over 20 years. Most of his career years were in Japan. He used to be an assistant director of a language program in Japan for three years. Jonathan joined the English language program at Mannar University about five years ago. He was teaching in the academic track in the men's campus when we met him. He was also engaged in developing online writing materials for the E-learning unit in the program.

John from the US is in his late 30s. John's specialty is in composition studies as he holds a degree in English with concentration on composition.

He taught several composition classes in the US before getting a job in the English language program at Mannar University in the men's campus several years ago. His interest centers around writing transfer. John also served as a part-time member of the curriculum and testing unit in the program. He is a well-trained item writer for writing exams in the academic track.

Shaun from Ireland is in his early 50s. He has a BA in Social Studies and an English as a Second Language (ESL) certificate from the UK. After working as a school counselor in the UK for over 15 years, he decided to take a job in Oman as a language instructor. Several years after that, he joined the English language program at Mannar University in the men's campus, where had been a coordinator and a language instructor for over half a decade. He had also put together several language-related workshops for teachers at the university. Alongside his teaching assignments, Shaun also provided support to the top administrators in the language program.

In short, the above teachers moved to Saudi Arabia with years of language and writing/composition teaching experience in other contexts. They spent an extended period of time teaching English in their own countries and then in EFL countries such as Japan, Korea and Oman before their current appointments in Saudi Arabia. They all hold relevant degrees and certificates that are required of English language teachers. Alongside teaching, these teachers also provide services to Mannar University including coordinating teaching units, developing online materials and running professional development workshops. The participants' profiles show that they are experienced, exposed and qualified teachers for the job. They showed a high degree of willingness to participate in our study, knowing that their participation would require in-depth and critical examination of their own teaching and pedagogical decisions involving assessment and writing instruction. Likewise, as they revealed to Abdullah, sharing their experiences and beliefs through the study helped them acknowledge their emotions and emotion(al) labor.

We got to know the teachers better through an intensive data collection exercise. During an academic semester, Abdullah observed two classes from each teacher: one 50-minute teaching session, and one 50-minute assessment feedback session after the mid-module writing exam. Observation notes and reflections were written down in Abdullah's journals during and after each session. Abdullah also video-recorded these sessions to capture the class vibe as well as teacher–student and student–student interactions to assist his observations and to correlate with his written notes. Then, Abdullah conducted semi-structured interviews with the teachers to ask about their views and experience regarding their classroom teaching and the assessment practice and policy in their English language program. Abdullah also asked the teachers about what he had observed in their sessions and sought their explanations and clarifications. The main aim of these interviews was to gain a more extended and deeper knowledge of the transnational EFL teachers' emotions and emotion(al) labor as they shared with us their beliefs, experiences, attitudes, concerns, suggestions and pedagogical practices.

The in-depth data collected with the teachers have revealed layers of challenges they have been facing in teaching writing and dealing with writing assessment at Mannar, as the rest of the article/chapter shows.

Emotion, Emotional Capital and Emotion(al) Labor Efforts to Communicate with Students

In this section, we show emotion(al) labor and emotional capital as expressed and felt in the participants' experiences of their day-to-day reality of teaching and assessment. In particular, we show how students' low English language proficiency combined with teachers' inability to speak Arabic could cause complex emotions and emotion(al) labor while also revealing emotional capital that is often hidden.

Previous studies have explored the challenges and difficulties encountered by Arab learners (including Saudis) and their teachers in EFL classrooms (Ahmed, 2018; Massri, 2019; Obeid, 2017). Arab learners who lack the basics of grammar find writing particularly difficult when it requires them to think in English and to perform a writing task (Doushaq, 1986; Javid & Umer, 2014; Mohammad & Hazarika, 2016). Many Arab students with weak language skills and knowledge also tend to develop a negative attitude towards foreign language writing (Shukri, 2014). Local EFL teachers with a basic knowledge of the context and of students' writing needs can cope with these challenges more effectively (Hyland, 2003), as compared to expatriate teachers who do not speak Arabic. While recruiters and institutions in Saudi Arabia are still inclined to employ non-Arabic-speaking international teachers to teach English, these reported problems continue to exist. These expatriate teachers often find it hard to teach writing and to conduct assessment with those students (Arnold, 2018; Ezza, 2017; Ghalib & Al-Hattami, 2015). This situation generates varied emotion(al) labor within and among teachers.

According to Abdullah's observation notes, the majority of students in all the observed classes struggled with the most basic language level in writing, although they were already at the highest levels (Levels 3 and 4) in the English academic track program.

> Their language proficiencies and writing skills were generally very low. Their vocabulary range was limited and basic, which required the teachers to spend most of the class time on word building and sentence level writing activities with students. Their language was not enough for effective or elaborate conversations that involved more complex explanations and a higher thinking level. (Abdullah's notes)

During the interviews with Abdullah, the teachers uniformly commented on the low language level among their Saudi students. They also revealed that they found it challenging to have to improve students' language proficiencies and writing skills and to communicate with them about feedback and assessment, particularly when many students had not acquired sufficient grammatical knowledge and vocabulary to perform writing tasks that go beyond the level of making sentences. For example, Shaun (with decades of experience in several educational systems and more than ten years of teaching English in the Gulf region), commented:

> The Saudi EFL learners lack the basic knowledge of the writing schemes. I guess they have a very weak schooling at their primary and secondary levels. Especially the lower level students always find it difficult to write a correct sentence. This presents lots of challenges to teaching and assessment. (Shaun, Interview)

The teachers all expressed their concerns and frustrations about the students' low language proficiencies and seeming lack of interest in learning about writing. Ian showed his disappointment about *'how once students go to write an essay in exams, everything they have already done vanishes'*. As he spoke to Abdullah, Ian raised his hands in a gesture of making something disappear and shrugged his shoulders in exasperation. Like Ian, Jonathan and John could not understand how students could do so poorly in writing. This frustrated them immensely. As a teacher of English himself, Abdullah admitted in his notes that *'few teachers want to teach writing'* because *'many students just don't care'*. This shared emotion and emotion(al) labor as a recognition of challenges should not be seen as teachers' failure and/or incompetence in managing and handling their negative emotions, as we later show when we juxtapose such emotion and emotion(al) labor in relation to prejudice, power, agency, discourse and institutional imposition (Benesch, 2020; Wetherell, 2015).

Students' low English language proficiencies and the teachers' inabilities to speak Arabic also made it unrealistic for teachers to engage students in peer assessment writing activities, as mandated by the university.

> Being a transnational teacher, it becomes so difficult to help them as their proficiency level does not allow them to comprehend my peer assessment activities and my lack of their L1 does not permit me to communicate or translate the words for them. I believe that lower level students should be taught by bilingual teachers who can speak Arabic or understand the basic needs of the students. (Shaun, Interview)

Ian also admitted that during his feedback sessions with students, he was frustrated with them for not being able to understand his explanations. He was frustrated with himself for not being able to answer their questions and to get his points across. The language barrier between him and his students was an obvious obstacle. As Shaun indicated, 'being a transnational teacher' is not seen as desirable capital in these teachers' case, particularly when it exposes their perceived weakness, incapability and 'lacking', which is at odds with the widely promoted desirable image of them as international teachers and native speakers of English. We elaborate on this point in subsequent sections.

Despite their dissatisfaction with students' low language proficiency and lack of interest in writing, the teachers still felt the need and responsibility to care. For example, they noticed students' habit of reproducing memorized sentences in exams and thus wanted to alert students to the danger of unintended plagiarism. As they tried to convey the message, however, they were also afraid that students would not understand the problem and hence misunderstand their good intention due to their limited language. Ian (with more than ten years' experience of teaching English in several countries), for instance, reported:

> Lower level students are good at rote learning. They often learn written sentences by heart and reproduce them in a writing exam. Assessing and grading such scripts is never easy. It is not easy to convince them that they have done something wrong or they must not memorize sentences. Their language is insufficient for me to explain to them that this is wrong. I'm nervous if they take it in the wrong way. (Ian, Interview)

Here, emotional capital and emotion(al) labor were displayed and expressed in the conduct of care and responsibility (Al-deen & Windle, 2016), under the self-awareness of doubt and vulnerability, and with certain feelings and affects from within the teachers (Phan & Bao, 2019; Wetherell, 2015).

In addition, as the teachers acknowledged they did not speak Arabic and had not learnt it, they also admitted that it would be better for bilingual teachers to teach Saudi students with limited English. This acknowledgement is consistent with the dominant projection of native-English-speaking teachers as '*monolinguals*'. They admitted being aware of '*this shortcoming*' and saw it as their '*weak point*' and a '*disadvantage*' in comparison with Saudi teachers or Arab teachers who could also speak Arabic, as they revealed further in the interviews. Their acknowledgement of the important role of bilingual teachers confirms the problem associated with the blanket recruitment of native speakers in many countries including Saudi Arabia (Akcan, 2016; Mahboob & Elyas, 2014). The teachers challenged the discourse that *native teachers are better* and challenged native-speakerism more broadly (Holliday, 2005). This awareness and sensibility can be seen as their emotional capital (Al-deen & Windle, 2016).

All in all, the teachers acknowledged their struggles and difficulties in their classroom teaching and in conducting peer assessment activities with students. Their emotional labor lies in their felt responsibility to help with their students' learning and is displayed in their helplessness because of the language barrier and other factors that we shall discuss in the subsequent sections. Ian, Shaun, John and Jonathan are *'qualified and experienced teachers'* with additional expertise in *'writing composition'* and *'test item writing'*. However, little of their capital was utilized and put to good use when their students could not benefit from their teaching and expertise. This reality led to frustration, disillusion and indifference, which the teachers attributed to the way *'the system operates'*. The findings here correspond with the teachers of English in Benesch's (2020) study and with many international teachers of English featured in the earlier chapters of this book, who also experienced professional unfulfillment because of undesirable institutional factors.

Emotion(al) Labor and the Ideology of Native-Speakerism

The participants also revealed hidden emotions and emotion(al) labor that they rarely expressed to anyone outside their closed circle. They admitted they were aware of the privilege and negative views attached to their White, male, native-speaker status (Appleby, 2013; Jenkins, 2019; Kubota & Lin, 2009; Stanley, 2013). Nonetheless, they reported being *'uncomfortable'* and *'undermined'* when this label was assumed to be their only identity. Moreover, the fixation on their privilege tended to *'overlook'* the fact that they were teachers with *'aspirations, feelings, emotions and problems'*. Accompanying *'the privilege'* had been *'struggles'* that they had *'no place to vent'* and *'no reasons to complain'* because of the attached privilege. This awareness and internalization made it *'awkward'* to even *'mention any problems'* they might have. This very emotional labor connects with Al-deen and Windle's (2016) discussion of the Muslim Iraqi immigrant mothers' involvement in their children's education in Australia in that their emotional labor is shaped by their acknowledged, unacknowledged, rejected, denied and undervalued emotional, social and cultural capital.

The teachers felt *'uncomfortable'* about being *'privileged'* as White native teachers of English yet *'inadequate'* and *'monolingual'* at the same time. They also felt burdened as *'native teachers of English'* when others thought they had *'the miracle and abilities to improve students' English regardless'*. This burden escalated when they felt they had *'failed to deliver because their students did not learn as much as they wanted them to'* (John). Negative teaching evaluations and lack of engagement and interest from their students also lowered their self-esteem and challenged their native-speaker status. They had to endure this emotion(al) labor in silence and found it *'difficult to share with anyone'*. They felt it was *'unfair'* that they did not create the situation, but were brought into the existing system and pushed to run alone without being asked for *'feedback, inputs or reflections'*. They felt they were *'left alone'* and wondered if this was because they were '*native teachers of English*', and that would somehow '*make others nervous and avoid them*'. Participating in this study gave them the opportunity to speak out loud what they had been enduring and experiencing, as they reported. Their emotions and emotion(al) labor had been unnoticed and unacknowledged by students, Saudi and Arab teachers and their own institution for all those years teaching in the program.

Putting the teachers' emotions in perspective and in their specific circumstances enables us to question the dominant discourse on White/Western native teachers of English which largely depicts them as being teachers who are unqualified, inexperienced and lacking knowledge who can get away with their native-speaker status (Bailey & Evison, 2020; Mahboob & Golden, 2013; Stanley, 2013). Here comes Benesch's (2019, 2020) reminder to engage emotion labor alongside critical examination of the associated prejudice, power and discourse. The teachers' complex multilayered emotions resulted from many factors, among which are established discourses surrounding the cultural politics of English and English language teaching and debates on native–non-native teachers of English (Fang & Widodo, 2019; Holliday, 2005; Pennycook, 1994, 1998/2017; Stewart, 2020; Wolff & De Costa, 2017). What we highlight more in this article/chapter are the contradictory connotations underlying privilege and how privilege is consumed, resisted and internalized alongside prejudice, discourse, power dynamics and sociopolitical factors.

At one level, these teachers' emotions and emotion(al) labor remind us of Kelley's complex account as a White male American scholar of Asian studies, in which he refers to a shared sentiment among area studies scholars that 'it was politically wiser … for a white male to predict his gradual extinction from the field and to declare that Asian Studies would soon be the domain of "heritage students," the children of immigrants' (Kelley, 2020: 283). Kelley's observation echoes much existing scholarship in TESOL, in which it is rare to find studies that put White native speakers at the center of inquiries without also attributing negative attributes to them and reminding them that they are on the wrong side. Indeed, Rivers (2017: 74) forcefully argues that 'the ideological conceptualization of native-speakerism allows only those identifying as "non-native speakers" access to the desirable status of victim and its accompanying discourse of moral righteousness'. Building on his long-established scholarship on native speakers of English, Rivers provocatively maintains that the field of TESOL has betrayed native-speaker teaching professionals. Rivers, hence, argues that this is a matter of injustice.

That the teacher participants felt injustice for predominantly being seen as White/Western native speakers of English shows how complex emotions and emotion(al) labor could easily be overlooked and simultaneously consumed by discourses and representation (Ahmed, 2004), particularly those about so-called privileged individuals/groups/populations

(Phan, 2014, 2017). This tendency is in and of itself a matter of injustice stemming from undermined emotion(al) labor, which corresponds to and expands Benesch's (2020) theorization of emotion labor as a discourse of injustice/unfairness.

At another level, the participants' emotions and their nuanced consumption of and resentment about this very discourse of privilege bring to the fore the entanglements of multiple related discourses underlying White, male, native-speakerism, and the ongoing debates between the pros and cons of native and non-native teachers of English in the sphere of education, and TESOL more specifically. These teachers' affective practice (Wetherell, 2015) sits well with their social interpersonal voices (Phan & Bao, 2019), as they are internalized, consumed, displayed, performed and rationalized.

Emotion(al) Labor in Response to Social, Religious and Cultural Difference

Islam is the only religion allowed in Saudi Arabia, and the country is generally known for its conservative tribal culture, although it is gradually opening up. International teachers must respect the fact that Saudi learners uphold the Islamic faith, values and customs (Alrahaili, 2018; Khafaji, 2004; Ministry of Education, 1970). The average Saudi EFL learner with an academic background and learning style particular to Saudi cultural, religious and educational settings often finds it difficult to respond to the varied teaching styles and pedagogies of language teachers coming from Western and other non-Arab countries (Bataineh & Reshidi, 2017; Richardson, 2004). In reality, many Saudi learners might find foreign traditions contradictory to the teachings of Islam (Ozog, 1989). The situation can become worse when employers and recruitment agencies in Saudi Arabia are inclined to hire TESOL professionals from English-speaking Western countries, believing that their native proficiency has a direct impact on the EFL learners' motivation and learning progress (Akcan, 2016; Mahboob & Elyas, 2014). This belief, while benefiting native-English-speaking teachers, also creates pressures on their part as well as on other teachers including Saudi teachers and students. This emotion(al) labor tends to be overlooked in the existing literature that places non-native English-speaking teachers at the center of inquiry and projects them as those who are at the receiving end of native-speakerism (Alghofaili & Elyas, 2017; Braine, 2010; Canagarajah, 1999; Phillipson, 1992; Song & Park, 2019). As we show below, the teacher participants in our study – Westerners, native speakers of English, experienced and qualified – also undergo their own emotion(al) labor which is often unacknowledged by those around them and by scholarly work.

The participants revealed that they were conscious of their status as Christian, non-Muslim and Western teachers. Likewise, they reported being aware of explicit and implicit expectations to respect local social, cultural and religious norms and traditions. Hence, they carefully chose their content materials for the writing tasks and the examples they quoted in their lessons to avoid any unnecessary problems. The teachers also revealed that they had been told by other colleagues that '*very religious Saudi students would complain to the administration*' if they considered any aspects of the teaching '*confrontational or insensible to their religious and cultural beliefs*'. When such incidents happen, '*teaching and learning could be affected in unpleasant ways*', confirmed Abdullah.

More and more Saudi higher education institutions tend to adopt a ready-made, custom-designed curriculum and ready-made materials for testing and assessment purposes developed by international publishers for use in their English language programs. Such a curriculum often presents a limited coverage of and relevance to the dominant Saudi cultural and educational context (Moskovsky & Picard, 2018; Shah & Elyas, 2019). In language classrooms, culturally sensitive topics, if not handled well, may lead to negative teaching and learning experiences (Hyland, 2003; Shukri, 2014). For example, Shukri (2014) discusses this issue in her review of the difficulties experienced by Saudi EFL learners in speaking about topics deemed appropriate in other cultural and social contexts such as those in Western societies. These difficulties stem from the religious and cultural affiliation of the Saudi learners. She argues that writing activities become even more difficult when students find writing topics alienating to their local cultural contexts. These topics include music, relationships, politics and sex, and they are considered culturally sensitive. Writing and discussion topics should not contradict the conservative Islamic teachings which are explicitly taught and practiced in educational institutions across Saudi Arabia. Therefore, international/transnational EFL teachers should be aware of the repercussions of discussing them in the classroom and should be cognizant of cultural prohibitions in order to avoid references that are inconsiderate of the officially endorsed values (El-Araby, 1983; Zhang, 2004). As observed by Abdullah and shown below, the participants were aware of the cultural difference and interacted appropriately with the students.

> I'm always aware of the fact that there are students who come from very religious backgrounds and they do not readily embrace Western cultures. There are students who love to talk about the West, they are quite open and liberal. However, I have to be careful as anything can go wrong and put me in trouble. This is a challenge, a cultural challenge no doubt, which affects the process of teaching, how I pick topics for writing essays and how I assess those writings. (Ian)

> It's never easy to teach in a place where students have a completely different culture to that of yours. I believe that students and teachers are both at a disadvantage. Understanding and appreciating each other's cultures can have a very positive impact on learning and teaching. (Jonathan)

The teachers' emotion(al) labor in recognizing social, cultural and religious difference and in making conscious efforts to avoid conflicts and misunderstanding is detected in the data above. It is also displayed in their understanding of their own limitations. Likewise, their emotion(al) labor is extended to their recognition of students' disadvantages when being taught by foreign teachers. At the same time, the data bring to the surface dichotomous emotional discourses underlying *local Saudi society* (very religious, conservative, closed) and *Western values* (open, liberal, appreciating diversity). This articulated difference carries the weight of deeply entrenched stereotypes and discourses surrounding the West and the rest in educational and transnational encounters (see Phan & Mohamad, 2020, for a detailed discussion). When teachers and students cannot engage each other in meaningful and in-depth conversations because of a language barrier, these discourses and stereotypes remain unchallenged.

The teachers also acknowledged that they felt uncomfortable and somewhat frustrated when they could not draw from their cultural knowledge and topics that they knew well so as to stimulate students' thinking and writing, largely because of the students' low language proficiency and their own reservations. Having to silence their core identity and familiar values so as to perform appropriately in their current workplace is an indicator of emotion(al) labor/discourse. Having to prove their ability to appreciate cultural difference and respond sensibly to students' cultural values is likewise another form of emotion(al) labor.

Reflecting on the constraints expressed by the teacher participants, Abdullah offers his own account, which illuminates the dilemma transnational teachers often experience.

> For me, teaching and assessing writing requires a decent knowledge about the local culture and students' interests. As a Western-trained Muslim teacher teaching in the US, I found it very challenging to discuss what I consider sensitive or taboo topics such as sexuality. I could not prevent it, and I could not discuss it because I had not thought I will ever discuss it with my students. How could I grade it and how could I improve a written argument on a topic I always avoided? My vision for my US students was different from the program vision and the students' vision. I found it difficult to compromise my own beliefs while in a more open culture like the US. My dilemma was the same as the Western transnational teachers in Saudi Arabia. The only difference, an essential one, is that they deal with a very conservative context and I dealt with a more open one. (Abdullah, Reflection 3)

Abdullah's reflection points to the importance of paying careful attention to the particularity of context, place and one's specific situation in studying transnational encounters, as argued in other studies (Karakas, 2020; Kelley, 2020; Nonaka, 2020; Phan & Mohamad, 2020; Phan *et al.*, 2020; Windle, 2020). Abdullah's dilemma did not get resolved, but not because he did not have any say or because he was discouraged by the US institution where he worked. Everything was open and free except Abdullah himself and the 'ideology as lived and felt' within him and his 'inter-individual consciousness' (Phan & Bao, 2019). Topics considered inappropriate to his religious beliefs were brought to him by his students whose assignments he had to grade and discuss. Yet, he found himself unable to engage given the resistance and unwillingness from within. On the other hand, the transnational teachers working at Mannar University in Saudi Arabia did not have any say in the curriculum and writing assessment policy and practice. They were expected to be respectful and observant of their students' religious and cultural values, while also having to refrain from drawing on their own 'Western' cultural repertoire as teaching resources. It seems that these teachers had to shoulder a tremendous emotional burden because of the situation they were in.

The emotion labor these teachers have endured partly resulted from the double-standard dominant discourse associated with White native teachers of English, whereby the desirability associated with their being White and native English speaking is coupled with the expectation that they should be good or even superior at teaching, as discussed earlier. Likewise, while the assumed desirability associated with Whiteness and English-speaking nativeness works to the institution's advantage in terms of marketization, appearance and internationalization, it does not do justice to the teachers and students, particularly when they are not part of the decision-making process (Phan, 2017). When this happens, only a fragment of their transnational emotional capital is utilized; how it is utilized is shaped by neoliberalism, the market and dominant discourses on the cultural politics of English language teaching.

Emotion(al) Labor and Top-Down Policy

As explained earlier, Mannar University requires that all English language teachers strictly follow a prescribed exam-driven curriculum and assessment procedure. The participants found this top-down policy and practice contradictory to their own pedagogical knowledge and their aspirations to help students learn. When teachers do not have any say and have to follow the set curriculum and assessment prescriptions, students do not learn and enjoy learning, as they collectively confirmed in the interviews with Abdullah.

> I must follow a pacing guide to teach the prescribed curriculum, even the page number. Of course, it comes from the top and we cannot have any objection to that. No enjoyment for me and for the students. (Shaun)

> Assessment of writing skills should reflect learners' improved performances which gives a sense of satisfaction to the students and teachers; however, I have never experienced any improvement or satisfaction. (Jonathan)

It's the top-down bureaucratic leadership structures and the top-down policy that creates issues. Since we cannot access the testing unit or those in decision-making positions, it's never easy to suggest improvements or changes. We pretend to teach, they pretend to learn. (Ian)

The participants reported that their teaching and assessment were confined to a pacing guide and restricted to fixed assessment rubrics provided from the top. They were not allowed to grade their students' exam papers but were required to give them feedback and consultation on their grades given by other teachers. They were critical of this teaching and assessment practice and unanimously found it destructive to language teaching and learning, particularly writing skills. With their professional training, prior teaching experience and knowledge of assessment, the teachers agreed that while writing assessment rubrics may assist with the development of writing skills if applied appropriately, they all opposed the way these rubrics were enforced at Mannar University. They described the writing assessment rubrics as being *'inconsistent'*, *'invalid'* and *'inappropriate'*, which makes writing, assessment and peer feedback practice *'a joke'*, *'mechanical'* and *'rather meaningless'*. Yet, the teachers are required to comply with the rules and are not supposed to express their disagreement or discontent, as Abdullah affirms from his insider knowledge working in Saudi Arabia.

The above situation has led to the teachers becoming the target of students' frustration and uncooperativeness when it comes to teaching and assessment. Such attitudes from students created low self-esteem and self-doubt among the teachers, making them feel *'unappreciated'* even *'more strongly'* in their own classrooms and at work when they *'were not supposed to express'* their frustration and discontent.

Take Ian's observed feedback session with students as an example. Ian admitted being frustrated with them for expressing their frustration through non-stop questions towards him whereas he was not the one grading their exam papers. He was also frustrated about their being unhappy about their grades and for not being able to understand his explanations of the *'ridiculous rubrics'*. He was frustrated with himself for not being able to answer their questions and to get his points across. The language barrier between him and his students, and the *'ridiculous'* assessment policy at Mannar made him suffer tremendously, as he revealed.

All through his interview with Abdullah, Jonathan was repeatedly sighing. He was frustrated with students memorizing their essays. He also seemed discouraged by what he perceived as 'the ridiculousness of essays and topics'.

> The feedback session was subdued, but the tension was still palpable in the room. Students seemed defeated about their grades given by another teacher and shrugged off poor performances. At the same time, Jonathan

did the best he could to present the rubric and explain it although he seemed aware that his efforts were not reaching the students. After repeatedly prompting the students to ask about their grades, his efforts seemed to dwindle with the growing futility of the exercise. (Observation notes)

As for John, he was also frustrated with the prescribed curriculum and assessments in Saudi Arabian institutions in general and at Mannar University in particular. He felt these were *'unfair to the teachers who were forced to use them'*. For Jonathan, *'the existing methods lack teachers' voice and input'*. He made it clear that *'no assessment instrument can be effective unless it has the input and deliberation from the classroom teachers'*. The participants also expressed that they were *'concerned'* about the students whose learning suffers from this whole problem, and whose *'writing seems very shallow and lacks depth'*. Shaun, for example, wondered if this was an indicator of how uncomfortable the students still were about their writing and assessment practice.

The teachers obviously felt a strong sense of injustice and unfairness against them and against their students. Their dissatisfaction, disillusionment and helplessness did not come from any lack of responsibility, care or concern. Instead, these came from their lack of power to negotiate and from the authority's uncritical submission to standardization and assessment prescriptions. The authority seemed *'far away minding its own business'* and teachers and students were left struggling, knowing there would not be anyone out there listening to them or wanting to fix the problem. Teachers and students were both powerless, although the mandatory feedback-giving practice gave a false impression of fairness and democratic participation. Benesch's (2020) conceptualization of emotion labor as *discourse of injustice* and *discourse of unfairness* speaks powerfully in the situation reported by the teachers that we have discussed thus far.

However, unlike the English language instructors in Benesch's (2020) study who expressed a sense of ambivalence (*discourse of inevitability*) when it came to standardized testing, the participants in our study were consistent with their criticisms and disapproval of it and of the rigid assessment rubrics they all had to follow. For them, these rubrics *'make little sense'*, *'have serious issues'* and *'are there to help students pass the writing tests and not to assess their writing ability'*. Basically, the rubrics serve as the safeguard of the university's top leadership instead of serving students' learning and teachers' teaching. The challenges international teachers face multiply when they hardly receive any support from the institution, particularly in ways that would allow them to have inputs in the curriculum and assessment practice in order to feel worthy of being a teacher and to help students learn knowledge and skills beyond testing. The emotion labor, echoing Benesch (2020), that these international TESOL teachers endure is in many ways unnoticed.

The social and cultural context of Mannar University seems inherently problematic and embeds injustice instead of promoting equality, communication and academic freedom – the values that have been advocated in education, applied linguistics and language education for decades (Benesch, 2020; Lynch, 2001; Shohamy, 1998). These values are what Ian, John, Jonathan and Shaun upheld and put into practice in their prior teaching back home. These values were also essential in the educational and professional training they had received, as they shared with Abdullah. Their desirable capital appeared to receive little appreciation and recognition in their current workplace; instead, their frustration and disillusion – often perceived as negative emotions – tended to dominate their experience at Mannar.

Being caught between the institution and students, these teachers are likely to receive criticism from both sides, whereby their *'monolingual'*, *'Western native-English-speaking'* and *'Christian'* identities could be blamed and negatively projected, as Abdullah observed. This problem, as we argue, takes away the teacher's agency while making the institution free from responsibility and accountability; hence change is not seen as necessary. This form of emotion(al) labor is evident in the teachers' resistance, dissatisfaction, unhappiness and disillusion, all of which speak strongly to Benesch's (2020) advocacy for recognizing teachers' emotion and emotion labor as being discursive and involving power, exclusion and injustice issues.

The teacher participants' frustration about and dissatisfaction with the situation resulted from their strong sense of care, responsibility and desire to make change through teaching, assessment and policy intervention. Their emotional capital, nevertheless, had hardly been recognized by their students and the institutions, and even by Saudi teachers like Abdullah. Collecting the data for this study has challenged his own prejudice and stereotypes about native teachers of English. Abdullah admitted that he had been biased by the abundant literature condemning this group of teachers and by the general jealousy among local teachers and TESOL critics for the high salaries their government and institutions pay native teachers. Indeed, deeply rooted and widely circulated discourses such as the ones Abdullah refers to can mask our understanding of 'the powerful' and prevent us from revisiting our own (pre)assumptions of certain groups in society, therefore perpetuating injustice (Rivers, 2017). Making explicit and critically examining these discourses help uncover layers of nuances and biases towards native teachers of English that have long been ignored. The relatability of discourse, prejudice, bias and reflection (Phan & Bao, 2019; Wetherell, 2015) offers useful analytical lenses, as we show in this study.

Abdullah's reflection presented below in response to the above findings offers insights into how teachers could adapt to difference, but shows that the extent to which such adaptation could succeed and is enabled depends hugely on the specific social, cultural, educational and ideological outlook of the context and those involved. Abdullah acknowledged that while he was hopeful of seeing many changes taking place in Saudi higher education, he felt helpless about the system's obsession with exam-driven policy and practice. He also showed much sympathy with the teacher participants, feeling that they all were on the same wavelength.

> While teaching in the US, I also had to abide by prescribed writing assessment tools in the US, but those assessment tools were not exam driven like the ones in Saudi Arabia. I came to understand that prescribed assessment tools are not always bad if they are assigned properly. I understand Western transnational teachers' frustration in dealing with only exams, rigid rubrics, and not having a voice in writing assessment design. As a Saudi writing assessment educator who was trained in the West, I too have no power to change the exam-driven context. Therefore, this reality should be made upfront to all new international teachers brought here. These teachers need a thorough induction into the Saudi context. These teachers may bring with them a wealth of knowledge and experience, but they have no place to show [that]. I'm exhausted but the long-lasting problem is worth fighting against. (Abdullah, Reflection)

Abdullah demonstrated his emotion capital and emotion(al) labor through relativizing institutional demands and self-positioning as an insider in relation to institutional constraints. At the same time, his acknowledgement of the problem, his empathy with the expatriate teachers and his strategic investment in particular forms of pedagogical labor are all manifestations of different kinds of emotion(al) labor. In the midst of all of this, the reality that Abdullah and other teachers face is their lack of power to negotiate despite their expressed strong agency to do so. The struggle to come to terms with accepting their absence of power to negotiate is another emotion discourse that teachers are subjected to.

In another reflection presented below on his teaching in the US, Abdullah also showed his emotion(al) labor in recognizing differences in expectations between students and teachers as a potential source of conflict. His painful adaptation to the teaching situation at his Saudi university is another display of emotion(al) labor.

> My American students wanted to learn how to develop their critical thinking through their writing as opposed to focusing simply on the structure of a paragraph or how to develop an acceptable essay, and I found it difficult to offer that on each writing assignment because I tended to focus too long on assessing low order skills in writing. They wanted feedback on their ideas and how to further develop their argument. Now that I have returned to Saudi Arabia to teach EFL students, I could relate to the dilemma and experiences shared by Shaun, Ian, John and Jonathan. Surely, I know my home context, but my teaching and assessing writing had changed. I struggled with neglecting all the knowledge and experience of teaching and assessing writing in the US that I had gained; and now I have had to, once again, become accustomed to assessing basic subskills of writing. So even with much teaching experience,

transnational teachers never find it easy to attend to students' basic language needs, assess their writing using fixed rubrics and have no say in how assessment is done, and at the same time compromise their teaching beliefs. (Abdullah, Reflection)

Further Thoughts and Reflections

As acknowledged by Bigelow (2019: 515), the past few years have seen 'the exciting and ever-present realm of emotion (or affect) in the research and practice of language teaching and learning'. Bigelow has also observed that:

> the examination and understanding of teachers' emotions has expanded considerably through layered, critical, and poststructural approaches to unpacking emotions which are carefully situated and recognize the many ways power can regulate emotion in different contexts. (Bigelow, 2019: 515)

In this article/chapter, we document in particular how transnationally trained TESOL teachers' emotions and emotion(al) labor could multiply through a mixture of all-at-once undesirable factors: lack of interest and negative attitudes towards foreign language writing among EFL students with weak language skills and basics of grammar; the difficulties faced by expatriate teachers employed to teach and assess writing performance by this group of learners (Arnold, 2018; Doushaq, 1986; Ezza, 2017; Ghalib & Al-Hattami, 2015; Hyland, 2003; Shukri, 2014); social and cultural difference; and the requirement to strictly follow the institution's prescribed curriculum and assessment policy and practice without any opportunities for teachers to give feedback and raise concerns. The existing literature, however, in an admirable attempt to empower non-native teachers of English and to counter native-speakerism and its underlying hegemonic discourses, has tended to overlook the varying affects experienced and practiced by these native teachers. It has also unintentionally perpetuated a discourse that native teachers of English are negligent of students' needs and unaware of cultural difference. At least the many native teachers of English in Phan (2014, 2017) and Phan and Barnawi (this volume) and in this current study do not fall into that category. Having tried to articulate difficult emotions caused by this strong prejudice against them, these teachers show us the importance of approaching emotion(al) labor as discourse and as a practice of intertwined affects (Ahmed, 2004; Benesch, 2019, 2020; Wetherell, 2015). Importantly, this approach enables researchers to understand how seemingly privileged individuals and groups display their own troubled emotions which are conditioned by their assumed powerful yet prejudiced status. In this process, we also recognize their unaddressed emotional capital (Al-deen & Windle, 2016) and their *ideology as lived and felt* (Phan & Bao, 2019).

The study discussed in this chapter signifies the importance for international teachers to learn Arabic, understand local Saudi culture and show respect for Islamic values, but this could also present a problem when non-Muslim international teachers feel they have to distance themselves from their own knowledge and cultural repertoire in teaching. If Saudi universities aim to continue to recruit TESOL professionals from outside the Saudi context, creating a mutually respectful and inclusive platform is important to prepare these transnational teachers for their fulfilling teaching which could enable more effective learning among Saudi EFL learners. Their transnational experiences and knowledge should be recognized as resources, not threats to local values and religion, particularly when these teachers showcase their cultural sensibilities and willingness to adapt. Put differently, this very emotion(al) labor and emotional capital ought to be appreciated.

The findings also indicate that these Western transnational teachers have encountered power shifts at several levels. When they are in the EFL context to teach English as native speakers, they become aware of their inability to communicate with and offer additional support to their Arabic-speaking students, whose weak linguistic knowledge adds another layer of difficulty to their teaching and writing assessment activities. Moreover, these teachers find the rubrics and assessment tools imposed by university authorities ineffective due to their lack of consistency and validity. This bureaucratic structure makes the transnational teachers aware of their own pedagogical restrictions in implementing any assessment tools they find effective. Experiencing such a power shift while in an unfamiliar cultural and social setting can affect these teachers' self-esteem and professional confidence – the kind of emotion labor that ought to result in institutional change and support. Therefore, this study recommends that top management involve teachers in the (re)development of the curriculum, including designing assessment activities and rubrics that would help them to grade the scripts in an objective manner as well as to help students see their learning progress. This process would also help build a community of transnational professionals who can rely on one another for support and ideas, which would benefit the institution as a whole. This is the activism transformation that Benesch (2020) calls for in studying and mobilizing teachers' emotion labor.

We would like to end the chapter/article with another reflection from Abdullah to show his moral support for the teacher participants and to show his critical engagement with his and the participants' emotion(al) labor, which, as he revealed, is 'W*orse, when you have to cope with it in isolation*'.

> Both cross-cultural similarities and key differences existed between the four transnational teachers in the Saudi context and my experience as a transnational teacher in the US. All of us had to cope with a prescribed curriculum and unfamiliar assessment tools. Even more salient was the

cultural contexts we found ourselves in. While I spent hours educating myself on pop culture in [the US] – a more open society, the teachers in the Saudi context adapted to a conservative, religious society. Each of us took it upon ourselves to adjust to unfamiliar cultural and societal circumstances while trying hard not to compromise our core values and beliefs. The respective education systems reflected this as well. On the surface Saudi students tend to be more submissive and typically accept grades without objection, but many American students challenge their teachers. Indeed, for the American students, revisions on their papers became a negotiation. However, while the transnational teachers in Saudi Arabia could relate to and count on one another if they wished for professional and emotional support, I did not have a transnational teachers' community to share my struggles with and to learn from. I was on my own in my teaching journey because I had issues that were dissimilar from my fellow composition teachers. I always wanted to find that sense of belonging because I wanted to prove to everyone that I was up to the job that I was assigned to do. This critical ethnographic study demonstrates a similar desire among the transnational EFL teachers at Mannar University. (Abdullah, Reflection)

We have treated our research participants' emotions and emotion(al) labor with care, complexity and ethical considerations. Abdullah's own emotion and emotion(al) labor play an important role in how he relates to the experiences of the teacher participants. We reiterate that the incorporation of Abdullah's reflections in the article/chapter proves how important and necessary research studies of this nature are in initiating and inspiring difficult dialogues with the self and conversations among researchers for support and for solidarity beyond constructed boundaries of race, religion, language, ethnicity and nationality. Through engaging with these dialogues and conversations, often-hidden nuances of emotion(al) labor in transnational mobilities could be revealed and engaged with, and hence could push scholarly discussion forward.

Notes

(1) King Abdulaziz University, Saudi Arabia.
(2) See https://journals.sagepub.com/doi/full/10.1177/1745499920946203

12 International TESOL Teachers Working in the Saudi 'Trust House': (Re)conceptualization of Key Constructs

Hear Us Out: Confessions and Difficult Questions We Wanna Raise

Up to this point, we hope we have been able to unpack many nuances behind the scenes as well as those that are at the core of Saudi TESOL. Likewise, we have discussed and offered multi-sided insights into the ways in which international English language teachers from different and mixed backgrounds working alongside one another in Saudi Arabia position themselves, negotiate, interact, adjust, make sense of their classroom and work dynamics, and validate their senses of selves and pedagogies in their day-to-day observations of their institutions and interactions at work. We have also shown how cultural, political, racial and religious issues, in many ways, affect the mobility, identity and professional trajectories of international TESOL teachers in general and in the context of Saudi HE institutions in particular. These issues can influence employers' perceptions and decisions regarding recruitment and contract renewals, to name a few.

In writing this book, we are humbled by the vast literature generated in TESOL, language education and applied linguistics cited throughout the book, such as the highly developed body of work on the cultural politics of English and ELT, the well-rounded scholarship along the lines of native and non-native speakers/teachers/learners/users, the extensive scholarship on English language teacher identity and positioning, and the abundant literature on Englishes, English as an international language, English as a lingua franca, English as a world/global language, English as an additional language and English as a language for intercultural communication. In the same vein, we are intrigued by the expanding volume of work on multilingualism and translanguaging, the well-developed body of work on second language acquisition, language teacher education, and teaching pedagogy and curriculum.

At the same time, we cannot deny the fact that there continues to be a strong desire among individuals and institutions to claim *authenticity* of some kind, as embedded in the data we have collected for this book. This desire is largely wrapped around contested constructs of race, ethnicity, language, nationality, religion, expertise, experience and professionalism. We see this phenomenon, again, as a manifestation of *double standard*, something we have briefly touched upon in an earlier chapter. One of us (Phan, 2016, 2017) has discussed and theorized this phenomenon in the larger context of TESOL, applied linguistics, education and mobility studies. Drawing on analogies between English and yoga, Phan (2016), for example, argues that the obsession with authenticity, nativeness and originality associated with English and with speakers of English is the same as the obsession expressed towards yoga and yoga instructors from India. We highlight Phan's (2016) detailed argument below:

> First, both English and yoga are internationally recognized as being desirable objects wanted by international citizens and are often linked to many positive attributes that could enhance one's lifestyle in many ways. Both, at the same time, are seen by many as a commodity that is often promoted as a necessity, an accessory, and a trend participated in by all age groups. Next, both English and yoga are multiple and controversial in their forms, ideologies, and teaching approaches. Then, as a matter of fact, whenever possible one tends to adhere both the English language and yoga to a 'native', 'original', and 'authentic' place, which one perceives as giving birth to a defined 'native', 'original' and 'authentic' population with an automatic and built-in ability to teach English and yoga respectively. As a result, with the English language, we have native English speakers, and with yoga, we have Indian yoga instructors, both of whom are being seen as the expert, the authority, and the guru. What's more, the reputation and trustworthiness attached to teachers of English with a qualification from a native-English-speaking country is as high as that attached to yoga instructors with some training and validation offered by Indian gurus and/or by yoga schools in India. Of course, all these assumptions have been challenged and their underlying controversies have been examined, at least in relation to English. Nevertheless, native teachers of English and Indian yoga instructors continue to be sought after. The sentiment towards English and native speakers of English is similar to that towards yoga and yoga instructors from India. Indeed, both yoga and English are deeply concerned with questions of authenticity, reliability, qualification, credentials, and identity. (Phan, 2016: 350)

Every actor is complicit in this double standard practice, and in perpetuating and (re)producing the obsession with authenticity, despite substantial scholarship to deconstruct this powerful notion. What implications does this have for our scholarly work and our fields? Are we hitting a wall and talking in circles? Are we stuck on keeping expanding aspirational scholarship, hoping and pretending that TESOL professionals are bringing the latest ideas and theories in the fields to their classrooms? Why is it that, after decades of producing critical theories and pedagogies and engaging with critical applied linguistics and language teacher preparations, native-speakerism continues to dominate practices on the ground? And why is multilingualism often not enacted in many classrooms, either? Is it time to revisit our critiquing mode and question the purposes and outcomes of the endless and energetic criticisms against native speakers? And what about race and religion? How are they played out within groups and between groups beyond the mere dichotomy of native and non-native teachers of English?

Indeed, many Saudi institutions are hugely diverse, with teachers coming from all over the world, and *'we all hold different views about race, and one's experience with racism is not necessarily the same as that of others. Many factors come with it too'*, as a teacher said. He then added, *'we're from everywhere, you name it, from the Philippines, India, Pakistan, Nepal, Malaysia, Jamaica, Morocco, Nigeria, South Africa, America, Canada, Australia, New Zealand, Britain, many European countries, Sudan, Libya, Egypt, Oman, Iraq, etc., just everywhere. And we disagree on many things'*.

There are in-group problems, then problems between groups, then problems between teaching staff and the administrators, and problems between sub-groups, etc. In all these group dynamics, one can find individuals like **Montreal** and those identifying with him, individuals like **Dave** and those who share his worldview and life experience, and individuals like **Tyrone** and **Jerome** who benefit from being American and native speakers of English while also feeling that they are discriminated against and marginalized by their Blackness (see Chapters 9 and 10). One can also find individuals like Sulaiman Jenkins who have not let racism and discrimination get in their way. Jenkins in particular has accomplished much during his time in Saudi Arabia. Growing up in Brooklyn, New York, his life experience is rich as well as central to many racial debates in America. His recent book on hip-hop entitled *Life is Raw: The Story of a Reformed Outlaw (Hip-Hop, Culture, and Education)*, published in November 2020, 'looks into the life of Mutah Beale, formerly known as Napoleon of the legendary Outlawz rap group who was affiliated with the late Tupac Shakur' (Amazon.com).[1] This book is one of several projects via which Jenkins 'hopes to produce significant pieces of writing that help America examine issues that are sensitive yet central to his lived experiences growing up in the inner city: namely, race relations, police brutality, drugs and gang violence, incarceration and the prison system, and employment discrimination'.[2]

Jenkins is becoming known among scholars in applied linguistics, especially those writing on race and identity and on native-speakerism matters (see, for example, an interview between Robert Lowe and Jenkins on race and speakerhood[3] released on 11 July 2020). He is an emerging voice on raciolinguistics and critical debates centered on African American TESOL teachers.

Then, the ways in which another Black teacher perceived the marginalization and discrimination he experienced seem to have little to do with his skin color. We are referring to **Othello** (Chapter 10). It is important to note that **Othello** did not anywhere hint that being Black was the problem for him. The racial White-Black and/or Black versus Others divide(s) was/were not present in his experience and reflection. White teachers and the West were not the target of his critique. Put differently, these seemingly obvious entities did not play any role in his suffering. Rather, he condemned the submission to American English and the efforts to reproduce the superiority of American English among other non-native, non-Western teachers of English, whom he labeled as *'extra Mutawa'*, whether by means of them imitating an American accent or by means of them condemning **Othello**'s Jamaican English. This very observation troubled **Othello** and also made him more confused about those colleagues who in theory should value their own ways of speaking English and respect different varieties of English around the world in general and in the diverse workplace in particular.

Relatedly, the construct of marginalization in the context of international TESOL teachers working across Saudi HE institutions such as the cases of the native teachers discussed in Chapters 9, 10 and 11, in light of Kumashiro (2000: 26–27), can also be understood as 'a social dynamic in which certain ways of being in this world, including certain ways of identifying or being identified, are normalized or privileged while other ways are disadvantaged or marginalized'. Nonetheless, we argue that marginalization is not a static state, as the accounts from these teachers show. Neither does it have a fixed meaning. Rather, what is perceived and experienced as marginalization is very much context driven, fluid and dependent as much on dominant discourses as on specific power relations at play at a specific time, space and place.

Although those feeling marginalized may often refer to polarities (i.e. Black versus White, Muslim versus non-Muslim, non-native versus native, etc.) to describe, portray and explain the experience and the dynamic around it, our examination of the teachers' complex accounts shows that the way marginalization materializes does not necessarily fixate on these polarities, but often crosses seemingly clearly defined constructs of race, ethnicity, language, religion, nationality, and the domain of marginalization itself. And importantly, as we have shown, marginalization does not spare White native-English-speaking teachers, either. The emotion labor they carry and struggle to overcome and navigate is most of the time overlooked, particularly when their perceived native-speaker privilege tends to be viewed and ridiculed one-sidedly as their by-default privilege with all its accompanying benefits and superior treatments. *White (male) native speakers of English: who cares?* – this position is dangerous, flawed and unproductive, as we argue and have shown in greater depth in Chapters 11 and 12 in particular.

Moving forward, we would also like to offer our theorizations of other important phenomena arising from the research projects featured in the book. Let us continue below.

Moving Forward

Now we would like to offer more elaborations on two key implications resulting from all the findings and arguments put forth thus far: *(i) limits of negotiability and (ii) competing discourses associated with trust in Saudi ELT and TESOL.*

We argue that these implications need to be unpacked, acknowledged and (re)theorized in order to develop more balanced understandings of the field in general and of international TESOL teacher transnational mobility in particular. The importance of engaging complexly with these two phenomena in any given social and educational context ought to be made explicit and enacted upon with depth and nuance.

Limits of Negotiability

Negotiation, as a social construct, in the field of TESOL/applied linguistics has been widely unpacked and discussed by scholars such as Canagarajah (1999), Farr (2015), Duff and Uchida (1997) and Johnston (2003). Recently, in their work on language and education in Europe, Ennser-Kananen and Saarinen (2021) note that it is imperative to understand the construct of 'negotiability' and its 'limits' in a given social and educational setting. Specifically, they argue that negotiation 'as a privilege [is] a politically charged, [and] socio-materially shaped concept'. Also, importantly, in order to critically conceptualize the construct of negotiability, we have to be aware of key questions: 'Who gets to negotiate? What? How? Under which circumstances? Why (not)?' (Ennser-Kananen & Saarinen, 2021: n.p.).

In this book, we make a modest attempt to theorize the limits of negotiability in relation to international TESOL teachers' mobility, with the intention of offering new perspectives to the construct. Throughout the book, we have showed that hundreds of international TESOL teachers with different linguistic, racial, religious, ideological and cultural backgrounds have worked across Saudi HE institutions. Saudi students, in the same vein, join their classrooms with certain expectations, cultural practices, norms, needs and values. At the same time, employers, local HE institutions and recruitment agencies across Saudi Arabia have their own varied systems of values and beliefs, interests and needs.

But before we continue to theorize the limits of negotiability, let us remind ourselves and the reader that international TESOL teachers' relocations to Saudi Arabia are guided by many factors, and the conditions under which negotiations take place also vary hugely. For instance, the majority of the teacher participants have confirmed many favorable conditions granted to them in this country, including *'generous monetary benefits'*, *'a holy land for religious pursuit'*, *'good remuneration and no income taxes'*, *'favorable working conditions'*, *'better payment'*, *'political stability and safety'*, *'a good place to raise family'* and *'an investment for the entire family'*. Some teachers have also considered Saudi Arabia to be a promising place to work, since it allows them to *'practice their profession'* and offers them *'new experiences and opportunities'*. Nonetheless, international TESOL teachers in general hold different positions on the idea that Saudi Arabia is the land of promise.

Specifically, in our findings, there were teachers who did not see a promising future in the KSA, owing to the *'lack of academic freedom'*, *'poor education quality'*, *'lack of professional development'*, *'lazy students and unmotivated Saudi teachers'*, *'excessive work politics'*, *'marginalization'*, *'discrimination'*, *'having little say in curriculum and assessment'*, and the like. One such participant, called **Daniel**, stated frankly: 'No, I am here to save up money and then I will leave. I don't want to take on the local work ethic.' We present more accounts from other teachers below:

> *I do not think I have a very bright future in Saudi Arabia. I am not willing to fall in line with the hierarchal management structure that is satisfied with delivering mediocre learning results year after year. I know what is possible with the caliber of students that XXXX attracts. I would not be able to look myself in the mirror in the morning if I did not do my very best with all my ability and knowledge to engage and educate my students to the best of my ability. I have a very difficult time following management instructions that I know will not lead to the optimum learning outcome for my students, and since a collaborative academic teaching environment does not presently exist at XXXX, I am unable to synchronize my teaching efforts with other like-minded teachers to improve the level of excellence at my university. I have a great amount of energy, will and motivation to be an agent of change, but the system punishes people who do not follow the rules exactly.* (**Jonson**)

> *In the present situation I don't see myself to be professionally or scholarly developing, so my future in the KSA seems not to be promising.* (**Salman**)

> *I don't see my future here. There is no clear rule or practice for granting nationality or even offering promotion in the career. Lack of educational facilities for expat children also reminds me that I have no future here.* (**Aziz**)

Being realistic, there are certain issues which don't allow us to think of making a prolific career here, especially family issues back in our homeland and children's high school education etc. (**Kurshaid**)

I am just a guest invited to help in the development of education of the country, to train their youngsters and bring them to higher achievement. It is not my place, as a guest, to demand anything now or in the future. (**Zar**)

No. I don't see any future as an English teacher in the KSA for expatriates. There is no real professional development here for them. They are not treated well in the everyday business. Fortunately, I feel I am lucky to have got some special treatment from the management. So it has not been too bad for me. (**Suhail**)

The above notes indicate that conditions of local realities play major roles in shaping international TESOL teachers' decisions and views, and the extent to which they can negotiate and make life and work decisions accordingly, as well as imagine their futures. Conditions of local realities often have a larger impact than factors in the wider context on these teachers' capacities to negotiate and to cultivate a sense of self and a professional trajectory for themselves. In actuality, many of these teachers have gone through endless struggles, uncertainties, pains and emotional labor, as we have shown in several chapters.

In a way, Saudi institutions can be simply conceptualized as 'rules and norms of behavior in use' (Banerjee & Bojsen, 2013: 20). These rules, norms and material conditions (be they formal or informal, explicit or implicit) could (positively or negatively or both) influence the interplay among actors and between actors (students, administrators, program directors, other academic leaders, and teachers) and institutions. Consequently, actors often compete, struggle and constantly negotiate and adjust in order to realize the benefits of particular institutions in relation to their own interests. The very practice of negotiation in this context can be interpreted through what Ribot and Peluso (2003) call 'access mechanisms' and 'access control'. In theory, international TESOL teachers working across Saudi HE institutions have access to local knowledge, value systems, languages, cultures and customs, and other institutional practices. They also have relational access (e.g. access to peers from their own countries) as well as access to international peers (e.g. Canadian, Indian, Pakistani, Jamaican, Sudanese and Jordanian working together). While 'access mechanisms' and 'access control' are socially, politically, religiously, culturally, linguistically and economically imbued, international TESOL teachers, in principle, have multiple options by which they could control, mediate, exploit, manipulate, block, limit and grant access for, to, and of others.

The construct of limits (control) is central to the conceptualization of the processes of negotiations and of the multilayered on-the-ground interactions among international TESOL teachers, between them and their Saudi students and institutions, and between them and the Saudi society more broadly. That is, 'if some actors are capable of controlling others they are also in a key position to negotiate and so are the institutions and mechanisms which enable them to be in control' (Banerjee & Bojsen, 2013: 21). Simply put, power relations, academic positions, ethnicity, nationality, race, religious affiliations and other forms of privilege play major roles in the processes of negotiation. Likewise, they play key roles in limiting such negotiations. Chapters 8, 9, 10 and 11 in particular offer more insights into the limits of negotiation with regard to institutional constraints, on-the-ground classroom realities, and racial, linguistic and religious matters.

Teachers' negotiations of their professional identity, wellbeing and emotion labor, in many ways, are largely affected by their workplace dynamic, their working conditions, and their relationships with the management, peers and students (Alshakhi & Phan, 2020; Benesch, 2019, 2020). At the same time, factors including race, language, religion and professional belief play crucial roles in teacher experience and how teachers view themselves and others. Language education, TESOL and applied linguistics are particularly contested sites in this regard, whereby teacher empowerment and multilingualism take place alongside racism, discrimination, marginalization, linguistic inequality and native-speakerism (De Costa, 2020; Jenkins, 2019; Kubota, 2018, 2020; Motha, 2014; O'Regan, 2021), whether at a particular location or on the move.

In the broader context of mobility, academic mobility and its associated negotiation prospect, all in all, embed, generate and respond to unexpected arrays of complexities and (un)desirable encounters, as we have consistently showed over two decades of scholarship on academic mobility and the mobility of knowledge, ideas and pedagogies across contexts and settings (Alshakhi & Phan, 2020; Barnawi & Phan, 2014; Chowdhury & Phan, 2014; Liu & Phan, 2021; Phan, 2001, 2008, 2014, 2017; Phan & Barnawi, 2015; Phan & Mohamad, 2020; Phan & Phung, 2020; Phan *et al.*, 2020). The mobility of TESOL professionals and their capacities to negotiate professionally on the move always entail power relations, discourses and prejudices that unfold in diverse ways, as is evident in the findings discussed throughout this book, and in existing scholarship (Barnawi & Ahmed, 2021; De Costa *et al.*, 2020; Nonaka, 2018; O'Regan, 2021; Park, 2018; Windle, 2020). All of these combined show us that engaging with possibilities is as important as engaging with the limits of negotiability.

Unpacking and Interrogating Trust

In writing this book, we have observed that trust, as an ongoing process, is a sociomaterially shaped as well as a culturally, politically, ideologically and institutionally charged construct. We have also noted two competing phenomena related to 'trust' in the field of TESOL: *(i) the seemingly unconditional trust in McTeachers with McQualifications in the Saudi HE market, and (ii) the conditional mentality of 'local-trusting-local' across Saudi HE institutions.* The construct of trust is seen in terms of self-worth, linguistic capability, credentials, individual qualifications and awarding bodies, academic leadership, and marketability status concerning non-native English-speaking teachers (NNESTs). In the following paragraphs we elaborate on these two seemingly contradictory phenomena.

The seemingly unconditional trust in *McTeachers with McQualifications* in the Saudi HE market

As revealed in the data, all native speakers of English in our studies are highly educated, and hold BA, MA and even PhD degrees. While some teachers hold relevant degrees in English Language Teaching and Learning (i.e. TESOL, TEFL, Applied Linguistics or other associated subjects) and enjoy years of experience teaching English in other countries, a high percentage of native-speaker teachers teaching English in Saudi HE institutions do not hold relevant degrees. Instead, they hold such degrees as Bachelor's of Science in Sociology and Education, BA in Music, BA in Political Science, Bachelor's of Science in Business Administration & Public Accounting, BA in Communication and Social Science, Law LLb (hons) and Criminology, and PhD in Educational Administration. These teachers have been appointed by their respective institutions across Saudi Arabia on the basis that they are native speakers of English and on the basis of their short TESOL teacher training courses (often several weeks long), such as ELT teacher training courses, summer TESOL training, SIT TESOL Certificates, CELTA (Certificate in Teaching English to Speakers of Other Languages), DELTA (Diploma in Teaching English to Speakers of Other Languages) and Cert-TESOL courses. These training courses are often obtained through online training (worth US$250), summer training (similar to a boot camp) and/or even by blended learning offered by leading mainstream institutions such as the University of Cambridge, Trinity College London and the University of Arizona, to name a few. Completing short TESOL teacher training courses like CELTA, DELTA and other TESOL certificates offered by leading mainstream institutions such as the above-mentioned ones continues to be the most effective route to join the English language teaching industry worldwide (Barnawi, 2016; Hobbs, 2013; Walker, 2001). Today, there are more than 100 Trinity-validated TESOL training providers globally, recognized by employers around the world. Likewise, the University of Cambridge has certified over 400 international branches in countries all over the world to offer CELTA training to nearly 10,000 trainees annually (Green, 2005; Hobbs, 2013). As one of us (Barnawi, 2016) has argued:

> The certificates awarded at the end of these courses, which are often heavily colored by the popular discourses of marketization and commercialization, have been perceived by consumers (teachers) as a form of

linguistic and economic capital. This is because although they offer consumers excellent career opportunities all over the world within a short period of time, they are geared solely toward practical aspects. (Barnawi, 2016: 85)

What is strikingly obvious is that a teacher's language background, education and subject matter are often overlooked in the process of hiring. On its official website, one of the online TESOL certificate providers called UNI-Prep advertises its training programs as follows:

> Are you interested in working as an English language teacher around the world? UNI-Prep's online TESOL Certificate program qualifies an individual to work as an English and ESL/EFL teacher internationally. The program is completely online and is 120-hours in length. Since the course is online, it allows you the option to study from anywhere in the world as long as you have a computer with an internet connection. In addition, there is no set schedule that you must follow, so you can study at your own schedule. Once you have registered in the course, you will be given a login and password allowing you access to the course 24/7 from any computer. Most students take two to four weeks to complete the full TESOL Certificate program, but you can take more or less time than this depending on how often and quickly you will study.[4]

Teachers with qualifications such as the above are referred to as *McTeachers with McQualifications* (Anderson, 2005). These teachers have continued to be hired in high numbers in Saudi Arabia. They have also been appointed to take charge of duties in their institutions that require much knowledge, experience and expertise in English language teaching, including curriculum design, program and course development, testing and assessment, and professional development.

As discussed earlier in the book, hiring agencies play an important role in soliciting and appointing TESOL teachers for Saudi institutions. Some work closely with institutions in the hiring process. While some local HE bodies are serious about their hiring requirements, others are just 'dying' to hire native speakers of English with a degree in any field coupled with a short ELT teacher training course, summer TESOL training, CELTA, DELTA and/or SIT TESOL Certificates. It is therefore not surprising to find that most native-English-speaking teachers, qualified or not, find it far too easy to get a teaching position in Saudi Arabia, as we presented in earlier chapters. Just to recap: most teachers reported that '*it was very easy to get the job here*' (**Adam**), '*it was easy to get a job here*' (**Sarah**), '*a piece of cake*' (**Mario**), '*it was the easiest place to get a job*' (**Dan**), '*it was never difficult*' (**Ben**).

Local-trusting-local: A fresh lens

Alongside the obvious and seemingly unconditional trust in native-English-speaking teachers found across Saudi institutions, there exists a parallel mentality, which we have termed and theorized as *local-trusting-local*. This mentality is largely unnoticed because of the overemphasis on native-English-speaking teachers in existing scholarship. Although scholars like Motha (2006: 496) have attributed the incessant 'spread of the English language across the globe' to the fact that it 'was historically connected to the international political power of White people, [as] English and Whiteness are thornily intertwined', we argue that non-native English teachers have actually played a major role in Saudi higher education institutions.

On the one hand, Saudi higher education institutions still uphold the concept that native English speakers are the ideal teachers, still prioritize teachers from English-speaking Western countries like the UK, the US, Canada and Australia, and still give preference to teachers with qualifications obtained from institutions in Western countries. On the other hand, the majority of Saudi higher education institutions also take into consideration important criteria such as relevant qualifications, teaching experience and the credentials of applicants when they are hiring. As such, hundreds of teachers of English from neighboring countries and from countries in Asia, Africa and elsewhere have also been hired. Evident in the findings we have presented, many such teachers have obtained their qualifications from non-Western institutions based in Asia, Africa, and other Middle Eastern countries such as Oman, Jordan, Egypt and Morocco. As a matter of fact, the number of English language teachers from Asia and other countries who do not necessarily identify English as their first or native language is significantly higher than that of native speakers, as is shown in earlier chapters. Additionally, unlike their Western counterparts, it was found that all the teachers from Asia and neighboring countries like Sudan, Jordan and Egypt working in Saudi institutions are multilingual and hold relevant qualifications such as a BA in English, an MA in Applied Linguistics, an MA in TESOL, an MA in TEFL, a PhD in Applied Linguistics, a PhD in English Literature and a PhD in English Education. In addition to their professional qualifications and relevant degrees, the majority of these teachers also hold certificates such as CETLA, TESOL and DELTA, and have several years of teaching experience in their home countries or elsewhere.

While acknowledging that a very high number of non-Western English language teachers have been employed in Saudi Arabia, we also want to emphasize that *the local-trusting-local mentality is conditional*. Evidently, despite their relevant professional qualifications, credentials and years of teaching experience in their home countries, it was found that the majority of these teachers were required to demonstrate their credentials in various ways and manners prior to their appointment, including a series of interviews, written exams and the like. As scholars like Canagarajah (1999), Ruecker (2018) and Selvi (2010), among others, have argued, prejudice against NNESTs is usually exercised in various forms and manners in both Western and non-Western countries. Ruecker and Ives (2014) further contend that some countries

> have developed a set of visa requirements oriented toward legitimizing teachers from inner-circle countries; alternatively, when moving beyond this narrow requirement, they demand more in the way of qualifications from teachers from other contexts where English is widely spoken, such as India [and/or other Asian countries]. (Ruecker & Ives, 2014: 737)

As a result, unlike their Western counterparts, the majority of teachers from Asia and other countries, who do not necessarily identify English as their first or native language, reported that it was more difficult for them to get employed in Saudi Arabia. This was either because of the non-availability of visas or because they had to go through a process of exams and interviews at their respective schools. These teachers, although highly qualified and enriched by prior training and teaching experience, are still facing various forms of prejudice demonstrated in the hiring process they have to go through. Once hired and after successfully demonstrating their credentials and qualifications, these teachers tend to have gained much trust from Saudi institutions and enjoy equal benefits to those granted to native teachers of English.

In the next section, we further theorize the *local-trusting-local phenomenon* in the larger context of TESOL which is beyond Saudi Arabia.

Situating Local-Trusting-Local in TESOL

In his book entitled *Passage to Juneau,* Jonathan Raban (1999, cited in Creswell, 2004: 6) explores how the collision between two world-views could lead to the creation of different meanings, epistemic ways of knowing and not knowing, tensions, interactions and intercultural conflicts. Raban captures the difference between the world-views of natives and colonists in their canoes along the coast between Seattle and Vancouver. He shows that while natives took complicated routes that lack apparent logic, the colonialists took direct routes on their journeys. In this regard, for the native canoeists, 'their [nonsensical] movements made perfect sense as they read the sea as a set of places associated with particular spirits and particular dangers'. For the colonialists, on the other hand, the sea was a 'blank space' throughout their routes (Raban, 1999). Raban further explains that:

> Two world-views were in collision; and the poverty of white accounts of these canoe journeys reflect the colonialists' blindness to the native sea. They didn't get it – couldn't grasp the fact that for Indians the water was a place, and the great bulk of the land was undifferentiated space. The whites had entered a looking-glass world, where their own most basic terms were reversed. Their whole focus was directed toward the land: its natural harbours, its limber, its likely spots for settlement and agriculture. They traveled everywhere equipped with mental chainsaws and at a

glance could strip a hill of its covering forest … and see there a future of hedges, fields, houses, churches. They viewed the sea as a medium of access to the all-important land …. one is very close to the world that emerges from Indian stories, where the forest is the realm of danger, darkness, exile, solitude, and self-extinction, while the sea and its beaches represent safety, light, home, society, and the continuation of life. (Raban, 1999: 13)

The above observations shared by Raban (1999) show the ways in which the knowledge of 'Other' local people has predominantly been understood in relation to the knowledge of the West or colonizers. Correspondingly, 'colonial constructions of [superior] Self and [inferior] Other, combined with factors such as race, gender, ethnicity, class, language, and others, have been constantly re/produced in TESOL', as Shin (2006: 147) notes. Shin (2006) further explains that:

The conjunction between TESOL and colonialism is evident in its name, which *others* [italics in the original] people (and their languages) who do not speak English as their first language. It privileges speaking English by assigning a superior status of 'teachers' to the speakers of the language (as opposed to SOLs who are taught to). That is, the meaning of using English is often associated with being 'superior'. (Shin, 2006: 151)

Indeed, scholars in the field of TESOL (for example, Barnawi, 2018; Canagarajah, 1999; Chowdhury & Phan, 2008; De Costa *et al.*, 2020; Kramsch, 1998; Kubota & Lin, 2009; Llurda, 2005; Motha, 2014; Pennycook, 1998/2017; Phan, 2008, 2017; Phillipson, 1992; Tupas, 2015) have consistently questioned the Self/Other binary as well as non-native English-speaking teachers (NNESTs) versus native-English-speaking teachers (NESTs), and called for further conceptualizations of such seemingly controversial issues. Nevertheless, Moussu (2018) argues, in spite of these ideological critiques of TESOL:

[T]he myth of the perfect native speaker still holds strong, and a great number of ESL [English as a Second Language] and EFL [English as a Foreign Language] schools across the world still advertise teaching positions 'for native speakers only.' These practices are now seen as discriminatory, and the native/non-native dichotomy (or 'native speaker fallacy' as it is sometimes called) is still discussed, researched, and criticized by linguists, TESOL scholars, and language professionals …. [M]ultiple institutions and professional associations have also published position statements against the discrimination of NNESs in the field of TESOL. The fact remains, however, that even with TESOL/TESL degrees in hand, NNESs are still perceived as lacking communicative competence and possessing limited knowledge and intuition about the English language, thus are not regarded as being suitable ESL/EFL teachers. (Moussu, 2018: 2)

What is evident in Moussu's (2018) argument above is a strong sense of lack of trust in terms of self-worth, linguistic capability, credentials and marketability status concerning NNESTs. This sense of lack of trust, whether from the perspective of qualifications, communicative competence or knowledge and intuition about the English language, is embedded in multiple intrinsic and extrinsic domains: among these teachers, against them from employers, parents and students, in comparison with NESTs, and in normalized discourses and practices in society and education that are deeply entrenched at every level. This lack of trust has been documented in historical, educational, social, cultural, promotional, political and literary accounts ever since English colonialism. It continued throughout the postcolonial and decolonization periods and has been expressed in different forms and intensities as globalization and neoliberalism have taken over (for instance, Alshakhi & Phan, 2020; Barnawi, 2018; Chun, 2017; De Costa & Norton, 2017; Hashimoto, 2000; Holliday, 2005; Kachru, 1996; Kubota, 1998; Park, 2018; Pennycook, 1994, 1998; Phan, 2017; Phillipson, 1992; Shin, 2016; Tsui & Tollefson, 2007; Tupas, 2015).

We would now like to shift the attention from this loudly expressed lack of trust in NNESTs in the current scholarship to a significantly overlooked reality and phenomenon in TESOL, which is *local-trusting-local*, in which local signifies non-Western English-speaking contexts and speakers of English who do not identify English as their native language. By *local-trusting-local* we are referring to the ways in which a seemingly native-speaker obsessed place and a very demanding English language teaching market for non-native teachers of English (e.g. Saudi Arabia, Hong Kong, Japan, Oman, Qatar) could also be so 'open' to non-native teachers of English and to the professional qualifications granted by other non-English-speaking countries. We define *local-trusting-local* as discourse and social practice occurring within and between NNESTs by means of having confidence in each other's qualifications, communicative competence and knowledge and intuition about the English language as well as their sociocultural, ideological, epistemological, pedagogical and sociolinguistic resources.

Indeed, the construct of trust has been defined differently by different scholars in such fields as philosophy, psychology, economics and sociology (e.g. Barber, 1983; Luhmann, 1979). For example, in Lewis and Weigert's (1985) definition, trust is:

> ... a property of collective units (ongoing dyads, groups, and collectivities), not of isolated individuals. Being a collective attribute, trust is applicable to the relations among people rather than to their psychological states taken individually. Therefore, we may say that trust exists in a social system insofar as the members of that system act according to and are secure in the expected futures constituted by the presence of each other or their symbolic representations. (Lewis & Weigert, 1985: 968)

As Tierney (2008: 30) notes, 'the trusted have incentives to fulfill the trust, and the trusters have information and knowledge that enables them to trust'. Trust requires highly complex rational expectations, judgements and justifications, based upon which individuals come to trust others. Trust is not merely an emotive state of mind or emotional reactions to others. Rather, it is built on give-and-take commitments from both sides.

> Trust is a two-party relationship in which an individual commits to an exchange before knowing whether the other individual will reciprocate. The focus of the exchange occurs within a structure of relationships where the motives for trust are instrumental. (Tierney, 2008: 30)

We see trust as an ongoing process that is a sociomaterially shaped as well as a culturally, politically, ideologically and institutionally charged construct. At the same time, *local-trusting-local* could involve 'an unavoidable element of risk and potential doubt' (Tierney, 2008: 30). This urges us to examine the functional aspect of *local-trusting-local* in order to understand its complexity. Among other key theorizations we have established so far such as those surrounding NESTs' emotion labor and their contested privileges, also central to our critical inquiry in this book is the reality and phenomenon of *local-trusting local* in non-English-speaking yet English-obsessed contexts such as Saudi Arabia. Informed by our data and all the discussions to this point, we are confident that we can make some attempts to understand and theorize how trust is negotiated within and between different local players (i.e. international NNESTs and their institutions in non-English-dominant contexts) in this age of academic mobility. What are the limits of negotiability within and between different players? What are the materialities of trust, particularly in the age of neoliberal academic mobility?

Trust in the age of (neoliberal) academic mobility

While the concept of 'trust' has been defined differently by different scholars in the professional literature as stated earlier (cf. Barber, 1983; Berscheid, 1994; Lewis & Weigert, 1985; Luhmann, 1979; Meyerson *et al.*, 1996; Tierney, 2008; Webb, 1996), these scholars have collectively acknowledged the importance of this concept in relation to how we interact with others (e.g. teacher–student, teacher–teacher, teacher–employer interactions, etc.). In this regard, 'social obligations, expectations, norms, and sanctions are [fundamental] arrangements used to build trust' (Tierney, 2008: 30). The presence of trust is mainly 'because the individuals have utilized the structures in a manner that fosters trusting relationships' (Tierney, 2008: 30). Seen in this light, trust is central to effective interpersonal relationships in different social and educational contexts.

In free market trust, Coleman (1997, cited in Salerno, 2018: 359) observes that trust is seen as 'a situation in an economy whereby its individuals and organizations have the confidence to cooperate with one another without government assistance' (Coleman, 1997). Trust is construed as a 'social product in neoliberal discourse … that could be bought and sold' (Coleman, 1997) within and between different players. From employer–employee perspectives, scholars like Reina and Reina (1999) postulate three categories for trust: (i) 'contractual trust' (i.e. faculty members fulfil the demands, expectations and other contractual obligations of their employers); (ii) 'competence trust' (in qualifications, communicative competence and knowledge to perform a given role); and (iii) 'communication trust'.

Conceptually, the heavy presence of NNESTs (from Asia, Africa, and other Arab neighboring countries) in the Arabian Gulf region is indicative of neoliberal trust; i.e. these teachers are seen as being able to contribute to the economic growth and to the development of human capital in countries in the region such as Saudi Arabia, Oman and Kuwait. For NNESTs working in these non-English-dominant contexts, creating trust in the mind of their employers is a 'costly investment' (to borrow Salerno's 2018 expression). At the same time, what is considered a 'good' teacher and 'good' teaching requires trust on the part of the institution, and from the teachers it employs to do the teaching, the peers in the workplace, and the students being taught. It is, hence, pivotal to understand what perceptions of 'good' teaching are held by all these actors. According to Macfarlane (2009: 221), 'loss of trust has negative economic as well as social and ethical implications for the university'. We argue that the absence of trust also has similar implications.

To build trust, NNESTs have to constantly and strategically negotiate their linguistic, pedagogical and communicative competence and knowledge and intuition about the English language, 'good' teaching and self-worth, as well as their sociocultural, ideological, epistemological, intercultural and sociolinguistic resources. In this picture, negotiation, broadly speaking, is seen as 'a process of communication between two or more parties that promotes mutual interests and reduces differences, whose goal is to reach an agreement based on different needs and approaches' (Lopez-Fresno *et al.*, 2018: 13). Employees (i.e. NNESTs) and employers, as they engage in a negotiation, look for mutual benefits and strengths, as both sides 'have each decided that they are dependent on the other to provide something that will improve their current situation and enable them to negotiate successfully' (Lopez-Fresno *et al.*, 2018: 13).

While this is happening, as discussed earlier, there are also limits of negotiability within and between different parties, especially where issues of power, prejudice, and stereotypes against NNESTs are alive and kicking. In many cases, there is not much room for negotiation (Ennser-Kananen & Saarinen, 2021). In light of what we have discussed in the previous chapters, stereotypes and prejudices against NNESTs working in Saudi Arabia can shape and reshape the results of negotiation and mutual benefits. In short, we argue that while trust in relation to negotiation 'is often considered vital for beneficial societal relations and actions'

(Clarke *et al.*, 2021: 258), the limits of negotiability among different players need to be critically unpacked and acknowledged.

The materiality of local-trusting-local in TESOL

In a given academic workplace, 'trust is related through elements such as power, control and other limitations, including statutory and hierarchical authority' (Kovač & Jesenko, 2008: 260–261). For NNESTs working in a non-English-dominant context like Saudi Arabia, relevant qualifications (e.g. MA in TESOL/Applied Linguistics coupled with certifications like CELTA or DELTA), previous teaching experience, religion, culture, knowledge of Arabic language, mannerisms, accent, student feedback, self-branding, appearance, commitment and proactive adjustment to constantly changing institutional expectations and demands symbolize the materials by which trust is realized.

We argue that the discursive relationship between the materiality of trust and the NNESTs working in non-English-dominant contexts needs to be further examined and theorized. This very line of inquiry needs to be approached from the perspective of the sociomateriality of trust. The contention is that the sociomateriality of trust could become more fragmented under the name of neoliberal trust. Neoliberal capitalism 'contain[s] the power to unite diverse populations [and a wide variety of materials resources] around issues of secular commercial law and consumer culture' (Salerno, 2018: 361). In this context, as Clarke *et al.* (2021: 259) argue, issues of 'trust and distrust can be mediated, not only through interpersonal relationships but through material resources' in this age of neoliberal mobility.

We also argue that this phenomenon of *local-trusting-local* offers a fresh lens through which to approach teacher identity and TESOL more broadly. This often overlooked and under-researched phenomenon invites further scholarly attention in the current debates surrounding native and non-native English-speaking TESOL teachers. Specifically, if we examine the tensions that exist within and between multilingual and monolingual TESOL teachers, while at the same time taking into account the dominant monolingual theories and pedagogies in the profession, there is an obvious need to reread the debates concerning multilingual versus monolingual TESOL teachers through the lens of *local-trusting-local*. Many of these multilingual non-native TESOL teachers have found what we call a *trust house* in Saudi HE institutions, where the value of their qualifications and multilingual pedagogical practices is recognized/acknowledged.

Nonetheless, the multilingual resources and advantages of the non-native English teachers participating in our study do not seem to be utilized in their classroom teaching and pedagogies at all, as we have shown in Chapters 6, 7 and 8. Therefore, we argue that much of the existing discussion and aspiration for multilingualism appears absent in Saudi

Arabian TESOL; this reality continues to legitimize the ideal teacher in the light of an English-only approach and practice. And hence, *local-trusting-local* operates and materializes in this very space, where multilingualism would be better understood in relation to *multi-Englishes* on the ground rather than the employment of other languages alongside English in one's classroom.

So, we hope that our book, while contributing to the growing scholarly efforts to resist 'the normalization of native speaker privilege' (Ruecker & Ives, 2014) in the professions of TESOL and applied linguistics, also helps 'break down the connection between racism and native speakerism' (Ruecker & Ives, 2014) and forces engagement with bold and difficult questions such as those questions we have raised and discussed thus far. We are hopeful that our book will stimulate nuanced thinking on many matters and issues that have appeared to settle in our fields.

Notes

(1) See https://www.amazon.com/gp/product/1645041077/ref=dbs_a_def_rwt_hsch_vapi_taft_p1_i0
(2) See https://www.amazon.com/Sulaiman-Jenkins/e/B08DK5XMFN%3Fref=dbs_a_mng_rwt_scns_share)
(3) See https://teflology-podcast.com/tag/native-speaker/; https://teflology-podcast.com/2020/11/07/interview-65-sulaiman-jenkins-on-race-and-speakerhood/
(4) see https://www.gooverseas.com/teach-abroad/united-states/uni-prep-institute/63174?page=11

Afterword

Ryuko Kubota

In 2018, tensions arose between Saudi Arabia and Canada due to cultural difference in understanding women's rights, creating not only diplomatic disasters between the two countries, but also leading the Saudi government to freeze all new trade and investment transactions with Canada, cancel scholarships for Saudi students studying in Canada, and order all its students in Canada to transfer to other countries. The number of affected Saudi students studying in Canada was estimated to be more than 16,000. As a professor teaching language education in a graduate program in Canada, I was worried about the wellbeing of our international students from the KSA. Fortunately, two female Master's students had graduated earlier that year, narrowly escaping the Saudi government's order. This event made our institution realize the fragility of international engagement with education.

A few years earlier, the Faculty of Education at our university was approached by a prestigious women's university in the KSA, asking about our interest in developing an offshore program including English language teacher education. Echoing the neoliberal desire of the Saudi government, which Phan Le Ha and Osman Barnawi outline in this volume, the proposal was undoubtedly prompted by the Saudi university's desire to expand their students' human capital through acquiring Western knowledge and linguistic skills. Despite our initial enthusiasm, a serious concern was raised about the legal restrictions that would be imposed on LGBT faculty and their partners, which would exclude them from participating in the program. After many hours of discussion, we decided not to move forward with the program. A major rationale was the need to protect the rights and freedom of LGBT members as well as related issues of academic freedom from a Western perspective.

Neoliberal Push and Ideological Pull

Underlying these two episodes is a clash of cultural values and ideological principles between the two societies. Interestingly, these episodes present both a contradiction and an alignment in spite of two different contexts: state diplomacy versus higher education. More specifically, while Canada supported the rights of a Saudi woman and all Saudi women, by extension based on a Western philosophy, the Faculty at my university did not approve a program that would support education for Saudi women. Nonetheless, both cases demonstrate an attempt to protect human rights based on a Canadian, or more broadly Western, principle. The Canadian justice-oriented principle stemming from the Western ideology denounced the Saudi policies and actions, leading to depriving Saudi and Canadian students and teachers – both women and men – of opportunities for mutual exchange and learning. This demonstrates that the practice of teaching and learning English based on the neoliberal promise of English can easily be thwarted by ideological conflicts.

These diverging and converging ideas and actions raise many questions: What is the ultimate purpose of teaching and learning English (or any other languages)? Aside from the categories of NES/NNES, who actually gets to teach English in the KSA? Who benefits or should benefit from international educational engagement? Is the current popularity of integrating social justice in language teaching and learning in English-dominant societies relevant to different places in the world?

ELT as a Contested Space of Ideology

One of the striking facts presented by the authors of this innovative volume is the high percentage of Asian TESOL teachers (77%) as opposed to NES counterparts (21%) working in Saudi institutions of higher education. On the surface, this is welcome since these ratios demonstrate Saudi universities' willingness to hire ethnically and linguistically diverse instructors. This diversity of English language teachers would broaden Saudi students' views on the ownership of English beyond the traditional image of English speakers as being those from Inner Circle locations only. Students would be able to conceptualize the space in which English is used as a 'multi-Englishes-speaking community' (p. 42).

However, the nature of this diversity is not inclusive but rather restricted. For example, readers are told that all teacher informants of the study, except one, were men. Although the actual gender proportion of all expatriate English language teachers in the KSA is unknown, there might be more men than women. Furthermore, as Abdullah Alshakhi and his informants commented, teachers are constrained by the Saudi cultural and religious norms in choosing teaching materials and they feel discouraged to address sensitive topics. One of these topics indeed provoked the controversy in the second Canadian episode presented earlier. We can speculate that not only do women expatriate teachers of English hesitate to move to the KSA to teach, but LGBT teachers of English are also unlikely to choose to work in the KSA due to a high possibility of risk (Moore, 2020). Furthermore, the narrative by Sulaiman Jenkins in this volume demonstrates how Arabic-speaking African American Muslim TESOL teachers (AAMTT) feel Othered and inferiorized due to the raciolinguistic normative assumptions about who authentic Americans are. In other words, the normative image of an American as a White, Christian, monolingual native speaker of English positions Arabic-speaking AAMTTs at odds. Here too, the normalized practice of hiring racialized multilingual non-NABA teachers in the KSA does not translate into the acceptance of racialized Arabic-speaking AAMTTs.

These issues make us wonder what the ultimate purpose of teaching and learning English is and what desires are held by learners, teachers, institutions and society (Motha & Lin, 2014). It seems that a significant impetus for ELT comes from a neoliberal desire for economic gain. For teachers who choose to work in the KSA, financial incentives – good salaries and fringe benefits – are a significant draw. For the government and institutions, English is perceived as a neoliberal tool for economic and technological advancement that helps them increase their competitive edge in the globalized world. Moreover, the slogan of 'More English and Less Islam' (p. 15) speaks to the aspiration for acquiring Western values, such as democracy, freedom, openness, peace and justice through teaching and learning English. Yet, this orientation contradicts the aforementioned state-sanctioned ideology that prohibits discussion of West-based liberal ideas. It seems that ELT in the KSA is a conflicting space in which multiple interests and desires collide.

Conflicting desires also underlie the discourses of ELT service providers. Clearly, the beneficiaries of the neoliberal push for learning English as a global language are not only learners who would gain socioeconomic mobility, but also providers of language instruction, teaching materials, language tests, and so on, who receive profit margins. In the opening episodes, Canada as well as Canadian educational programs financially suffered from the loss of Saudi learners of English. The decision not to pursue an offshore program in collaboration with the Saudi women's university meant not only a missed financial opportunity, but also a missed international experience of teaching and learning.

This lost opportunity for intercultural exchange and learning, especially for the sake of protecting and promoting Canadian human rights, raises a question in relation to popularized discourses of internationalization as well as diversity, inclusion and social justice in higher education. In the field of languages education, there has also been an increased awareness of the need to pay attention to social justice (e.g. Hastings & Jacob, 2016; Randolph & Johnson, 2017), antiracism (e.g. Kubota, 2021; Motha, 2020) and queer inquiry (e.g. Nelson, 2016; Paiz, 2019). From a Western perspective, this trend humanizes learners and encourages them to critically engage with sociopolitical and ideological issues, rather than adhering to a purely pragmatic orientation to language learning. Yet, this approach is largely founded on a Western conceptualization of human rights, individual freedom and the valorization of various forms of diversity (Pennycook & Makoni, 2019). Thus, upholding the Western ideal of the protection of human rights, no matter how it is intended, could ironically undermine gender equity for Saudi women or transnational educational opportunities, although some may argue that gender equity itself is a Western idea, or that study abroad in the West is a contemporary form of (self)colonization. Ideological difference in the notion of justice across societies in the world makes it difficult for ELT professionals to address issues beyond pragmatic aspects of language learning.

Conclusion

The neoliberal spread of ELT can be observed in every corner of the world. Yet, the question of who teaches in what way for what purposes does not have a single answer. As a critical scholar working in the Global North and promoting antiracism and social justice for ELT, I feel humbled by the realities and perspectives presented in this book. They have enlightened me about the positive trend of many multilingual NNESTs of color being hired, but at the same time questioned the normativity and universality of the critical stances that are increasingly promoted in the West. There are many other non-Western societies that embrace diverse cultural, historical and political standpoints regarding social, racial and sexual justice. Our journey to learn, unlearn and relearn the meaning of ELT has just begun in the Gulf region and it will continue to explore other parts of the world.

References

Adamson, B. (2004) Fashions in language teaching methodology. In A. Davies and C. Elder (eds) *The Handbook of Applied Linguistics* (pp. 604–622). Oxford: Blackwell.

Agha, A. (2006) *Language and Social Relations*. Cambridge: Cambridge University Press.

Ahmed, A. (2018) Assessment of EFL writing in some Arab world university contexts: Issues and challenges. In A. Ahmed and H. Abouabdelkader (eds) *Assessing EFL Writing in the 21st Century Arab World* (pp. 1–19). London: Palgrave MacMillan.

Ahmed, S. (2004) *The Cultural Politics of Emotion*. New York: Routledge.

Akcan, S. (2016) Novice non-native English teachers' reflections on their teacher education programmes and their first years of teaching. *Profile Issues in Teachers' Professional Development* 18 (1), 55–70.

Aker, M.F. (2016) A study of black teachers' perceptions of the academic achievement of black male students in elementary schools in rural Georgia. Unpublished doctoral dissertation, Georgia Southern University. *Electronic Theses and Dissertations* No. 1375. See https://digitalcommons.georgiasouthern.edu/etd/1375

Alam, M.S. (2006) *Challenging the New Orientalism: Dissenting Essays on the War against Islam*. North Haledon, NJ: Islamic Publications International.

Al-deen, T. and Windle, J. (2016) 'I feel sometimes I am a bad mother': The affective dimension of immigrant mothers' involvement in their children's schooling. *Journal of Sociology* 53 (1), 110–126.

Alenazi, O. (2014) The employment of native and non-native speaker EFL teachers in Saudi higher education institutions: Programme administrators' perspective. Unpublished doctoral dissertation, Newcastle University.

Alghofaili, N.M. and Elyas, T. (2017) Decoding the myths of the native and non-native English speakers teachers (NESTs & NNESTs) on Saudi EFL tertiary students. *English Language Teaching* 10 (6), 1–11. See https://eric.ed.gov/?id=EJ1143457

Al-Hajailan, T. (1999) Evaluation of English as a foreign language textbook for third grade secondary boys' schools in Saudi Arabia. Unpublished doctoral dissertation, Mississippi State University.

Alim, H.S. (2016) Introducing raciolinguistics: Racing language and languaging race in hyperracial times. In H.S. Alim, J.R. Rickford and A.F. Ball (eds) *Raciolinguistics: How Language Shapes our Ideas about Race* (pp. 1–32). New York: Oxford University Press.

Alim, H.S., Rickford, J.R. and Ball, A.F. (eds) (2016) *Raciolinguistics: How Language Shapes our Ideas about Race*. New York: Oxford University Press.

Al-Issa, A. (2011) Advancing English language teaching research in Gulf Cooperation Council States universities. *The Modern Journal of Applied Linguistics* 3 (2), 60–77.

Al-Kinani, M. (2019) Foreign universities to open branch campuses in Saudi Arabia. *Arab News*, 29 October. See https://www.arabnews.com/node/1576231/amp

Alrahaili, M. (2018) Cultural and linguistic factors in the Saudi EFL context. In C. Moskovsky and M. Picard (eds) *English as a Foreign Language in Saudi Arabia* (pp. 93–110). London: Routledge.

Alseweed, M.A. (2012) University students' perceptions of the influence of native and non-native teachers. *English Language Teaching* 5 (12), 42–53. doi:10.5539/elt.v5n12p42

Alshakhi, A. and Phan, L.H. (2020) Emotion labor and affect in transnational encounters: Insights from Western-trained TESOL professionals in Saudi Arabia. *Research in Comparative and International Education* 15 (3), 305–326. doi:10.1177/1745499920946203

Alshammari, A. (2020) Job advertisements for English teachers in the Saudi Arabian context: Discourses of discrimination and inequity. *TESOL Journal* 12 (2), e542. doi.org/10.1002/tesj.542

Altbach, P.G. and Knight, J. (2007) The internationalization of higher education: Motivations and realities. *Journal of Studies in International Education* 11 (3–4), 290–305. doi:10.1177/1028315307303542

Amin, N. (1997) Race and the identity of the nonnative ESL teacher. *TESOL Quarterly* 31 (3), 580–583.

Anderson, C. (2005) The commodification of education: The case of TESOL. Paper presented at the Annual BAAL Meeting, Bristol University.

Aneja, G.A. (2016) (Non) native speakered: Rethinking (non) nativeness and teacher identity in TESOL teacher education. *TESOL Quarterly* 50 (3), 572–596.

Arnold, L.R. (2018) Today the need arises: Arabic student writing at the turn of the 20th century. In X. You (ed.) *Transnational Writing Education: Theory, History, and Practice* (pp. 95–112). New York: Routledge.

Aronin, L. and Singleton, D. (2008) Multilingualism as a new linguistic dispensation. *International Journal of Multilingualism* 5 (1), 1–16. doi:10.2167/ijm072.0

Appleby, R. (2010) *ELT, Gender and International Development: Myths of Progress in a Neocolonial World*. Bristol: Multilingual Matters.

Appleby, R. (2013) Desire in translation: White masculinity and TESOL. *TESOL Quarterly* 47 (1), 122–147.

Atkinson, R. (1993) *Crusade: The Untold Story of the Gulf War*. New York: Houghton-Mifflin.

Bailey, L. and Evison, J. (2020) Neither backpackers nor locals: The professional identities of TESOL teachers in East Asia studying on an MA TESOL. *European Journal of Applied Linguistics and TEFL* 9 (1), 209–224.

Baker, W. (2015) Research into practice: Cultural and intercultural awareness. *Language Teaching* 48 (1), 130–141. doi:10.1017/S0261444814000287

Ball, S.J. (2016) Neoliberal education? Confronting the slouching beast. *Policy Futures in Education* 14 (8), 1046–1059. doi:10.1177/1478210316664259

Banerjee, N. and Bojsen, K.P.M. (2013) Negotiability, and limits to negotiability–land use strategies in the SALCRA Batang Ai resettlement scheme, Sarawak, East Malaysia. *Geografisk Tidsskrift – Danish Journal of Geography* 105 (1), 17–28. doi:10.1080/00167223.2005.10649523

Barber, B. (1983) *The Logic and Limits of Trust*. New Brunswick, NJ: Rutgers University Press.

Barcelos, A. and Aragão, R. (2019) Emotions in language teaching: A review of studies on teacher emotions in Brazil. *Chinese Journal of Applied Linguistics* 41 (4), 506–531. doi:10.1515/cjal-2018-0036

Barnawi, O. (2011) Reading texts in an active and reflective manner: Examining critical literacy. Paper presented at the 3rd Annual Conference on Higher Education Pedagogy, Virginia.

Barnawi, O.Z. (2016) Re-reading your CELTA training course: A case study of four international teachers working at a Saudi HE institution. *English Language Teaching* 9 (9). See elt.ccsenet.org

Barnawi, O.Z. (2018) *Neoliberalism and English Language Education Policies in the Arabian Gulf*. London: Routledge.

Barnawi, O.Z. (2021) EMI-cum-acceleration policy in the contemporary transnational HE market: Experiences of Saudi engineering students. *Australian Review of Applied Linguistics* 44 (2), 208–228. doi:10.1075/aral.20092.bar

Barnawi, O.Z and Ahmed, A. (eds) (2021) *TESOL Teacher Education in a Transnational World: Turning Challenges into Innovative Prospects*. London and New York: Routledge.

Barnawi, O. and Al-Hawsawi, S. (2017) English education policy in Saudi Arabia: English language education policy in the Kingdom of Saudi Arabia: Current trends, issues and challenges. In R. Kirkpatrick (ed.) *English Language Education Policy in the Middle East and North Africa* (pp. 199–222). Cham: Springer.

Barnawi, O.Z. and Phan, L.H. (2014) From Western TESOL classroom to home practice: A case study with two 'privileged' Saudi teachers. *Critical Studies in Education* 56 (2), 259–276. doi:10.1080/17508487.2014.951949

Barnawi, O.Z. and Phan, L.H. (2020) 'Saudi women are finally allowed to sit behind the wheel': Initial responses from TESOL classrooms. In J.A. Windle, D. de Jesus and L. Bartlett (eds) *The Dynamics of Language and Inequality in Education: Social and Symbolic Boundaries in the Global South* (pp. 141–157). Bristol: Multilingual Matters.

Bataineh, R.F. and Reshidi, A.E. (2017) The cultural gap in EFL secondary stage curricula and instructional practices as perceived by Saudi students, teachers and supervisors. *International Journal of Teaching and Education* 5 (2), 1–21.

Bauman, Z. (2004) Identity. In *Conversations with Benedetto Vecchi*. Cambridge: Polity Press.

Baurain, B. (2004) Teaching as a moral enterprise. *Teacher's Edition* 15, 35.

Baurain, B. (2007) Christian witness and respect for persons. *Journal of Language, Identity & Education* 6 (3), 201–219. doi:10.1080/15348450701454221

Baurain, B. (2015) *Religious Faith and Teacher Knowledge in English Language Teaching*. Newcastle upon Tyne: Cambridge Scholars Publishing.

Bax, S. (2003) The end of CLT: A context approach to language teaching. *ELT Journal* 57 (3), 278–287.

Baxter, J. (2016) Positioning language and identity: Poststructuralist perspectives. In S. Preece (ed.) *The Routledge Handbook of Language and Identity* (pp. 34–49). New York: Routledge.

Benesch, S. (2017) *Emotion and English Language Teaching: Exploring Teachers' Emotion Labor*. London and New York: Routledge.

Benesch, S. (2019) Exploring emotions and power in L2 research: Sociopolitical approaches. *The Modern Language Journal* 103 (2), 530–533. doi:10.1111/modl.12575

Benesch, S. (2020) Emotions and activism: English language teachers' emotion labor as responses to institutional power. *Critical Inquiry in Language Studies* 17 (1), 26–41. doi:10.1080/15427587.2020.1716194

Benke, E. and Medgyes, P. (2005) Differences in teaching behaviour between native and non-native speaker teachers: As seen by the learners. In E. Llurda (ed.) *Non-native Language Teachers* (pp. 195–215). Boston, MA: Springer US.

Bérešová, J. (2017) The impact of the CEFR on teaching and testing English in the local context. *Theory and Practice in Language Studies* 7 (11), 959–964. doi:10.17507/tpls.0711.03

Berscheid, B. (1994) Interpersonal relationships. *Annual Review of Psychology* 45, 79–129. doi:10.1146/annurev.ps.45.020194.000455

Bialystok, E., Craik, F.I.M. and Luk, G. (2008) Lexical access in bilinguals: Effects of vocabulary size and executive control. *Journal of Neurolinguistics* 21 (6), 522–538. doi:10.1016/j.jneuroling.2007.07.001

Bigelow, M. (2019) (Re)considering the role of emotion in language teaching and learning. *The Modern Language Journal* 103 (2), 515–516. doi:10.1111/modl.12569

Block, D. (2007) *Second Language Identities*. London: Continuum.

Block, D. (2008a) *Multilingual Identities in a Global City*. London: Palgrave.

Block, D. (2008b) Multilingual identities and language practices in a global city: Four London case studies. *Journal of Language, Identity & Education* 7 (1), 1–4. doi:10.1080/15348450701804672

Block, D., Gray, J. and Holborow, M. (2012) *Neoliberalism and Applied Linguistics*. New York: Routledge.

Blommaert, J. (2010) *The Sociolinguistics of Globalization*. Cambridge: Cambridge University Press.

Blommaert, J. (2013) *Ethnography, Superdiversity and Linguistic Landscapes: Chronicles of Complexity*. Bristol: Multilingual Matters.

Blommaert, J. and Dong, J. (2010) Language and movement in space. In N. Coupland (ed.) *The Handbook of Language and Globalization* (pp. 366–385). Malden, MA: Wiley-Blackwell.

Bolitho, R. and Rossner, R. (2020) *Language Education in a Changing World: Challenges and Opportunities*. Bristol: Multilingual Matters.

Bonwell, C.C. and Eison, J.A. (1991) Active learning: Creating excitement in the classroom. *1991 ASHE-ERIC Higher Education Reports*. Washington DC: School of Education and Human Development, George Washington University.

Bourdieu, P. (1986) The forms of capital. In J.G. Richardson (ed.) *Handbook of Theory and Research for the Sociology of Education* (pp. 241–58). Westport, CT: Greenwood.

Bourdieu, P. (1991a) *Language and Symbolic Power*. Cambridge: Polity Press.

Bourdieu, P. (1991b) *Language and Symbolic Power*. Cambridge, MA: Harvard University Press.

Braine, G. (2010) *Nonnative speaker English Teachers: Research, Pedagogy, and Professional Growth*. London: Routledge.

Bright, D. and Phan, L.H. (2011) Learning to speak like us: Identity, discourse, and teaching English in Vietnam. In L.J. Zhang, R. Rubdy and L. Alsagoff (eds) *Asian Englishes: Changing Perspectives in a Globalized World* (pp. 121–140). Upper Saddle River, NJ: Pearson.

Bristol, T.J. and Mentor, M. (2018) Policing and teaching: The positioning of black male teachers as agents in The Universal Carceral Apparatus. *Urban Review: Issues and Ideas in Public Education* 50 (2), 218–234.

Brown, K. (2010) Teachers as language-policy actors: Contending with the erasure of lesser-used languages in schools. *Anthropology & Education Quarterly* 41 (3), 298–314. doi:10.1111/j.1548-1492.2010.01089.x

Brutt-Griffler, J. and Samimy, K. (1999) Revisiting the colonial in the postcolonial: Critical praxis for nonnative-English-speaking teachers in a TESOL program. *TESOL Quarterly* 33 (3), 413–431. doi:10.2307/3587672

Bunnell, T. and Poole, A. (2021) *Precarity and Insecurity in International Schooling: New Realities and New Visions*. Bingley: Emerald Group.

Burton, D. and Robinson, J. (1999) Cultural interference: Clashes of ideology and pedagogy in internationalizing education. *International Education* 28 (2), 5–30.

Byram, M., Nichols, A. and Stevens, D. (2001) *Developing Intercultural Competence in Practice*. Berlin: De Gruyter.

Canagarajah, S. (1999) *Resisting Linguistic Imperialism in English Teaching*. Oxford: Oxford University Press.

Canagarajah, S. (2002) Globalization, methods, and practice in periphery classrooms. In D. Block and D. Cameron (eds) *Globalization and Language Teaching* (pp. 134–150). London: Routledge.

Canagarajah, S. (2011a) Codemeshing in academic writing: Identifying teachable strategies of translanguaging. *The Modern Language Journal* 95 (3), 401–417. doi:10.1111/j.1540-4781.2011.01207.x

Canagarajah, S. (2011b) Translanguaging in the classroom: Emerging issues for research and pedagogy. *Applied Linguistics Review* 2, 1–28. doi:10.1515/9783110239331.1

Canagarajah, S. and Liyanage, I. (2012) Lessons from pre-colonial multilingualism. In M. Martin-Jones, A. Blackledge and A. Creese (eds) *The Routledge Handbook of Multilingualism*. London and New York: Routledge.

Carlin, E., Léglise, I., Migge, B. and Tjon Sie Fat, P. (2014) Looking at language, identity, and mobility in Suriname. In E. Carlin, I. Léglise and P. Tjon Sie Fat (eds) *In and Out of Suriname* (pp. 1–12). Leiden: Brill.

Carter Andrews, D.J., Bartell, T. and Richmond, G. (2016) Teaching in dehumanizing times: The professionalization imperative. *Journal of Teacher Education* 67 (3), 170–172. doi:10.1177/0022487116640480

Cenoz, J. (2013) Defining multilingualism. *Annual Review of Applied Linguistics* 33, 3–18. doi:10.1017/S026719051300007X

Cheung, Y.L., Said, S.B. and Park, K. (eds) (2015) *Advances and Current Trends in Language Teacher Identity Research*. London: Routledge.

Choak, C. (2012) Asking questions: Interviews and evaluations. In S. Bingley and F. Cullen (eds) *Research and Research Methods for Youth Practitioners* (pp. 90–112). London: Routledge.

Chowdhury, R. (2003) International TESOL training and EFL contexts: The cultural disillusionment factor. *Australian Journal of Education* 47 (3), 283–302.

Chowdhury, R. (2008) Teacher training and teaching practice: The changing landscape of ELT in secondary education in Bangladesh. In T. Ferrel, U.N. Singh and R.A. Giri (eds) *English Language Education in South Asia: From Policy to Pedagogy* (pp. 147–159). Delhi: Cambridge University Press.

Chowdhury, R. and Phan, L.H. (2008) Reflecting on Western TESOL training and communicative language teaching: Bangladeshi perspectives, *Asia Pacific Journal of Education* 28 (3), 305–316. doi:10.1080/02188790802236006

Chowdhury, R. and Phan, L.H. (2014) *Desiring TESOL and International Education: Market Abuse and Exploitation*. Bristol: Multilingual Matters.

Chun, C. (2016) Exploring neoliberal language, discourses and identities. In S. Preece (ed.) *The Routledge Handbook of Language and Identity* (pp. 558–571). London: Routledge.

Chun, C.W. (2017) *The Discourses of Capitalism: Everyday Economists and the Production of Common Sense*. London: Routledge.

Chun, S.Y. (2014) EFL learners' beliefs about native and non-native English-speaking teachers: Perceived strengths, weaknesses, and preferences. *Journal of Multilingual and Multicultural Development* 35 (6), 563–579. doi:10.1080/01434632.2014.889141

Clark, E. and Paran, A. (2007) The employability of non-native-speaker teachers of EFL: A UK survey. *System* 35 (4), 407-430.

Clarke, M. (2008) *Language Teacher Identities: Co-constructing Discourse and Community*. Clevedon: Multilingual Matters.

Clarke, R.E., Briggs, J., Armstrong, A., MacDonald, A., Vines, J., Flynn, E. and Salt, K. (2021) Socio-materiality of trust: Co-design with a resource limited community organisation. *CoDesign* 17 (3), 258–277. doi:10.1080/15710882.2019.1631349

Coffman, J. (1995) Does the Arabic language encourage radical Islam? *Middle East Quarterly*, December, 51–57. See http://www.meforum.org/article/276

Cogo, A. (2012) ELF and super-diversity: A case study of ELF multilingual practices from a business context. *Journal of English as a Lingua Franca* 1 (2), 287–313. doi:10.1515/jelf-2012-0020

Coleman, S. (1997) International students in the classroom: A resource and an opportunity. *International Education* 26 (2), 52–61.

Collins, F.L. and Ho, K.C. (2018) Discrepant knowledge and interAsian mobilities: Unlikely movements, uncertain futures. *Discourse: Studies in the Cultural Politics of Education* 39 (5), 679–693. doi:10.1080/01596306.2018.1464429

Collins, J. and Slembrouck, S. (2007) Reading shop windows in globalized neighbourhoods: Multilingual literacy practices and indexicality. *Journal of Literacy Research* 39 (3), 335–356.

Conteh, J. and Meier, G. (eds) (2014) *The Multilingual Turn in Languages Education: Opportunities and Challenges*. Bristol: Multilingual Matters.
Cook, M., Robinson, C., Fierro, M., Morgan, D., Reid, A., Irwin, R., Robinson, F. and Hefner, R. (2010) *The New Cambridge History of Islam*. Cambridge: Cambridge University Press.
Cook, V. (1992) Evidence for multicompetence. *Language Learning* 42, 557–591.
Cope, B. and Kalantzis, M. (2009) 'Multiliteracies': New literacies, new learning. *Pedagogies: An International Journal* 4, 164–195.
Corbyn, Z. (2009) Saudi Arabia begins putting minds to challenges of future. *Times Higher Education*, 24 September. See http://www.timeshighereducation.co.uk/408293.article (accessed 10 October 2013).
Coskun, A. (2013) Native speakers as teachers in Turkey: Non-native pre-service English teachers' reactions to a nation-wide project. *Qualitative Report* 18, 1–21.
Cottee, S. (2015) Pilgrims to the Islamic State: What Westerners migrating to ISIS have in common with Westerners who sympathized with communism. *The Atlantic*, 24 July. See https://www.theatlantic.com/international/archive/2015/07/isis-foreign-fighters-political-pilgrims/399209/
Council of Europe (2001) *Common European Framework of Reference for Languages: Learning, Teaching, Assessment*. Cambridge: Cambridge University Press/Council of Europe.
Coupland, N. (ed.) (2010) *The Handbook of Language and Globalization*. Malden, MA: Wiley-Blackwell.
Crabtree, R. and Sapp, D.A. (2004) Your culture, my classroom, whose pedagogy? Negotiating effective teaching and learning in Brazil. *Journal of Studies in International Education* 8 (1), 105–132. doi:10.1177/1028315303260826
Creswell, J.W. (2007) *Research Design: Qualitative, Quantitative, and Mixed Methods Approaches* (2nd edn). Thousand Oaks, CA: Sage.
Creswell, J. (2014) *Research Design: Qualitative, Quantitative, and Mixed Methods Approaches* (4th edn). Thousand Oaks, CA: Sage.
Creswell, J. (2018) *Qualitative Inquiry and Research Design: Choosing among Five Approaches* (4th edn). Thousand Oaks, CA: Sage.
Cummins, J. (2007) Rethinking monolingual instructional strategies in multilingual classrooms. *Canadian Journal of Applied Linguistics* 10 (2), 221–240. See https://journals.lib.unb.ca/index.php/CJAL/article/view/19743
Czaika, M. and Haas, H. de (2014) The globalization of migration: Has the world become more migratory? *International Migration Review* 48 (2), 283–323.
Dabashi, H. (2008) *Islamic Liberation Theology: Resisting the Empire*. London: Routledge.
Davies, A. (2003) *The Native Speaker: Myth and Reality*. Clevedon: Multilingual Matters.
De Costa, P. (2020) Linguistic racism: Its negative effects and why we need to contest it. *International Journal of Bilingual Education and Bilingualism* 23 (7), 833–837. doi: 10.1080/13670050.2020.1783638
De Costa, P. and Norton, B. (2017) Introduction: Identity, transdisciplinarity, and the good language teacher. *The Modern Language Journal* 101 (S1), 3–14.
De Costa, P.I., Rawal, H. and Li, W. (2018) Broadening the second language teacher agenda: International perspectives on teacher emotions. *Chinese Journal of Applied Linguistics* 41 (4), 401–409.
De Costa, P.I., Park, J.S.-Y. and Wee, L. (2019) Linguistic entrepreneurship as affective regime: Organizations, audit culture, and second/foreign language education policy. *Language Policy* 18 (3), 387–406. doi:10.1007/s10993-018-9492-4
De Costa, P., Green-Eneix, C. and Li, W. (2020) Problematizing EMI language policy in a transnational world: China's entry into the global higher education market. *English Today* 1–8. doi:10.1017/S026607842000005X
De Costa, P., Green-Eneix, C. and Li, W. (2021) Embracing diversity, inclusion, equity and access in EMI-TNHE: Towards a social justice-centered reframing of English language teaching. *RELC Journal* 52 (2), 227–235. doi:10.1177/00336882211018540

De Fina, A. (2013) Top-down and bottom-up strategies of identity construction in ethnic media. *Applied Linguistics* 34 (5), 554–573.

De Fina, A. (2016) Linguistic practices and transnational identities. In S. Preece (ed.) *The Routledge Handbook of Language and Identity* (pp. 163–178). New York: Routledge.

De Fina, A. and Perrino, S. (2013) Transnational identities. *Applied Linguistics* 34 (5), 509–515. doi:10.1093/applin/amt024

de Groot, A.M.B. (2011) *Language and Cognition in Bilinguals and Multilinguals: An Introduction.* Hove: Psychology Press.

De Jong, E.J. and Harper, C.A. (2005) Preparing mainstream teachers for English-language learners: Is being a good teacher good enough? *Teacher Education Quarterly*, Spring, 101–124.

Dervin, F. (2012) Cultural identity, representation and othering. In J. Jackson (ed.) *The Routledge Handbook of Language and Intercultural Communication.* London and New York: Routledge.

Díaz, N.R. (2015) Students' preferences regarding native and non-native teachers of English at a university in the French Brittany. *Procedia – Social and Behavioral Sciences* 173, 93–97. doi:10.1016/j.sbspro.2015.02.036

Dobao, A.F. (2012) Collaborative writing tasks in the L2 classroom: Comparing group, pair, and individual work. *Journal of Second Language Writing* 21 (1), 40–58. doi:10.1016/j.jslw.2011.12.002

Doushaq, H.M. (1986) An investigation into stylistic errors of Arab students learning English for academic purposes. *English for Specific Purposes* 5 (1), 27–39.

Drennan, D. (2015) Islamophobia and adoption: Who are the civilized? *Journal of Social Distress and the Homeless* 24 (1), 7–25.

Duff, P. (2015) Transnationalism, multilingualism, and identity. *Annual Review of Applied Linguistics* 35, 57–80. doi:10.1017/S026719051400018X

Duff, P.A. and Uchida, Y. (1997) The negotiation of teachers' sociocultural identities and practices in postsecondary EFL classrooms. *TESOL Quarterly* 31 (3), 451–486.

El-Araby, S.A. (1983) *Teaching Foreign Languages to Arab Learners.* Tokyo: Institute for the Study of Languages and Cultures of Asia and Africa.

Ennser-Kananen, J. and Saarinen, T. (2021) Challenging constitutional bilingualism with 'What if …': Counterfactual histories and at-risk minorities in Finland. In C. Cunningham and C.J. Hall (eds) *Vulnerabilities, Challenges and Risks in Applied Linguistics* (pp. 81–96). Bristol: Multilingual Matters. https://doi.org/10.21832/9781788928243-007

Evison, J. and Bailey, L. (2019) Going beyond US and THEM: Exploring the pronoun use of professionalizing English language teachers in East Asia. *English Language Teacher Education and Development (ELTED) Journal* 22, 1–8.

Ewing, K.P. (1990) The illusion of wholeness: Culture, self, and the experience of inconsistency. *Ethos* 18 (3), 251–278. See http://www.jstor.org/stable/640337

Ezza, E.-S.Y. (2017) Criteria for assessing EFL writing at Majma'ah University. In S. Hidri and C. Coombe (eds) *Evaluation in Foreign Language Education in the Middle East and North Africa* (pp. 185–200). Cham: Springer International. doi:10.1007/978-3-319-43234-2_11

Fang, F. and Baker, W. (2018) 'A more inclusive mind towards the world': English language teaching and study abroad in China from intercultural citizenship and English as a lingua franca perspectives. *Language Teaching Research* 22 (5), 608–624. doi:10.1177/1362168817718574

Fang, F. and Widodo, H.P. (eds) (2019) *Critical Perspectives on Global Englishes in Asia: Language Policy, Curriculum, Pedagogy and Assessment.* Bristol: Multilingual Matters.

Farr, F. (2015) *Practice in TESOL.* Edinburgh: Edinburgh University Press.

Finlan, A. (2003) *The Gulf War 1991.* Oxford: Osprey.

Flores, N. (2013) The unexamined relationship between neoliberalism and plurilingualism: A cautionary tale. *TESOL Quarterly* 47 (3), 500–520.

Flores, N. and Rosa, J. (2015) Undoing appropriateness: Raciolinguistic ideologies and language diversity in education. *Harvard Educational Review* 85 (2), 149–171.

Flubacher, M.-C. and Del Percio, A. (eds) (2017) *Language, Education and Neoliberalism: Critical Studies in Sociolinguistics*. Bristol: Multilingual Matters.

Foley, J. (2021) CLT using CEFR and EIL in Southeast Asia and East Asia in the English language classroom. *RELC Journal*. doi:10.1177/0033688221998079

Foucault, M. (1997) Technologies of the self. In P. Rabinow (ed.) *Ethics: Subjectivity and Truth*. Essential Works of Foucault 1954–1984, Vol. 1 (pp. 223–252). New York: New Press.

García, O. and Li, W. (2017) *Translanguaging: Language, Bilingualism and Education*. Cham: Springer.

García, O. and Lin, A.M.Y. (2017) Translanguaging in bilingual education. In O. García A. Lin and S. May (eds) *Bilingual and Multilingual Education: Encyclopedia of Language and Education* (3rd edn). Cham: Springer. doi:10.1007/978-3-319-02258-1_9

Gao, S. and Park, J. (2015) Space and language learning under the neoliberal economy. *L2 Journal* 7 (3), 78–96.

Gardner, S. and Martin-Jones, M. (eds) (2012) *Multilingualism, Discourse, and Ethnography*. London: Routledge.

Ghalib, T.K. and Al-Hattami, A.A. (2015) Holistic versus analytic evaluation of EFL writing: A case study. *English Language Teaching* 8 (7), 225–236. doi:10.5539/elt.v8n7p225

Giroux, H. (2009) Neoliberalism, youth and the leasing of higher education. In D. Hill and R. Kumar (eds) *Global Neoliberalism and Education and its Consequences* (pp. 30–53). New York: Routledge.

Giroux, H. (2014) *Neoliberalism's War on Higher Education*. Chicago, IL: Haymarket Books.

Glasser, S.B. (2003) Qatar reshapes its schools, putting English over Islam. *Washington Post*, 2 February. See https://www.washingtonpost.com/archive/politics/2003/02/02/qatar-reshapes-its-schools-putting-english-over-islam/cc2ce372-30b0-48cf-bcc3-35fd23c906f8/

Golombek, P. and Jordan, S.R. (2005) Becoming 'Black Lambs' not 'Parrots': A poststructuralist orientation to intelligibility and identity. *TESOL Quarterly* 39 (3), 513–533.

Gomes, C. (2022) *Parallel Societies of International Students: Connections, Disconnections and a Global Pandemic*. London: Routledge.

Graves, K. and Garton, S. (2017) An analysis of three curriculum approaches to teaching English in public-sector schools. *Language Teaching* 50 (4), 441–482. doi:10.1017/S0261444817000155

Green, T. (2005) Staying in touch: Tracking the career paths of CELTA graduates. *Research Notes* 19, 7–11.

Gumperz, J. (1982) *Discourse Strategies*. Cambridge: Cambridge University Press.

Habbash, M. (2011) Status change of English and its role in shaping public education language policy and practice in Saudi Arabia: A postmodernist critical perspective. Unpublished doctoral dissertation, University of Exeter.

Hagopian, E. (ed.) (2004) *Civil Rights in Peril: The Targeting of Arabs and Muslims*. Chicago, IL: Haymarket Books.

Halkes, R. and Oslon, J.K. (1984) *Teacher Thinking: A New Perspective on Persisting Problems in Education*. Lisse: Swets & Zeitlinger.

Hall, S. (2000) Who needs identity? In P. Du Gay, J. Evans and P. Redman (eds) *Identity: A Reader* (pp. 15–30). London: Sage/Open University.

Hamid, M.O. and Rahman, A. (2019) Language in education policy in Bangladesh: A neoliberal turn? In A. Kirkpatrick and A.J. Liddicoat (eds) *The Routledge International Handbook of Language Education Policy in Asia* (pp. 382–398). London: Routledge.

Han, H. (2011) Social inclusion through multilingual ideologies, policies and practices: A case study of a minority church. *International Journal of Bilingual Education and Bilingualism* 14 (4), 383–398. doi:10.1080/13670050.2011.573063

Hannah-Jones, N. (2019) Our democracy's founding ideals were false when they were written. Black Americans have fought to make them true. *New York Times Magazine*, 14 August. See https://www.nytimes.com/interactive/2019/08/14/magazine/black-history-american-democracy.html

Hardt, M. and Negri, A. (2000) *Empire*. Cambridge, MA: Harvard University Press.

Harris, R. (1998) *Introduction to Integrationist Linguistics*. Oxford: Pergamon.

Hartse, J. and Jiang, D. (eds) (2015) *Perspectives on Teaching English at Colleges and Universities in China*. Alexandria, VA: TESOL Press.

Harvey, D. (1993) From space to place and back again: Reflections on the condition of postmodernity. In J. Bird, B. Curtis, T. Putnam and L. Tickner (eds) *Mapping the Futures: Local Cultures, Global Change* (pp. 3–29). London: Routledge.

Harvey, D. (2005) *Spaces of Neoliberalization: Towards a Theory of Uneven Geographical Development*. Stuttgart: Franz Steiner Verlag.

Hashimoto, K. (2000) 'Internationalisation' is 'Japanisation': Japan's foreign language education and national identity. *Journal of Intercultural Studies* 21 (1), 39–51.

Hastings, C. (2015) *Perspectives on Teaching English for Specific Purposes in Saudi Arabia*. Alexandria, VA: TESOL Press.

Hastings, C. and Jacob, L. (eds) (2016) *Social Justice in English Language Teaching*. New York: TESOL Press.

Heckman, F. (1993) Multiculturalism defined seven ways. *The Social Contract Press* 3 (4), 245–246.

Held, D. and Ulrichsen, K. (2012) Introduction. In H. David and U. Kristian (eds) *The Transformation of the Gulf: Politics, Economics and the Global Order* (pp. 1–18). London: Routledge.

Hickey, M. (2018) Thailand's 'English fever', migrant teachers and cosmopolitan aspirations in an interconnected Asia. *Discourse: Studies in the Cultural Politics of Education* 39 (5), 738–751. doi:10.1080/01596306.2018.1435603

Hicks, S.K. (2013) On the (out)skirts of TESOL networks of homophily: Substantive citizenship in Japan. In S.A. Houghton and D.J. Rivers (eds) *Native-Speakerism in Japan: Intergroup Dynamics in Foreign Language Education* (pp. 147–158). Bristol: Multilingual Matters.

Hillman, S., Graham, K.M. and Eslami, Z.R (2021) EMI and the international branch campus: Examining language ideologies, policies, and practices. *Australian Review of Applied Linguistics* 44 (2), 229–252. doi:10.1075/aral.20093.hil

Hiro, D. (1992) *Desert Shield to Desert Storm: The Second Gulf War*. London: Routledge.

Hoang, L.A. (2020) *Vietnamese Migrants in Russia: Mobility in Times of Uncertainties*. Amsterdam: Amsterdam University Press.

Hobbs, V. (2013) 'A basic starter pack': The TESOL Certificate as a course in survival. *ELT Journal* 67 (2), 163–174. doi:10.1093/elt/ccs078

Hochschild, A.R. (1979) Emotion work, feeling rules, and social structure. *American Journal of Sociology* 85 (3), 551–575. doi:10.1086/227049

Hochschild, A. (1983) *The Managed Heart: Commercialization of Human Feeling*. Berkeley, CA: University of California Press.

Hollander, P. (1981) *Political Pilgrims: Travels of Western Intellectuals to the Soviet Union, China, and Cuba 1928–1979*. New York: Harper Colophon Books.

Hollander, P. (2017) *Political Pilgrims: Western Intellectuals in Search of the Good Society* (4th edn). New York: Routledge.

Holliday, A. (2005) *The Struggle to Teach English as an International Language*. Oxford: Oxford University Press.

Holliday, A. (2008) Standards of English and politics of inclusion. *Language Teaching* 41 (1), 119–130. doi:10.1017/S0261444807004776

Hopkyns, S. (2020) *The Impact of Global English on Cultural Identities in the United Arab Emirates: Wanted not Welcome*. New York: Routledge.

Horner, B., NeCamp, S. and Donahue, C. (2011) Toward a multilingual composition scholarship: From English only to a translingual norm. *College Composition and Communication* 63 (2), 269–300. See http://www.jstor.org/stable/23131585

Hsu, T.H.-L. (2019) Rater attitude towards emerging varieties of English: A new rater effect? *Language Testing in Asia* 9 (5), 1–21. doi:10.1186/s40468-019-0080-0

Hyland, K. (2003) *Second Language Writing*. Cambridge: Cambridge University Press.

International Consultants for Education and Fairs (2016) Report: Saudi scholarship programme to sharpen focus on top universities. Retrieved from https://monitor.icef.com/2016/02/report-saudi-scholarship-programme-to-sharpen-focus-on-top-universities/

Ilieva, R. (2010) Non-native English-speaking teachers' negotiations of program discourses in their construction of professional identities within a TESOL program. *The Canadian Modern Language Review* 66 (3), 343–369. doi:10.3138/cmlr.66.3.343

Ilieva, R. and Waterstone, B. (2013) Curriculum discourses within a TESOL program for international students: Affording possibilities for academic and professional identity. *TCI: Transnational Curriculum Inquiry* 10 (1), 16–37.

Ilieva, R., Li, A. and Li, W. (2015) Negotiating TESOL programs and EFL teaching contexts in China: Identities and practices of international graduates of a TESOL program. *Comparative and International Education* 44 (2), Art. 3. See https://ir.lib.uwo.ca/cgi/viewcontent.cgi?article=1364&context=cie-eci

Inoue, N. and Stracke, E. (2013) Non-native English speaking postgraduate TESOL students in Australia: Why did they come here? *University of Sydney Papers in TESOL* 8, 29–56.

Iqbal, A. (2003) Mastering the madrassas. *Washington Times*, 17 August. See http://www.washtimes.com/world/20030817-123032-5826r.htm (accessed 24 February 2005).

Irham, I., Huda, M., Sari, R. and Rofiq, Z. (2021) ELF and multilingual justice in English language teaching practices: Voices from Indonesian English lecturers. *Asian Englishes* 23 (2), 1–16. doi:10.1080/13488678.2021.1949779

Jain, R., Yazan, B. and Canagarajah, S. (eds) (2021) *Transnational Identities and Practices in English Language Teaching: Critical Inquiries from Diverse Practitioners*. Bristol: Multilingual Matters.

James A. Baker III Institute for Public Policy of Rice University (2014) The Gulf States and Israeli-Palestinian conflict resolution. Baker Institute Policy Report No. 61. See https://www.bakerinstitute.org/files/8185/

Jandt, F.E. (2020) *An Introduction to Intercultural Communication: Identities in a Global Community* (10th edn). Thousand Oaks, CA: Sage.

Javid, C.Z. and Umer, M. (2014) Saudi EFL learners' writing problems: A move towards solution. *Proceeding of the Global Summit on Education GSE 2014, Kuala Lumpur, Malaysia* (pp. 164–180). See https://www.scirp.org/(S(lz5mqp453edsnp55rrgjct55))/reference/referencespapers.aspx?referenceid=1731991

Jenkins, J. (2006) Current perspectives on teaching world Englishes and English as a lingua franca. *TESOL Quarterly* 40 (1), 157–181.

Jenkins, J. (2012) English as a lingua franca from the classroom to the classroom. *ELT Journal* 66 (4), 486–494. doi:10.1093/elt/ccs040

Jenkins, S. (2017) The elephant in the room: Discriminatory hiring practices in ELT. *ELT Journal* 71 (3), 373–376.

Jenkins, S. (2019) Examining the (im)mobility of African American Muslim TESOL teachers in Saudi Arabia. *Transitions: Journal of Transient Migration* 3 (2), 157–175.

Johnston, B. (2003) *Values in English Language Teaching*. Mahwah, NJ: Lawrence Erlbaum.

Jupp, J. (1995) From 'white Australia' to 'part of Asia': Recent shifts in Australian immigration policy towards the region. *International Migration Review* 29 (1), 207–228.

Kabir, A.H. and Chowdhury, R. (2021) *The Privatisation of Higher Education in Postcolonial Bangladesh: The Politics of Intervention and Control*. London: Routledge.

Kachru, B. (1996) The paradigms of marginality. *World Englishes* 15, 241–255. doi:10.1111/j.1467-971X.1996.tb00112.x

Kachru, B.B., Kachru, Y. and Nelson, C.L. (eds) (2006) *The Handbook of World Englishes*. Oxford: Blackwell.

Kagawa, F. (2005) Emergency education: A critical review of the field. *Comparative Education* 41 (4), 487–503.

Karakas, A. (2020) Disciplining transnationality? The impact of study abroad educational experiences on Turkish returnee scholars' lives, careers and identity. *Research in Comparative and International Education* 15 (3), 252–272. doi:10.1177/1745499 920946223

Karim, A., Shahed, F.H., Mohamed, A.R., Rahman, M.M. and Ismail, S.A.M.M. (2019) Evaluation of the teacher education programs in EFL context: A testimony of student teachers' perspective. *International Journal of Instruction* 12 (1), 127–146. doi:10.29333/iji.2019.1219a

Karmani, S. (2005) English, 'terror', and Islam. *Applied Linguistics* 26 (2), 262–267.

Ke, I.C. (2021) *Globalization and English Education in Taiwan: Curriculum, Perceptions, and Pedagogies*. London: Routledge.

Kearns, E.M., Betus, A. and Lemieux, A. (2019) Why do some terrorist attacks receive more media attention than others? *Justice Quarterly* 36 (6), 985–1022. doi:10.1080/07418825.2018.1524507

Kelley, L.C. (2020) The decline of Asian Studies in the West and the rise of knowledge production in Asia: An autoethnographic reflection on mobility, knowledge production and academic discourses. *Research in Comparative and International Education* 15 (3), 273–290. doi:10.1177/1745499920946224

Khafaji, A.I.A. (2004) An evaluation of the materials used for teaching English to the secondary level in male public high schools in Saudi Arabia. Unpublished Master's thesis, University of Exeter.

Kiczkowiak, M. and Lowe, R.J. (2021) Native-speakerism in English language teaching: 'Native speakers' more likely to be invited as conference plenary speakers. *Journal of Multilingual and Multicultural Development*. doi:10.1080/01434632.2021.1974464

Kim, T. (2017) Academic mobility, transnational identity capital, and stratification under conditions of academic capitalism. *Higher Education* 73, 981–997. doi:10.1007/s10734-017-0118-0

King, K. and Ganuza, N. (2005) Language, identity, education, and transmigration: Chilean adolescents in Sweden. *Journal of Language, Identity & Education* 4 (3), 179–199.

Kinninmont, J. (2015b) *Iran and the GCC: Unnecessary Insecurity*. London: Chatham House, the Royal Institute of International Affairs. See https://www.chathamhouse.org/sites/default/files/field/field_document/20150703IranGCCKinninmont.pdf

Kırkgöz, Y. and Karakaş, A. (eds) (2021) *English as the Medium of Instruction in Turkish Higher Education: Policy, Practice and Progress*. Cham: Springer.

Klees, S., Samoff, J. and Stromquist, N. (eds) (2012) *The World Bank and Education: Critiques and Alternatives*. Boston, MA: Sense Publishers.

Kostogriz, A. and Bonar, G. (2019) The relational work of international teachers: A case study of a Sino-foreign school. *Transitions: Journal of Transient Migration* 3 (2), 127–144.

Kovač, J. and Jesenko, M. (2008) The significance and role of trust in an organization within the processes of communication and control. *Izvorni znanstveni rad Primljeno* 28 (4), 259–277.

Kramsch, C. (1993) *Context and Culture in Language Teaching*. Oxford: Oxford University Press.

Kramsch, C. (1998) *Language and Culture*. Oxford: Oxford University Press.

Kramsch, C. (2009) *The Multilingual Subject*. Oxford: Oxford University Press.

Kubota, M. (2004) Native speaker: A unitary fantasy of a diverse reality. *The Language Teacher* 28 (1), 3–30.

Kubota, R. (1998) Ideologies of English in Japan. *World Englishes* 17 (3), 295–306.

Kubota, R. (2002) The author responds: (Un) raveling racism in a nice field like TESOL. *TESOL Quarterly* 36 (1), 84–92.

Kubota, R. (2004) Critical multiculturalism and second language education. In B. Norton and K. Toohey (eds) *Critical Pedagogies and Language Learning* (pp. 30–52). Cambridge: Cambridge University Press.

Kubota, R. (2014) The multi/plural turn, postcolonial theory, and neoliberal multiculturalism: Complicities and implications for applied linguistics. *Applied Linguistics* 37 (4), 474–494. doi:10.1093/applin/amu045

Kubota, R. (2018) Racial, ethnic, and cultural stereotypes in teaching English. In J.I. Liontas (ed.) *The TESOL Encyclopedia of English Language Teaching*. Hoboken, NJ: Wiley.

Kubota, R. (2020) Confronting epistemological racism, decolonizing scholarly knowledge: Race and gender in applied linguistics. *Applied Linguistics* 41 (5), 712–732. doi:10.1093/applin/amz033

Kubota, R. (2021) Critical antiracist pedagogy of English as an additional language. *ELT Journal* 75 (3), 237–246.

Kubota, R. and Lin, A. (2006) Race and TESOL: Introduction to concepts and theories. *TESOL Quarterly* 40 (3), 471–493.

Kubota, R. and Lin, A. (eds) (2009) *Race, Culture, and Identities in Second Language Education: Exploring Critically Engaged Practice*. London: Routledge.

Kumar, D. (2012) *Islamophobia and the Politics of Empire*. Chicago, IL: Haymarket Books.

Kumaravadivelu, B. (2001) Toward a postmethod pedagogy. *TESOL Quarterly* 35 (4), 537–560.

Kumaravadivelu, B. (2003) Forum on critical language pedagogy: A postmethod perspective on English language teaching. *World Englishes* 22, 539–550. doi:10.1111/j.1467-971X.2003.00317.x

Kumaravadivelu, B. (2006) *Understanding Language Teaching: From Method to Postmethod*. Mahwah, NJ: Lawrence Erlbaum.

Kumashiro K.K. (2000) Toward a theory of anti-oppressive education. *Review of Educational Research* 70 (1), 25–53. doi:10.3102/00346543070001025

Kuske, E.A. (2015) The development of and diversity in the nativised variety of English on Guam Unpublished paper presented at the CUSO Workshop: Conducting Sociolinguistic Research on Englishes Near and Far, Schloss Muenchenwiler, 27–29 March. See https://boris.unibe.ch/75725/ (accessed 10 February 2022).

Kymlicka, W. (2010) The rise and fall of multiculturalism? New debates on inclusion and accommodation in diverse societies. *International Social Science Journal* 61 (199), 97–112.

Kymlicka, W. (2011) Multicultural citizenship within multination states. *Ethnicities* 11 (3), 281–302. doi:10.1177/1468796811407813

Lane, N. (2012) *The Islamophobia Industry: How the Right Manufactures Fear of Muslims*. London: Pluto Press.

Lasagabaster, D. and Sierra, J.M. (2002) University students' perceptions of native and non-native speaker teachers of English. *Language Awareness* 11 (2), 132–142. doi:10.1080/09658410208667051

Le, T.T.H. and Phan, L.H. (2013) Problematizing the culture of learning English in Vietnam: Revisiting teacher identity. In L. Jin and M. Cortazzi (eds) *Researching Cultures of Learning* (pp. 248–264). Hampshire and New York: Palgrave MacMillan. See https://link.springer.com/chapter/10.1057/9781137296344_13

Lee, J.H. (2020) Relationships among students' perceptions of native and non-native EFL teachers' immediacy behaviours and credibility and students' willingness to communicate in class. *Oxford Review of Education* 46 (2), 153–168. doi:10.1080/03054985.2019.1642187

Lee, J.W. (ed.) (2022) *The Sociolinguistics of Global Asias*. London: Routledge.

Lewis, J.D. and Weigert, A. (1985) Trust as a social reality. *Social Forces* 63 (4), 967–985. doi:10.2307/2578601

Li, Y. and Dervin, F. (2018) Interculturality in a different light: Modesty towards democracy in education? *Intercultural Communication Education* 1 (1), 12–26.

Lin, A.M.Y. (2015) Researcher positionality. In F. Hult and D. Johnson (eds) *Research Methods in Language Policy and Planning: A Practical Guide* (pp. 21–32). Chichester: Wiley-Blackwell.

Lin, A. and Li, D.C.S. (2012) Codeswitching. In M. Martin-Jones, A. Blackledge and A. Creese (eds) *The Routledge Handbook of Multilingualism* (pp. 470–481). London: Routledge.

Lin, R.P. and Shi, L. (2021) Translingual identity and professional legitimacy of two Western-educated English writing instructors in Taiwan. *Journal of Language, Identity & Education*. doi:10.1080/15348458.2021.1974865

Liu, D. (1998) Ethnocentrism in TESOL: Teacher education and the neglected needs of international TESOL students. *ELT Journal* 52 (1), 3–10. doi:10.1093/elt/52.1.3

Liu, J. and Berger, C. (2015) *TESOL: A Guide*. London: Bloomsbury.

Liu, M. and Phan, L.H. (2021) 'We have no Chinese classmates': International students, internationalization, and medium of instruction in Chinese universities. *Australian Review of Applied Linguistics* 44 (2), 180–207. doi:10.1075/aral.20091.liu

Llurda, E. (ed.) (2005) *Non-native Language Teachers*. Boston, MA: Springer.

Lopez-Fresno, P., Savolainen, T. and Miranda, S. (2018) Role of trust in integrative negotiations. *Electronic Journal of Knowledge Management* 16 (1), 13–22.

Lowe, R.J. and Lawrence, L. (2018) Native-speakerism and 'hidden curricula' in ELT training: A duoethnography. *Journal of Language and Discrimination* 2 (2), 162–187. doi:10.1558/jld.36409

Luhmann, N. (1979) *Trust and Power*. Chichester: Wiley.

Luke, A. (2004) Two takes on the critical. In B. Norton and K. Toohey (eds) *Critical Pedagogies and Language Learning* (pp. 21–29). Cambridge: Cambridge University Press.

Lynch, B.K. (2001) Rethinking assessment from a critical perspective. *Language Testing* 18 (4), 351–372.

Macaro, E., Curle, S., Pun, J., An, J. and Dearden, J. (2017) A systematic review of English medium instruction in higher education. *Language Teaching* 51 (1), 36–76. doi:10.1017/S0261444817000350

Macfarlane, B. (2009) *A Leap of Faith*: The Role of Trust in Higher Education Teaching. 名古屋高等教育研究 第 9 号.

Mahboob, A. (2004) Native or non-native: What do the students think? In L.D. Kamhi-Stein (ed.) *Learning and Teaching from Experience: Perspectives on Nonnative English-speaking Professionals* (pp. 121–147). Ann Arbor, MI: University of Michigan Press.

Mahboob, A. (ed.) (2010) *The NNEST Lens: Non-native English Speakers in TESOL*. Newcastle upon Tyne: Cambridge Scholars.

Mahboob, A. and Elyas, T. (2014) English in the Kingdom of Saudi Arabia. *World Englishes* 33 (1), 128–142.

Mahboob, A. and Golden, R. (2013) Looking for native speakers of English: Discrimination in English language teaching job advertisements. *Voices in Asia Journal* 1 (1), 72–81.

Mahboob, A., Uhrig, K., Newman, K.L. and Hartford, B.S. (2004) Children of a lesser English: Nonnative English speakers as ESL teachers in English language programs in the United States. In L. Kamhi-Stein (ed.) *Learning and Teaching from Experience: Perspectives on Nonnative English-speaking Professionals* (pp. 100–120). Ann Arbor, MI: University of Michigan Press.

Maisel, S. (2009) *Tribes and the Saudi Legal-System: An Assessment of Coexistence*. Washington, DC: Middle East Institute. See https://www.mei.edu/publications/tribes-and-saudi-legal-system-assessment-coexistence

Mandall, R. (2016) *Creating an African American Identity and a New Nation*. Princeton, NJ: African American Intellectual History Society. See https://www.aaihs.org/creating-an-african-american-identity-and-a-new-nation/ (accessed 2 December 2018).

Marga, A. (2010) Globalization, multiculturalism and brain drain. *Journal of Organisational Transformation & Social Change* 7 (1), 105–115. doi:10.1386/jots.7.1.105_1

Margic, B. and Sirola, D. (2014) 'Jamaican and Irish for fun, British to show off': Attitudes of Croatian university students of TEFL to English language varieties: How entrenched are students' attitudes to national varieties of English? *English Today* 30 (3), 48–53. doi:10.1017/S0266078414000261

Massri, R. (2019) The perceptions and beliefs of Saudi preparatory year program learners towards learning English: A case study. *Arab World English Journal (AWEJ)* 10 (3), 220–232. See https://awej.org/images/Volume10/Volume10Number3September2019/15.pdf

Matsuda, A. (2002) 'International understanding' through teaching World Englishes. *World Englishes* 21 (3), 436-440.

Matsuda, A. (ed.) (2017) *Preparing Teachers to Teach English as an International Language*. Bristol: Multilingual Matters.

Matthes, J., Kaskeleviciute, R., Schmuck, D., von Sikorski, C., Klobasa, C., Knupfer, H. and Saumer, M. (2020) Who differentiates between Muslims and Islamist terrorists in terrorism news coverage? An actor-based approach. *Journalism Studies* 21 (15), 2135–2153. doi:10.1080/1461670X.2020.1812422

May, S. (ed.) (2014) *The Multilingual Turn: Implications for SLA, TESOL and Bilingual Education*. New York: Routledge.

Mazzetti, M. and Kirkpatrick, D.D. (2015) Saudi Arabia leads air assault in Yemen. *The New York Times*, 26 March. See https://www.nytimes.com/2015/03/26/world/middleeast/al-anad-air-base-houthis-yemen.html

McEwen, N., Swenden, W. and Bolleyer, N. (2012) Intergovernmental relations in the UK: Continuity in a time of change? *British Journal of Politics and International Relations* 14 (2), 323–343.

McKinley, J., Rose, H. and Zhou, S. (2021) Transnational universities and English medium instruction in China: How admissions, language support, and language use differ in Chinese universities. *RELC Journal* 52 (2), 236–252. doi:10.1177/00336882211020032

McNamara, T. (2011) Multilingualism in Education: A poststructuralist critique. *The Modern Language Journal* 95 (3), 430–441.

Medgyes, P. (1992) Native or non-native: Who's worth more? *ELT Journal* 46 (4), 340–349. doi:10.1093/elt/46.4.340

Medgyes, P. (2011a) Nonnative speaker English teachers: Research, pedagogy, and professional growth. *ELT Journal* 65 (2), 190–192. doi:10.1093/elt/ccr009

Medgyes, P. (2011b) When the teacher is a non-native speaker. In M. Celce Murcia, D. Brinton and M.A. Snow (eds) *Teaching English as a Second or Foreign Language* (pp. 429–442). Boston, MA: National Geographic Learning.

Medina-López-Portillo, A. (2014) Preparing TESOL students for the ESOL classroom: A cross-cultural project in intercultural communication. *TESOL Journal* 5 (2), 330–352.

Meer, N. (2015) Looking up in Scotland? Multinationalism, multiculturalism and political elites. *Ethnic and Racial Studies* 38 (9), 1477–1496. doi:10.1080/01419870.2015.1005642

Menard-Warwick, J. (2009) The cultural and intercultural identities of transnational English teachers: Two case studies from the Americas. *TESOL Quarterly* 42 (4), 617–640.

Menard-Warwick, J. (2014) *English Language Teachers on the Discursive Faultlines: Identities, Ideologies and Pedagogies*. Bristol: Multilingual Matters.

Merriam, S.B. (1998) *Qualitative Research and Case Study Applications in Education*. San Francisco, CA: Jossey-Bass.

Merriam, S.B., Johnson-Bailey, J., Lee, M.Y., Kee, Y., Ntseane, G. and Muhamad, M. (2001) Power and positionality: Negotiating insider/outsider status within and across cultures. *International Journal of Lifelong Education* 20 (5), 405–416.

Metz, H.C. (1993) *Saudi Arabia: A Country Study*. Washington, DC: Federal Research Division of the Library of Congress. See https://www.loc.gov/item/93028506/ (accessed 12 December 2018).

Meyerson, D., Weick, K. and Kramer, R. (1996) Swift trust and temporary groups. In R. Kramer and T. Tyler (eds) *Trust in Organizations: Frontiers of Theory and Research* (pp. 166–195). Thousand Oaks, CA: Sage. doi:10.4135/9781452243610.n9

Miller, D. (1995) *On Nationality*. Oxford: Oxford University Press.

Ministry of Education (1970) *Education Policy of Saudi Arabia*.

Mohammad, T. and Hazarika, Z. (2016) Difficulties of learning EFL in KSA: Writing skills in context. *International Journal of English Linguistics* 6 (3), 105–117.

Moore, A.R. (2020) Queer inquiry: A loving critique. *TESOL Quarterly* 54, 1122–1130. doi:10.1002/tesq.597

Moore, D. and Gajo, L. (2009) Introduction – French voices on plurilingualism and pluriculturalism: Theory, significance and perspectives. *International Journal of Multilingualism* 6 (2), 137–153. doi:10.1080/14790710902846707

Morgan, B. (2004) Teacher identity as pedagogy: Towards a field-internal conceptualization in bilingual and second language education. *International Journal of Bilingual Education and Bilingualism* 7 (2), 172–188.

Moskovsky, C. and Picard, M. (eds) (2018) *English as a Foreign Language in Saudi Arabia*. London: Routledge.

Motha, S. (2006) Racializing ESOL teacher identities in US K–12 public schools. *TESOL Quarterly* 40 (3), 495–518. doi:10.2307/40264541

Motha, S. (2014) *Race, Empire, and English Language Teaching: Creating Responsible and Ethical Anti-Racist Practice*. New York: Teachers College Press.

Motha, S. (2020) Is an antiracist and decolonizing applied linguistics possible? *Annual Review of Applied Linguistics* 40, 128–133.

Motha, S. and Lin, A. (2014) 'Non-coercive rearrangements': Theorizing desire in TESOL. *TESOL Quarterly* 48, 331–359.

Motha, S., Jain, R. and Tecle, T. (2012) Translinguistic identity-as-pedagogy: Implications for language teacher education. *International Journal of Innovation in English Language Teaching and Research* 1 (1), 13–28.

Moussu, L. (2018) Shortcomings of NESTs and NNESTs. In J.I. Liontas (ed.) *The TESOL Encyclopedia of English Language Teaching* (1st edn) (pp. 1–6). Hoboken, NJ: Wiley-Blackwell.

Muhammad, P.R. (2013) *Muslims and the Making of America*. Los Angeles, CA: Muslim Public Affairs Council Policy. See https://www.mpac.org/publications/policy-papers/muslims-and-the-making-of-america.php (accessed 2 December 2018).

Mullock, B. (2009) Motivations and rewards in teaching English overseas: A portrait of expatriate TEFL teachers in South-East Asia. *Prospect* 24 (2), 4–19. See http://www.ameprc.mq.edu.au/docs/prospect_journal/volume_24_no_2/Barbara_Mullock.pdf

Nagatomo, D.H. (2015) How being an 'insider' or an 'outsider' shapes EFL teachers' professional identity: One teacher's story from Japan. *Asian EFL Journal* 17 (3), 111–130.

Naidoo, R. and Williams, J. (2015) The neoliberal regime in English higher education: Charters, consumers and the erosion of the public good. *Critical Studies in Education* 56 (2), 208–223. doi:10.1080/17508487.2014.939098

Nasr, S. (2004) *The Heart of Islam: Enduring Values for Humanity*. San Francisco, CA: Harper One.

Nelson, C.D. (2016) The significance of sexual identity to language learning and teaching. In S. Preece (ed.) *The Routledge Handbook of Language and Identity* (pp. 351–365). Abingdon: Routledge.

Nelson, C. and Appleby, R. (2014) Conflict, militarization, and their after-effects: Key challenges for TESOL. *TESOL Quarterly* 49 (2), 309–332.

Nieto, S. (2010) *Language, Culture, and Teaching: Critical Perspectives* (2nd edn). New York: Routledge.

Nonaka, C. (2018) *Transcending Self and Other Through Akogare [Desire]: The English Language and the Internationalization of Higher Education in Japan*. Bristol: Multilingual Matters.
Nonaka, C. (2020) Transnational identity: The struggles of being and becoming a Japanese female professor in a neo-*kokusaika* phase of Japan. *Research in Comparative and International Education* 15 (3), 234–251. doi:10.1177/1745499920946201
Obeid, R. (2017) Second language writing and assessment: Voices from within the Saudi EFL context. *English Language Teaching* 10 (6), 174–181.
Ong, A. (2007) Neoliberalism as a mobile technology. *Transactions of the Institute of British Geographers* 32 (1), 3–8.
O'Regan, J. (2014) English as a lingua franca: An immanent critique. *Applied Linguistics* 35 (5), 533–552. doi:10.1093/applin/amt045
O'Regan, J.P. (2021) *Global English and Political Economy*. London: Routledge.
Ottaway, M., Brown, J., Hamzawy, A., Sadjadpour, K. and Salem, P. (2008) *The New Middle East*. Washington, DC: Carnegie Endowment for International Peace.
Owens, C.D. (2017) Traveling yellow peril: Race, gender, and empire in Japan's English teaching industry. *American Studies* 55 (4), 29–49.
Ozog, A.C.K. (1989) English for Islamic purposes – a plea for cross-cultural consideration. In V. Bickley (ed.) *Language Teaching and Learning Styles within and across Cultures* (pp. 398–403). Hong Kong: Institute of Language in Education.
Pae, T. (2016) Effects of the differences between native and non-native English-speaking teachers on students' attitudes and motivation toward learning English. *Asia Pacific Journal of Education* 37 (2), 163–178. doi:10.1080/02188791.2016.1235012
Paiz, J.M. (2019) Queering practice: LGBTQ+ diversity and inclusion in English language teaching. *Journal of Language, Identity & Education* 18, 266–275.
Paradis, J. (2007) Early bilingual and multilingual acquisition. In P. Auer and W. Li (eds) *Handbook of Multilingualism and Multilingual Communication* (pp. 15–44). Berlin: Mouton de Gruyter.
Park, G. (2013) Situating the discourses of privilege and marginalization in the lives of two East Asian women teachers of English. *Race Ethnicity and Education* 18 (1), 108–133. doi:10.1080/13613324.2012.759924
Park, G. (2018) *Narratives of East Asian Women Teachers of English: Where Privilege Meets Marginalization*. Bristol: Multilingual Matters.
Park, J. (2021) Political economy of language and language learning: Beyond neoliberal commodification. Paper presented as part of the invited colloquium on 'Political Economy of Language and Language Learning: Beyond Neoliberal Commodification', AAAL 2021 Conference, Houston, TX, 20–23 March.
Park, J.S.-Y. and Wee, L. (2012) *Markets of English: Linguistic Capital and Language Policy in a Globalizing World*. New York: Routledge.
Patrick, F. (2014) Making the transition to a 'knowledge economy' and 'knowledge society': Exploring the challenges for Saudi Arabia. In A.W. Wiseman, N.H. Alromi and S.A. Alshumrani (eds) *Education for a Knowledge Society in Arabian Gulf Countries* (pp. 229–251). Bingley: Emerald Group. doi:10.1108/S1479-367920 140000024018
Pavlenko, A. (2003) 'I never knew I was a bilingual': Reimagining teacher identities in TESOL. *Journal of Language, Identity & Education* 2 (4), 251–268.
Pavlenko, A. (2008) Multilingualism in post-Soviet countries: Language revival, language removal, and sociolinguistic theory. *International Journal of Bilingual Education and Bilingualism* 11 (3), 275–314.
Pavlenko, A. and Blackledge, A. (eds) (2004) *Negotiation of Identities in Multilingual Contexts*. Clevedon: Multilingual Matters.
PBS (Public Broadcasting Company) (2013) *The African Americans: Many Rivers to Cross*. Arlington, VA: Public Broadcasting Company. See https://www.pbs.org/show/african-americans-many-rivers-cross/ (accessed 2 December 2018).

Pennington, M.C. (2014) Teacher identity in TESOL: A frames perspective. In Y.L. Cheung, S.B. Said and K. Park (eds) *Advances and Current Trends in Language Teacher Identity Research*. London and New York: Routledge.

Pennycook, A. (1994) *The Cultural Politics of English as an International Language*. London: Routledge.

Pennycook, A. (1995) English in the world/the world in English. In J.W. Tollefson (ed.) *Power and Inequality in Language Education* (pp. 34–58). Cambridge: Cambridge University Press.

Pennycook, A. (1998/2017) *English and the Discourses of Colonialism*. London: Routledge.

Pennycook, A. (2010) Critical and alternative directions in applied linguistics. *Australian Review of Applied Linguistics* 33 (2), 1–16.

Pennycook, A. and Makoni, S. (2019) *Innovations and Challenges in Applied Linguistics from the Global South*. Abingdon: Routledge.

Petrol, M. (2009) Transnational teachers of English in Mexico. *The High School Journal* 92 (4), 115–128. See https://www.jstor.org/stable/40364009

Pham, H.H. (2004) Trained in the West, teaching in the East: Vietnamese teachers returning from TESOL courses abroad. Unpublished PhD thesis, University of Melbourne. See https://hdl.handle.net/11343/39930 (accessed 14 November 2021).

Phan, L.H. (2001) How do culturally situated notions of 'polite' forms influence the way Vietnamese postgraduate students write academic English in Australia? *Australian Journal of Education* 45 (3), 296–308. doi:10.1177/000494410104500307

Phan, L.H. (2004) University classrooms of English in Vietnam: Contesting the stereotypes. *English Language Teaching Journal* 58 (1), 50–57.

Phan, L.H. (2008) *Teaching English as an International Language: Identity, Resistance and Negotiation*. Clevedon: Multilingual Matters.

Phan, L.H. (2014) The politics of naming: Critiquing 'learner-centred' and 'teacher as facilitator' in English language and humanities classrooms. *Asia-Pacific Journal of Teacher Education* 42 (4), 392–405. doi:10.1080/1359866X.2014.956048

Phan, L.H. (2016) English and identity: A reflection and implications for future research. *Journal of Asian Pacific Communication* 26 (2), 348–355. doi:10.1075/japc.26.2.10pha

Phan, L.H. (2017) *Transnational Education Crossing 'Asia' and 'the West': Adjusted Desire, Transformative Mediocrity, and Neo-colonial Disguise*. London: Routledge.

Phan, L.H. (2021) Locating English and its economic value within sociopolitical conditions, ideology, aspirations, and celebrated models of success. Paper presented as part of the invited colloquium on 'Political Economy of Language and Language Learning: Beyond Neoliberal Commodification', AAAL 2021 Conference, Houston, TX, 20–23 March.

Phan, L.H. and Bao, D. (2019) Multiple classrooms of life: Engaging multi-faceted reflections on 'changing English', ideology and 'sparkle' moments. *Changing English* 26 (3), 238–251.

Phan, L.H. and Barnawi, O.Z. (2015) Where English, neoliberalism, desire and internationalization are alive and kicking: Higher education in Saudi Arabia today. *Language and Education* 29 (6), 545–565. doi:10.1080/09500782.2015.1059436

Phan, L.H. and Le, T.L. (2013) Living the tensions: Moral dilemmas in English language teaching. In T. Seddon, J. Ozga and J. Levin (eds) *Routledge World Year Book of Education 2013* (pp. 220–235). New York: Routledge.

Phan, L.H. and Mohamad, A. (2020) The making and transforming of a transnational in dialogue: Confronting dichotomous thinking in knowledge production, identity formation, and pedagogy. *Research in Comparative and International Education* 15 (3), 197–216. doi:10.1177/1745499920946222

Phan, L.H. and Phung, T. (2020) COVID-19 opportunities for internationalization at home. *University World News*, 29 August. See https://www.universityworldnews.com/post.php?story=20200828113510793

Phan, L.H., Kelley, L.C and Curaming, R.A. (2020) Transnationally-trained scholars working in global contexts: Knowledge production, identity, epistemology, and career trajectories. *Research in Comparative and International Education* 15 (3), 189–196. doi:10.1177/1745499920946226

Phillipson, R. (1992) *Linguistic Imperialism.* Oxford: Oxford University Press.

Phillipson, R. (2001) English for globalization or for the world's people? *International Review of Education* 47 (3), 185–200.

Phillipson, R. (2010) *Linguistic Imperialism Continued.* London and New York: Routledge.

Piller, I. (2016) Monolingual ways of seeing multilingualism. *Journal of Multicultural Discourses* 11 (1), 25–33.

Piller, I. and Cho, J. (2013) Neoliberalism as language policy. *Language in Society* 42 (1), 23–44. doi:10.1017/S0047404512000887

Pincas, A. (1962) Structural linguistics and systematic composition teaching to students of English as a foreign language. *Language Learning: A Journal of Research in Language Studies* 12 (3), 185–194.

Piper, N. and Withers, M. (2018) Forced transnationalism and temporary labour migration: Implications for understanding migrant rights. *Identities* 25 (5), 558–575.

Planken, B. (2005) Managing rapport in lingua franca sales negotiations: A comparison of professional and aspiring negotiators. *English for Specific Purposes* 24 (4), 381–400. doi:10.1016/j.esp.2005.02.002.

Pluralism Project (n.d.) African-American Islam reformed: 'Black Muslims' and the universal Ummah. *The Pluralism Project, Harvard University.* See http://pluralism.org/religions/islam/islam-in-america/african-american-islam-reformed-black-muslims-and-the-universal-ummah/ (accessed 12 December 2018).

Polat, N., Mahalingappa, L. and Kayi-Aydar, H. (eds) (2021) *The Preparation of Teachers of English as an Additional Language around the World: Research, Policy, Curriculum and Practice.* Bristol: Multilingual Matters.

Poole, A. (2019) International education teachers' experiences as an educational precariat in China. *Journal of Research in International Education* 18 (1), 60–76.

Poole, A. (2021) *International Teachers' Lived Experiences: Examining Internationalised Schooling in Shanghai.* Cham: Palgrave Macmillan.

Porter, L. (2016) 17 famous black Muslims. *Essence.* See https://www.essence.com/celebrity/famous-black-muslims/ (accessed 12 December 2018).

Preece, S. (ed.) (2016) *The Routledge Handbook of Language and Identity.* London: Routledge.

Prior, M.T. (2019) Elephants in the room: An 'affective turn,' or just feeling our way? *The Modern Language Journal* 103 (2), 516–527. doi:10.1111/modl.12573

Qadeer, A. (2019) Saudi EFL learners' perceptions about the teaching of English by native and non-native English teachers. *Arab World English Journal* 11 (3: Special Issue: The Dynamics of EFL in Saudi Arabia), 137–153. doi:10.24093/awej/efl1.11

Raban, J. (1999/2011) *Passage to Juneau: A Sea and its Meanings.* New York: Vintage Books.

Randolph Jr, L.J. and Johnson, S.M. (2017) Social justice in language classroom: A call for action. *Dimension* 2017, 99–121.

Rao, Z. (2009) Chinese students' perceptions of native English-speaking teachers in EFL teaching. *Journal of Multilingual and Multicultural Development* 31 (1), 55–68. doi:10.1080/01434630903301941

Reina, D.S. and Reina, M.L. (1999) Trust and betrayal in the workplace: Building effective relationships in your organization. *Advances in Developing Human Resources* 2 (1), 121.

Reuveny, R. and Prakash, A. (1999) The Afghanistan war and the breakdown of the Soviet Union. *Review of International Studies* 25 (4), 693–708.

Reynie, D. (ed.) (2021) *Islamist Terrorist Attacks in the World 1979–2021.* Paris: Fondation pour l'innovation politique. See https://www.fondapol.org/en/study/islamist-terrorist-attacks-in-the-world-1979-2021/ (accessed 10 February 2022).

Ribot, J. and Peluso, N.L. (2003) A theory of access. *Rural Sociology* 68 (2), 153–181.

Richards, J.C. and Lockhart, C. (1996) *Reflective Teaching in Second Language Classrooms*. Cambridge: Cambridge University Press.

Richardson, P.M. (2004) Possible influences of Arabic-Islamic culture on the reflective practices proposed for an education degree at the Higher Colleges of Technology in the United Arab Emirates. *International Journal of Educational Development* 24 (4), 429–436.

Rivers, D.J. (2017) Native-speakerism and the betrayal of the native speaker language-teaching professional. In D.J. Rivers and K. Zotzmann (eds) *Isms in Language Education: Oppression, Intersectionality and Emancipation* (pp. 74–97). Berlin: De Gruyter Mouton.

Rizvi, F. and Choo, S. (2020) Education and cosmopolitanism in Asia: An introduction. *Asia Pacific Journal of Education* 40 (1), 1–9. doi:10.1080/02188791.2020.1725282

Rizvi, F. and Lingard, B. (2010) *Globalizing Education Policy*. New York: Routledge.

Rose, H., Syrbe, M., Montakantiwong, A. and Funada, N. (2020) *Global TESOL for the 21st Century: Teaching English in a Changing World*. Bristol: Multilingual Matters.

Rubdy, R. and Alsagoff, L. (eds) (2014) *The Global-Local Interface and Hybridity: Exploring Language and Identity*. Bristol: Multilingual Matters.

Ruecker, T. (2018) Employment landscape for NESTs and NNESTs: Non-native English-speaking teachers (NNESTs). In *The TESOL Encyclopedia of English Language Teaching*. Wiley Online Library. See https://onlinelibrary.wiley.com/doi/10.1002/9781118784235.eelt0015

Ruecker, T. and Ives, L. (2014) White native English speakers needed: The rhetorical construction of privilege in online teacher recruitment spaces. *TESOL Quarterly* 49 (4), 733–756.

Rupp, R. (2009) Higher education in the Middle East: Opportunities and challenges for US universities and Middle East partners. *Global Media Journal* 8 (14).

Sahan, K. (2021) Implementing English-medium instruction: Comparing policy to practice at a Turkish university. *Australian Review of Applied Linguistics* 44 (2), 129–153. doi:10.1075/aral.20094.sah

Said, E. (1997) *Covering Islam: How the Media and the Experts Determine How We See the Rest of the World*. New York: Vintage Books.

Said, E. (2002) *Reflections on Exile and Other Essays*. Cambridge, MA: Harvard University Press.

Saito, K. and Lyster, R. (2012) Effects of form-focused instruction and corrective feedback on L2 pronunciation development of /ɹ/ by Japanese learners of English. *Language Learning* 62, 595–633.

Salerno, R.A. (2018) Neoliberal ideology and the centrality of trust. *Comparative Sociology* 17 (3–4), 354–368. doi:10.1163/15691330-12341464

Sand, A. (2013) Jamaican English. In B. Kortmann and K. Lunkenheimer (eds) *The Mouton World Atlas of Variation in English* (pp. 210–221). Berlin: De Gruyter Mouton. doi:10.1515/9783110280128.210

Sarıgül, M. (2018) Native English-speaking teachers in foreign language teaching in Turkey: A brief historical overview. *Journal of Multilingual and Multicultural Development* 39 (4), 289–300. doi:10.1080/01434632.2017.1375508

Saunders, D. (2007) The impact of neoliberalism on college students. *Journal of College and Character* 8 (5), 1–9. doi:10.2202/1940-1639.1620

Savski, K. (2021) Negotiating boundaries while becoming a TESOL practitioner in Southern Thailand. In R. Jain, B. Yazan and S. Canagarajah (eds) *Transnational Identities and Practices in English Language Teaching: Critical Inquiries from Diverse Practitioners* (pp. 227–239). Bristol: Multilingual Matters.

Schneider, E. (2020) *English Around the World: An Introduction* (2nd edn). Cambridge: Cambridge University Press. doi:10.1017/CBO9780511781711

Schumann, J.H. (2019) Sources of definitional problems in the study of emotion: Nonphysical aspects of mind. *The Modern Language Journal* 103 (2), 536–539. doi:10.1111/modl.12577

Schwartz, F., Almasmari, H. and Fitch, A. (2015) Saudi Arabia launches airstrikes on Houthi rebels in Yemen. Wall Street Journal, 25 March. See https://www.wsj.com/articles/saudi-arabia-launches-military-operations-in-yemen-1427275251?tesla=y&mod=e2tw (accessed 24 April 2016).

Selvi, A.F. (2010) All teachers are equal, but some teachers are more equal than others: Trend analysis of job advertisements in English language teaching. *WATESOL NNEST Caucus Annual Review* 1 (1), 155–181.

Selvi, A.F. (2014) Myths and misconceptions about nonnative English speakers in the TESOL (NNEST) movement. *TESOL Journal* 5 (3), 573–611.

Selvi, A.F. and Yazan, B. (eds) (2021) *Language Teacher Education for Global Englishes: A Practical Resource Book*. London: Routledge.

Shah, M.A. and Elyas, T. (2019) TESOL at the crossroads: Representation of source cultures in TESOL textbooks. *Cogent Education* 6 (1), Art. 1643524. doi:10.1080/2331186X.2019.1643524

Sharkey, J. (2004) ESOL teachers' knowledge of context as critical mediator in curriculum development. *TESOL Quarterly* 38 (2), 279–299.

Sheehi, S. (2011) *Islamophobia: The Ideological Campaign Against Muslims*. Atlanta, GA: Clarity Press.

Shin, H. (2006) Rethinking TESOL from a SOL's perspective: Indigenous epistemology and decolonizing praxis in TESOL. *Critical Inquiry in Language Studies* 3 (2–3), 147–167. doi:10.1080/15427587.2006.9650844

Shin, H. (2016) Language 'skills' and the neoliberal English education industry. *Journal of Multilingual and Multicultural Development* 37 (5), 509–522.

Shin, H. and Park, J.S.-Y. (2016) Researching language and neoliberalism. *Journal of Multilingual and Multicultural Development* 37 (5), 443–452. doi:10.1080/01434632.2015.1071823

Shohamy, E. (1998) Critical language testing and beyond. Plenary talk at American Association of Applied Linguistics (AAAL) Meeting, Orlando, Florida, 1997. *Studies in Educational Evaluation* 24 (4), 331–345.

Shohamy, E. and Gorter, D. (eds) (2009) *Linguistic Landscape: Expanding the Scenery*. New York: Routledge.

Shukri, N.A. (2014) Second language writing and culture: Issues and challenges from the Saudi learners' perspective. *Arab World English Journal* 5 (3), 190–207.

Simpson, W. and O'Regan, J. (2018) Fetishism and the language commodity: A materialist critique. *Language Sciences* 70, 155–156. See 10.1016/j.langsci.2018.05.009

Song, J. and Park, J.S.-Y. (2019) The politics of emotions in ELT: Structure of feeling and anxiety of Korean English teachers. *Changing English* 26 (3), 252–262.

Stake, R.E. (1995) *The Art of Case Study Research*. Thousand Oaks, CA: Sage.

Stanley, P. (2013) *A Critical Ethnography of 'Westerners' Teaching English in China: Shanghaied in Shanghai*. London: Routledge.

Stewart, A. (2020) *Language Teacher Recognition: Narratives of Filipino English Teachers in Japan*. Bristol: Multilingual Matters.

Sung, C.C.M. (2015) Hong Kong English: Linguistic and sociolinguistic perspectives. *Language and Linguistics Compass* 9 (6), 256–270. doi:10.1111/lnc3.12142

Sung, C.C.M. (2020) English as a lingua franca in the international university: Language experiences and perceptions among international students in multilingual Hong Kong. *Language, Culture and Curriculum* 33 (3), 258–273. doi:10.1080/07908318.2019.1695814

Taylor, S.V. and Sobel, D.M. (2011) *Culturally Responsive Pedagogy: Teaching Like Our Students' Lives Matter*. Bingley: Emerald Group.

Thompson, G., Aizawa, I., Curle, S. and Rose, H. (2022) Exploring the role of self-efficacy beliefs and learner success in English medium instruction. *International Journal of Bilingual Education and Bilingualism* 25 (1), 196–209. doi:10.1080/13670050.2019.1651819

Tierney, W.G. (2008) Trust and organizational culture in higher education. In J. Välimaa and O.H. Ylijoki (eds) *Cultural Perspectives on Higher Education*. Dordrecht: Springer. doi:10.1007/978-1-4020-6604-7_3

Toom, A. (2019) Shaping teacher identities and agency for the profession: Contextual factors and surrounding communities. *Teachers and Teaching* 25 (8), 915–917. doi:10.1080/13540602.2019.1703619

Tran, T. (2002) In impoverished Afghanistan, English becomes international language of jobs and opportunity. *Global Policy Forum*, 21 August. See http://www.globalpolicy.org (accessed 12 December 2018).

Tribble, S. (1997) *Writing. Language Teaching: A Scheme for Teacher Education*. Oxford: Oxford University Press.

Tsou, S.-Y. and Chen, Y. (2019) Taiwanese university students' perceptions toward native and non-native English-speaking teachers in EFL contexts. *International Journal of Teaching and Learning in Higher Education* 31 (2), 176–183.

Tsui, A. and Tollefson, J. (eds) (2007) *Language Policy, Culture, and Identity in Asian Contexts*. Mahwah, NJ: Lawrence Erlbaum.

Tuan, Y.F. (1977) *Space and Place: The Perspective of Experience*. Minneapolis, MN: University of Minnesota Press.

Tupas, R. (ed.) (2015) *Unequal Englishes*. New York: Palgrave McMillan.

Turki, B. (2014) The Kuwait Fund for Arab Economic Development and its activities in African countries, 1961–2010. *Middle East Journal* 68 (3), 421–435.

Ubani, M. (2013) Threats and solutions: Multiculturalism, religion and educational policy. *Intercultural Education* 24 (3), 195–210. doi:10.1080/14675986.2013.797701

Üstünlüoglu, E. (2007) University students' perceptions of native and non-native teachers. *Teachers and Teaching* 13 (1), 63–79. doi:10.1080/13540600601106096

Varghese, M., Morgan, B., Johnston, B. and Johnson, K.A. (2005) Theorizing language teacher identity: Three perspectives and beyond. *Journal of Language, Identity & Education* 4 (1), 21–44. doi:10.1207/s15327701jlie0401_2

Vertovec, S. (1999) Conceiving and researching transnationalism. *Ethnic and Racial Studies* 22 (2), 447–462. doi:10.1080/014198799329558

Vertovec, S. (2009) *Transnationalism*. London/New York: Routledge.

Viete, R. and Phan, L.H. (2007) The growth of voice: Expanding possibilities for representing self in research writing. *English Teaching: Practice and Critique* 6 (2), 39–57.

Vološinov, V. (1929/1986) *Marxism and the Philosophy of Language* (L. Matejka and I.R. Tutunik, trans.). Cambridge: Harvard University Press. (Original work published 1929.)

Vološinov, V.N. (1929/2017) *Chu Nghia Marx va Triet Hoc Ngon Ngu* (T.L. Ngo, trans.). Ha Noi: Vietnam National University Press. (Original work published 1929.)

Vu, H.H. and Phan, L.H. (2020) Interrogating troubling issues in Vietnam's English language teacher education. In A. Tsui (ed.) *English Language Teaching and Teacher Education in East Asia: Global Challenges and Local Responses* (pp. 217–234). Cambridge: Cambridge University Press. doi:10.1017/9781108856218.012

Wahyudi, R. (2021) A transnational TEGCOM practitioner's multiple subjectivities and critical classroom negotiations in the Indonesian university context. In R. Jain, B. Yazan and S. Canagarajah (eds) *Transnational Identities and Practices in English Language Teaching: Critical Inquiries from Diverse Practitioners* (pp. 240–258). Bristol: Multilingual Matters.

Walker, A. (2017) Critical autobiography as research. *The Qualitative Report* 22 (7), 1896–1908.

Walker, J. (2001) Client views of TESOL service: Expectations and perceptions. *International Journal of Educational Management* 15 (4), 187–196. doi:10.1108/09513540110394438

Walkinshaw, I. and Duong, O. (2014) Native and non-native English language teachers: Student perceptions in Vietnam and Japan. *Sage Open* 4 (2), 1–9. doi:10.1177/2158244014534451

Wang, Y. (2019) The role of English in the internationalization of Chinese higher education: A case study of English medium instruction in China. In K. Murata (ed.) *English-medium Instruction from an English as a Lingua Franca Perspective: Exploring the Higher Education Context* (pp. 201–218). New York: Routledge.

Watson-Gegeo, K.A. (1988) Ethnography in ESL: Defining the essentials. *TESOL Quarterly* 22 (4), 575–592. doi:10.2307/3587257

Webb, E. (1996) Trust and crisis. In R. Kramer and T. Tyler (eds) *Trust in Organizations: Frontiers of Theory and Research* (pp. 288–301). Thousand Oaks, CA: Sage.

Wetherell, M. (2015) Trends in the turn to affect: A social psychological critique. *Body & Society* 21 (2) 139–166. doi:10.1177/1357034X14539020

Widin, J. (2010) *Illegitimate Practices: Global English Language Education*. Bristol: Multilingual Matters.

Wilkins, S. (2010) Higher education in the United Arab Emirates: An analysis of the outcomes of significant increases in supply and competition. *Journal of Higher Education Policy and Management* 32 (4), 389–400.

Windle, J. (2020) Recontextualizing race, politics and inequality in transnational knowledge circulation: Biographical resignifications. *Research in Comparative and International Education* 15 (3), 291–304. doi:10.1177/1745499920946202

Windle, J.A., de Jesus, D. and Bartlett, L. (eds) (2020) *The Dynamics of Language and Inequality in Education: Social and Symbolic Boundaries in the Global South*. Bristol: Multilingual Matters.

Wolcott, H.F. (1994) *Transforming Qualitative Data: Description, Analysis, and Interpretation*. Thousand Oaks, CA: Sage.

Wolff, D. and De Costa, P.I. (2017) Expanding the language teacher identity landscape: An investigation of the emotions and strategies of a NNEST. *The Modern Language Journal* 101, 76–90.

Wong, M.S. and Mahboob, A. (eds) (2018) *Spirituality and English Language Teaching: Religious Explorations of Teacher Identity, Pedagogy and Context*. Bristol: Multilingual Matters.

Wong, M.S., Kristjiansson, C. and Dörnyei, Z. (eds) (2013) *Christian Faith and English Language Teaching and Learning: Research on the Interrelationship of Religion and ELT*. New York: Routledge.

Woods, P. (2005) 'The hedgehog and the fox': Approaches to English for peace-keeping in Central and Eastern Europe and Central Asia. In H. Coleman, J. Gulyamova and A. Thomas (eds) *National Development, Education and Language in Central Asia and Beyond* (pp. 94–99). Tashkent: British Council Uzbekistan.

Yazan, B. and Rudolph, N. (eds) (2018) *Criticality, Teacher Identity, and (In)equity in English Language Teaching and Research: Issues and Implications*. Cham: Springer.

You, X. (ed.) (2018) *Transnational Writing Education: Theory, History, and Practice*. London and New York: Routledge.

Yuan, R. and Lee, I. (2021) *Becoming and Being a TESOL Teacher Educator: Research and Practice*. London: Routledge.

Zafer, A. (2002) A survey of Saudi school teachers' and college professors' perspectives on topics and roles to emphasize in English as a foreign language in teacher preparation course. Unpublished doctoral dissertation, University of Kansas.

Zhang, J. and Jun Zhang, L. (2021) Learners' satisfaction with native and non-native English-speaking teachers' teaching competence and their learning motivation: A path-analytic approach. *Asia Pacific Journal of Education* 41 (3), 558–573. doi:10.1080/02188791.2020.1833834

Zhang, Y. (2004) A study of English writing by native Chinese freshman: Teaching English requires the teaching of culture(s). *Asian EFL Journal* 6 (4), 1–26.

Index

Act, 49, 103, 141, 147–148
Actors, 7–8, 28, 32, 35, 41, 76, 137, 156, 186–187, 195
Adamson, 4, 6
Africa, 7, 26–27, 50, 62, 74, 123, 136, 141, 146, 182, 190, 195
Alshakhi, 4, 6, 13, 43, 73, 77, 84, 92, 157–158, 160, 187, 193, 199
Analyze, 131
Analysis, 4, 9, 15, 19, 31, 74, 129, 132, 155, 160
Arabian Gulf, 3, 8, 18–20, 27, 36, 56, 195
Arabic, 7, 12, 14, 16–17, 22–23, 36, 41, 67–68, 84, 86, 105–106, 113, 117, 122, 128, 131–133, 135, 138, 164–166, 178, 196, 199–200
Assessment, 12, 24, 36, 75, 76, 85, 88, 90–102, 112, 118, 160–167, 170, 172–178, 185, 189
Assumption, 4, 12–13, 16, 80, 82, 117, 137, 144, 157, 175, 181, 200
Attached, 10, 14, 17, 167, 181
Awareness, 5, 51, 58, 114, 127, 147, 166–167, 200

Backgrounds, 2–4, 7, 9, 11–12, 16, 27–28, 31–33, 35, 37, 40, 42, 45, 48, 59, 74, 79–80, 82, 84, 89, 91, 118, 140, 145–146, 149, 154, 159, 162, 170, 180, 184
Bank, 27, 73
Barnawi, 73–74, 76, 78, 82, 89, 92, 104–105, 109, 112, 118, 121, 138, 145, 148, 159, 177, 187–189, 193, 198
BBC, 15–16
Being, 3, 5, 12, 15, 19, 26, 28, 32–33, 36, 43–45, 50, 54, 57, 59–60, 64, 67–71, 77, 83–85, 98, 100, 102, 106, 110, 114, 116–117, 119, 122, 125–128, 131–138, 141, 143–145, 147–148, 151–153, 155, 159–161, 165–175, 181–183, 186, 192–193, 195, 199, 201
Between, 10–14, 16, 19–20, 23, 28, 32, 34–35, 40, 44–45, 60, 69, 75–76, 79, 81, 83, 87, 93, 96–97, 99, 101–102, 106, 112, 114–115, 117, 119, 122–126, 129–130, 132, 134, 138, 145–146, 148, 154–155, 165, 169, 173, 175–176, 178, 181–183, 186–187, 191–198
Benesch, 10, 42–46, 165, 167–169, 174–175, 177–178, 187
Black, 122, 126–127, 129, 131–136, 138, 140–145, 147, 183
Boko, 14
Book, 187, 189, 191, 194, 197, 201
Bourdieu, 26, 130
Brothers, 135

Call, 9, 15–17, 19–20, 28, 30, 49, 79, 114, 136, 141, 144, 154, 178, 186, 196
Capital, 5, 24–25, 36–38, 43, 45–46, 117, 122–124, 130, 143, 149, 154, 160, 164–167, 172, 175–178, 189, 195, 198
Cenoz, 38, 41
Certain, 5–6, 9, 14, 16–17, 32, 43–45, 49, 69, 71, 81, 85, 91, 97, 109, 117, 130, 134, 137, 146, 166, 175, 183–186
Change, 39, 93, 95, 109, 115, 123, 134, 151, 175–176, 178, 185
Classroom, 4–5, 9–13, 28, 31, 33, 35, 40–41, 50, 60, 70, 76, 81–84, 88–102, 104–120, 142, 145, 160, 163, 166, 170, 174, 180, 187, 196–197
Concepts, 4, 30, 39, 43, 46–47, 97, 113, 125–126, 128

Index 225

Commercialization, 8, 34, 78, 188
Communicative, 36, 52, 76, 89–92, 97–98,
    102, 104, 107–108, 111–112,
    115–116, 118–119, 192–193, 195
Communities, 9, 14–15, 22–23, 31, 40,
    44, 53, 127
Community, 4, 7, 11, 22, 26, 37, 38, 42,
    99, 146, 150, 178, 199
Competence, 32–33, 41, 98–99, 106,
    112, 122, 136–137, 143, 145, 147,
    151, 153, 192–193, 195
Common, 16, 36, 40, 46, 73, 76, 82, 88,
    90–91, 107–109, 143, 146, 149,
    152, 161
Complex, 4, 8–9, 11, 18, 28, 31–32,
    35–36, 40, 42–43, 45–46, 49,
    60, 112, 125, 141, 144–145, 149,
    156–157, 160, 164, 168, 183, 194
Conceptual, 30–31, 43, 121
Conceptually, 39, 195
Conditions, 4, 11, 28, 33–36, 38, 43, 49,
    69, 71, 89, 93–94, 112, 120, 124,
    128, 185–187
Consequences, 31, 39
Constructs, 25, 36, 43, 45, 105, 109, 119,
    144, 146, 180–183
Culture, 6–7, 20, 39–40, 54, 56, 61–62,
    66–67, 86, 89, 95, 98, 102, 114,
    122–123, 125, 127–128, 132–141,
    145–148, 152, 158, 161, 169–171,
    178–179, 182, 196
Cultivate, 32, 82, 120, 186
Current, 7–8, 17–19, 26, 33, 36, 42, 50,
    53–56, 59, 62–70, 75–79, 90, 96,
    100, 112, 123–124, 151, 160, 163,
    171, 175, 177, 193, 195–196, 199
Curricula, 15, 17, 19, 23–25, 27, 31,
    36–37, 65, 74–76, 82, 129
Committed, 20–21, 37, 93, 100, 116,
    148–149, 162

Data, 4, 11–13, 47, 51–52, 57–59, 61–62,
    71–72, 84–86, 89, 95, 98, 104,
    114, 118, 120, 122, 130–131, 137,
    140, 158, 160, 162–164, 171, 175,
    181, 188, 194
Debates, 8, 14, 16, 18, 20, 30, 46–47, 51,
    87, 108, 111, 113–114, 168–169,
    182–183, 196
Development, 24–25, 52, 54, 62–63, 65,
    67–68, 75, 77, 100, 102, 142, 145,
    163, 173, 178, 185–186, 189, 195

Demand, 17, 27, 37, 46, 73, 119, 123,
    128, 144–145, 148, 158–159,
    186, 191
Dialogic, 45
Different, 1–3, 7, 9–13, 22, 26–28,
    30–35, 37, 39–42, 45, 47, 49,
    51, 54, 60, 65–66, 69–71, 74,
    78, 80–82, 87–90, 96–98, 102,
    104–120, 158–162, 170–171,
    176–178, 180, 182–185, 191,
    193–196, 198–199
Directional, 45
Disagree, 173, 182
Discussed, 6, 13, 15, 17, 21, 36, 42–43,
    46, 51, 74, 79, 82, 88, 99, 102,
    105, 108–110, 117, 120, 122, 142,
    144, 155, 157, 172, 174, 178,
    180–181, 183–184, 187, 189, 192,
    195, 197
Dong, 30–33, 36, 62, 81
Drawing, 6, 10, 43, 85, 126, 130, 160,
    172, 181
Dynamic, 28, 37, 44–46, 59, 82, 89, 101,
    104–120, 124, 136, 138, 149, 160,
    168, 180, 182–183, 187

Economic, 5, 18–23, 25–27, 33–37,
    55–56, 59, 70, 74–75, 78, 80, 122,
    124–125, 127, 189, 195, 200
Education, 3, 6–10, 12–13, 17, 19–20,
    22–26, 30–31, 34–37, 42–45, 47,
    50, 52, 57, 59, 61, 63, 65, 67–68,
    70–78, 82, 87–89, 92, 105, 108,
    115, 117–120, 122, 130, 140–142,
    145, 147–148, 157, 159, 167,
    169–170, 175–176, 179–182,
    184–190, 193, 198–200
Efficient, 58
Effective, 7, 28, 90–91, 97–100, 104,
    108–113, 118, 164, 174, 178,
    188, 194
Empower, 177
English, 1–11, 14–28, 30–31, 34–42,
    45–46, 50–71, 73–200
Englishes, 42–43, 72, 82, 116–117, 122,
    147–149, 156, 180, 197, 199
Ethics, 44, 79, 110, 152
Example, 4, 7, 15, 19–20, 24, 36, 40, 42,
    59, 65–66, 70, 77–78, 80, 84, 87,
    89–101, 119, 141, 146, 149–150,
    153, 161, 165–166, 170, 173–174,
    181, 183, 192

Experience, 4, 6–13, 23, 28, 30, 33–34, 37, 41–42, 46–47, 49–71, 74–77, 79–84, 88–127, 130–200

Face to face, 64
Factor, 9, 15, 43–44, 49, 61–72, 80, 83, 85–86, 89, 100, 102, 124, 138, 160, 167–168, 177, 182, 185–187, 192
False, 36, 141, 176
Field, 6, 8–9, 12, 17, 35–38, 40–41, 44–45, 47, 57–60, 105, 117, 123, 128–129, 138, 154, 156, 168, 182, 184
Financial, 3, 18, 22–23, 25, 27, 51–58, 61–68, 128, 134, 200
follow, 43, 49–50, 79, 85, 93, 135, 141, 161, 172, 174, 177, 189
Forms, 12, 24–26, 30–32, 38, 42, 45, 49, 59, 74, 79, 81–82, 84, 87, 93, 95, 108, 119, 122, 138, 141, 143, 156, 160, 176, 181, 187, 190–191, 193
Fragmented, 49, 196
Fulfil, 57, 195

Gave, 12, 19, 53, 75, 77, 82, 106, 108, 132, 140, 143, 168, 174
Goods, 8, 20, 24, 36, 76–77, 123
Group, 9, 14–15, 17, 20, 27, 45, 49, 60, 72, 82, 83–84, 91–93, 105–108, 111, 113–115, 125–127, 145, 152–153, 160, 175, 177, 182
Ground realities, 7, 11, 31, 47, 49, 76, 88–103, 116, 144, 148
Growing body, 88, 117
Governments, 3, 15, 19–20, 34–35, 38
Govern, 39

Hardships, 125
Happens, 104, 119–120, 172
Happy, 80
Highlight, 48, 86, 116, 122–123, 126, 155, 168, 181
Hire, 57–58, 136, 155, 169, 189, 199
Home, 4–5, 9, 51, 53–54, 56, 61–63, 65–68, 70–71, 85–86, 94, 110, 115, 118, 133–134, 151, 159, 175–176, 190, 192
Human, 24–25, 33–34, 39, 44–45, 65, 100, 124, 126, 130, 132, 141, 195, 198–200

Identification, 40, 110, 119, 121, 128, 131, 143, 149
Identified, 6, 17, 45, 50–51, 57, 71, 90, 122, 125, 131, 133, 183
Identity, 5–6, 8, 11, 38, 40, 71, 82, 89, 110, 117, 120–140, 143, 146–147, 154, 159–160, 167, 171, 180–181, 183, 187, 196
Identifiable, 127
Immobilities, 31, 121
Incompatible, 125
Individuals, 10–11, 31–34, 37–38, 40, 44–45, 81, 102, 117, 124, 129, 131, 140, 146, 156, 158, 168, 177, 181–182, 193–194
Injustices, 82, 128–129
Intense, 122
International, 1–28, 30–40, 42
Islamic, 15–23, 122–125, 127, 131, 133–135, 148, 169–170, 178

Jerome, 131–136, 142, 144, 182
Jenkins, 6, 10, 13, 31, 38, 89, 116, 121–124, 129, 137–138, 141, 143, 145, 154, 159, 167, 182–183, 187
Job, 8, 26–27, 36, 38, 52–70, 88–89, 136, 148–149, 163, 179, 189
Joint, 24
Jordan, 21, 23, 27, 37, 38, 51, 61–62, 80–81, 146, 190
Joy, X
Just, 1–3, 14, 25, 28, 48, 57, 65, 81, 88, 92, 120, 124, 132, 135, 140–141, 145, 151–152, 165, 182, 186, 189, 201

Kingdom of Saudi Arabia, 8, 21, 36, 53, 61, 73, 121, 128
Karmani, 15–17
Kinninmont, 21
knowledge, 4–6, 9, 20, 24–25, 27–28, 33, 35, 37, 59–60, 63, 68, 77–79, 88–89, 92, 102, 104, 108, 110, 113, 117–118, 120, 123, 128–129, 133, 140, 150, 158, 161, 164–165, 168, 171–174, 176, 178, 185–187, 189, 192–193, 195–196, 198
Kuwait, 18–19, 21, 27, 66, 195

Labor, 10, 30, 42–47, 71, 93, 134, 143, 156–158, 160–161, 163–179, 183, 186–187, 194

Language, 3–11, 15–20, 22–23, 26–28, 30–31, 33–38, 40–43, 45, 47, 49–52, 54–58, 60–63, 65–68, 70–78, 81–102, 105–120, 122–123, 125–133, 135, 140–147, 151, 154–155, 158–175, 177–193, 195–200

Levels, 3, 9, 20, 23, 26, 34, 40, 51, 66, 71, 73, 76, 86, 88–90, 98, 108, 116–119, 124, 131, 137–138, 158–159, 161, 164–165, 178

Linguistic, 4–10, 12, 26–28, 30–43, 47–48, 50, 52, 55–58, 63–68, 71, 74, 82, 87, 89–90, 96, 99, 102, 105, 108, 112, 115–117, 120–132, 140, 142–143, 147, 149, 153–154, 156, 159, 175, 178, 181–200

Literacy, 35, 73–74, 76, 119

Literature, 4–7, 9, 39–40, 55–56, 59, 62, 64–67, 70–71, 84, 88–89, 100, 113–115, 120, 124–125, 132, 138, 141, 149, 157–160, 169, 175, 177, 180, 190, 194

Lives, 4, 49, 75, 98–100, 129, 146

Local, 3, 7–8, 11, 17, 19, 22–25, 27–28, 35, 57, 59–60, 64, 66, 69, 71, 73–74, 80, 88, 89, 91, 110, 113, 133–135, 145, 148, 158, 164, 170–171, 175, 178, 184–186, 188–194

Market, 9, 18–19, 25–27, 33, 35–36, 38, 40, 45, 49–52, 54–55, 57, 60–61, 71, 73–74, 76, 118, 129, 136, 172, 188–191, 193–194

Member, 4, 19, 37, 65–68, 127, 163, 193, 195, 198

Method, 58, 70, 75, 89, 96, 98, 104–106, 110–111, 117

Mind, 32, 44, 51, 54, 56, 105, 145, 151, 155, 194

Mobility, 4, 6, 9, 26–28, 30–42, 49, 55, 59, 71, 110, 120, 122–141, 154, 156–157, 161, 180–181, 184, 187, 194

Mobilities, 6, 10, 30–31, 42, 48–58, 61–72, 74, 121, 158, 160, 179

Motives, 51, 61, 194

Monolingualism, 42, 114–115

Multilingual, 37–42, 50, 66, 89, 116, 149, 190, 196

Multiple, 4, 8–9, 11, 33, 41, 43–46, 49, 51–52, 57, 59, 74, 81, 106, 127, 134, 156, 159, 169, 181, 186, 193

Napoleon Beale, 127

Native, 5–8, 10, 30–31, 37–38, 42, 46, 50–52, 56–58, 60–61, 68, 70–71, 78–87, 93, 101, 113–118, 122, 128–129, 133, 136–138, 140, 145, 147–150, 152–179

Nationalism, 4, 8–9, 36–38, 122–126, 131, 138

Non-native, 5, 7, 30–31, 37, 42, 46, 51, 61, 68, 70–71, 78–87, 98–99, 101, 113–114, 116–118, 129, 149, 152–154, 168–169, 177, 180, 182–183, 190

Norms, 8, 10, 13, 22, 32–33, 39, 43, 114, 117–118, 170, 184, 186, 194, 199

Nuanced accounts, 116

Pedagogies, 4–6, 11, 13, 19, 23, 27–28, 31, 33–37, 62, 74, 89, 93–94, 99, 101–103, 116–119, 140, 161, 169, 180, 182, 187, 196

Pedagogical, 5, 9–10, 12, 28, 30–33, 37, 39, 48, 58, 60, 70–71, 76, 88–97, 100–105, 107–109, 111–115, 117–118, 120, 142, 147–148, 150–151, 156, 159, 163–164, 172, 176, 178, 193, 195–196

Peninsula Shield Force, 21

Persistent, 5, 82

Phan, 2–6, 8–13, 15–16, 24, 26–27, 31, 33–38, 42–43, 46, 51, 73–74, 77–79, 82, 84, 89, 92, 97, 102, 104–105, 110, 118–121, 138, 146, 148, 157–172, 175, 177, 181, 187, 192–193, 198

Philippines, 15, 27, 62–63, 68, 81, 98–100, 110, 112, 117, 182

Place, 5–6, 9, 14, 18, 30–33, 35–36, 43

Platform, 14–15, 138, 178

Political, 6, 14–18, 21, 25, 32–33, 35, 39–40, 43–44, 52–53, 61, 89, 126–127, 133, 180, 185, 188

Power, 8, 10, 17–18, 37–38, 43–46, 76, 78, 114–115, 129–130, 137, 153, 156, 160, 165, 168, 174–178, 183

Practice, 5–6, 10, 14, 34, 37, 40, 42–47, 60, 65, 71, 90, 91–92, 94–95, 98, 101, 107, 109, 111, 117, 119, 128, 149, 154, 158, 160, 163, 169, 172–177, 181
Privilege, 45, 138, 142, 154, 156, 167–169, 184, 187
Private, 3, 33, 62, 138, 141
Prophet, 14, 23
Program, 3, 25, 28, 52, 67, 70–71, 77, 88, 92, 97, 101, 105, 109, 141, 149, 158, 161–164
Project, 13, 17, 24, 35, 59–60, 81, 118, 127, 146
Public, 3, 19–20, 22–24, 34, 51–53, 67, 113, 119, 131, 138, 141, 150, 188

Raciolinguistics, 121–123, 129, 132, 183
Racism, 9, 38, 45, 82, 87, 122, 128–130, 138, 144–145, 182, 187, 197
Reactions, 15, 23, 82–87, 194
Regions, 15, 31, 85
Reproduce, 43, 78, 137, 157, 166, 183
Represent, 7, 19, 31, 80, 105, 117, 123, 127, 192
Research, 6, 11–14, 26, 32, 34–35, 37–38, 43–44, 52, 54, 56, 63, 70, 74, 88–91, 98, 104, 121–122, 130
Respect, 6, 22, 28, 37, 39, 79–81, 83, 85
Restructure, 24, 125–126, 132–133
Rich, 11, 17–21, 24, 27, 34, 48–49, 59, 89, 126, 132, 182
Rural, 7, 22

Saudi, 1–13, 16, 18, 19, 21–28, 31–36, 40, 42–43, 47, 49–195
Scholarship, 8, 10, 25, 30, 37–38, 42–45, 50, 69, 116–117, 121, 129, 138, 146–149, 153, 156, 168, 180–182, 187, 190, 193
Skin color, 132, 137, 140, 143, 156, 183

Social, 6, 8, 10, 15, 18–20, 26, 28, 31–36, 38–49
Speakers, 5–8, 10, 30–31, 37–38, 42, 46, 50–52, 56–58, 60–61, 68, 70–71, 78–87, 93, 101, 113–118, 122, 128–129, 133, 136–138, 140, 145, 147–150, 152–179
Superior, 97, 136, 172, 184, 192
Suitable classroom, 145
Symbolic capital, 149
System, 12, 15, 20, 22–26, 46, 78, 116, 134, 141, 150, 167
Symptoms of oppression, 142

Teacher, 3, 5–13, 37, 48, 51–100, 104–110, 113, 115–182
Teaching, 1–28, 34–37, 41, 46, 50–184
TESOL, 1–28, 30–182
Testing, 34, 45, 67, 158, 163, 170, 173–174
Time, 3, 5, 7, 10, 14–15, 17–28, 31, 33–41, 47, 49, 55
Transnational, 8–11, 38, 42–43, 45, 48–49, 51, 72, 74, 89, 121–122, 124–137, 157–179
Travel, 12, 16, 25, 52, 55, 62, 85, 128, 130, 140, 144
Trust, 180–197

Weak, 44, 164–166, 177–178
Westerners, 7, 17, 80, 140, 150–155, 159, 169
Western, 4–8, 10, 15, 17, 19–20, 24–26, 34–38, 59, 74, 77, 80, 82–84, 93, 110, 134, 142, 149, 151–159, 168
White, 10, 125–130, 134–140, 149–156, 167–169, 172, 183–184
Witnessed, 15
Windle, 31, 43–45, 166, 171, 177, 187
Woman, 44, 198
World War, 16
Woods, 16

Lightning Source UK Ltd.
Milton Keynes UK
UKHW051438160622
404528UK00016B/191